TOOL SCHOOL

The Complete Guide to
Using Your Tools
from Tape Measures to Table Saws

MONTE BURCH

SKYHORSE PUBLISHING

Safety

Safety is always a very important consideration when using tools, whether hand, portable electric, or stationary shop tools. And don't think even simple hand tools can't cause problems. As you read through this book, you'll discover a lifelong collection of woodworking incidents to avoid. The first step is to thoroughly read and make sure you understand the owner's manuals of any tools you intend to use before you begin. Follow all the manufacturers' safety instructions. Do not use tools without the appropriate guards, where possible. Do not change, adjust, or work on any power tools without unplugging them or removing batteries and assuring they do not have power. Keep your hands a safe distance from blades and cutters as suggested by owner's manuals. Always wear eye, ear, and, in instances where needed, dust protection devices. In addition to being a woodworking writer, I'm a professional musician, and believe me, safety is a very important part of my woodworking techniques. I can also speak of experience with ear protection. A lifetime of playing in rock and country bands and running power equipment, early on without proper protection, has almost completely taken away my hearing.

Do not attempt techniques or operations unless you understand them completely, even those explained in this book. And do not take shortcuts. Make sure you keep tools sharp and in proper operating condition. Please be safe, but enjoy woodworking, it's a very enjoyable hobby and avocation.

Metric Conversion Chart

to convert	to	multiply by
Inches	Centimeters	2.54
Centimeters	Inches	0.4
Feet	Centimeters	30.5
Centimeters	Feet	0.03
Yards	Meters	0.9
Meters	Yards	1.1

Skyhorse Publishing books may be purchased in bulk at special discounts for sales promotion, corporate gifts, fund-raising, or educational purposes. Special editions can also be created to specifications. For details, contact the Special Sales Department, Skyhorse Publishing, 307 West 36th Street, 11th Floor, New York, NY 10018 or info@skyhorsepublishing.com.

Skyhorse® and Skyhorse Publishing® are registered trademarks of Skyhorse Publishing, Inc.®, a Delaware corporation.

Visit our website at www.skyhorsepublishing.com.

10 9 8 7 6 5 4 3 2

Library of Congress Cataloging-in-Publication Data is available on file.

ISBN: 978-1-62873-702-8

Printed in China

About the Author

Monte Burch was an editor for **Workbench** magazine through the late 1960s and early 1970s. He has been a freelance how-to woodworking writer/photographer and is the author of over 70 how-to outdoor and other nonfiction books, including a number that were **Popular Science** monthly main selections, such as **The Home Cabinetmaker** and **Complete Guide to Building Log Homes**. Over a million copies of his books have been sold. Monte lives on a 350-acre farm with over half the land in managed timberlands. His home has a full woodworking shop and photo studio.

TABLE OF CONTENTS

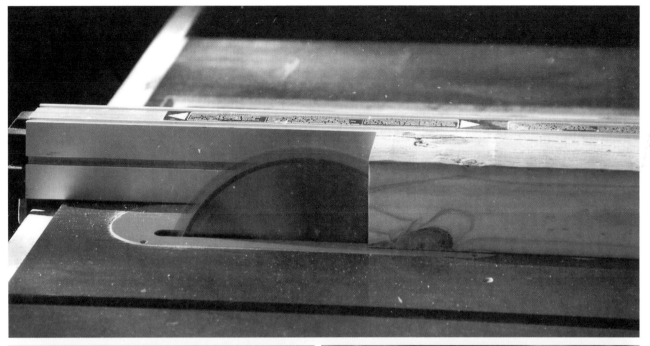

3

STATIONARY TOOLS 146

INTRODUCTION

IF YOU'RE NEW TO TOOLS and are curious about what tools to purchase, as well as the basics of how to use them, this book will enlighten you in your purchases and learning. It's best to start small, with only a few hand tools, and learn to use them properly. Then graduate to a portable electric tool or two, and finally begin adding stationary power tools.

Longtime woodworkers will find new methods, procedures, and tool uses in this book. The knowledge, drawings, and photos are not meant to take the place of tool manufacturers' instruction books on their specific tools. Make sure you read and understand all procedures and safety instructions for each tool. Some of the tools shown are handed down or purchased old-timers—some are, at the time of printing, the latest and greatest. Regardless, the basics of what constitutes a good-quality tool remain the same, and their uses are also fairly standard.

I hope this *Tool School* book introduces you and encourages you to a lifetime of woodworking enjoyment.

1

HAND TOOLS

WOODWORKERS AND CARPENTERS have been in my family for generations. We have inherited a beautiful walnut bureau constructed by an ancestor for his wife around the turn of the century. When you examine it, including the turned side pedestals, it's hard to imagine the massive furniture piece was constructed entirely with hand tools with the exception of the turnings, which were created on a foot-operated lathe.

If you spend any time in museums, you'll appreciate the work with hand tools alone on projects, such as a Philadelphia Highboy, as well as any number of Chippendale pieces. I learned woodworking at my father's side, and his first lessons were, of course, with hand tools. His thoughts were the basics should be with hand tools, and then you graduate to powered tools.

When I later began to teach woodworking, I followed his advice with my students. There is also something "connecting" in creating a project using only hand tools, especially when using an old tool handed down from fathers or grandfathers or purchased at a flea market. On the other hand, some hand tools are still the primary tool of use.

HAMMERS AND NAILS

A hammer, in the form of a rock, was probably mankind's first "tool." Today hammers are just as important and are available in a wide range of types and sizes that are suited to specific chores. Hammers are also some of the most misused and abused tools. Although we often treat hammers as such, there is no such thing as a universal hammer. Hammers include nail or claw hammers, ball-peen hammers, sledges, blacksmith's hammers, magnetic hammers, and soft-face mallets. Choosing the proper hammer for each chore is important not only for safety, but also for the life of the hammer, the ease of use, and success in the chore. The most common hammers for woodworkers are nail or claw hammers.

Types of Hammers

Claw hammers should be used only with nonhardened common or finishing nails. These hammers are available in two styles: curved-claw with 16- or 20-ounce weights, used for general carpentry, and lighter 10- or 12-ounce weights, used for finish carpentry or cabinetry. Straight-claw hammers are sometimes called ripping hammers. The straight claw provides more leverage for pulling larger nails when doing framing or remodeling work. Straight-claw hammers commonly come in 20-, 24-, 28-, or 32-ounce sizes. The most common hammer is a curved-claw 16-ounce model. This hammer can be used for just about any carpentry, millwork, furniture construction, or home repair and maintenance. This size hammer can also drive everything from small brads to heavy nails, and the curved claw provides easy nail pulling of small- to medium-size nails.

Two other common sizes, however, can make specific chores easier. A 12- or 13-ounce hammer is ideal for cabinetry, millwork, and furniture building with small nails where it's important not to mar the wood finish. A 20- or 24-ounce framing hammer is best if doing extensive house framing or remodeling. The larger hammer also has a longer handle for better balance and force in driving large nails. These hammers are available with a curved claw, but more commonly come with a straight claw, called a ripping claw. The ripping claw can be used to pry up boards, remove large nails, and perform other building and remodeling chores. Hammers are also like many other items, such as golf clubs. Even if you have a number of

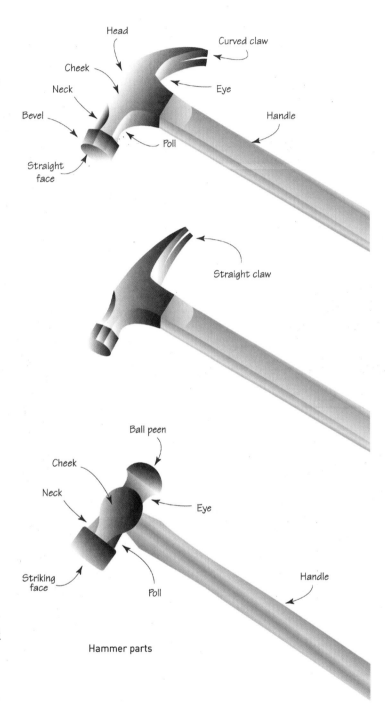

Hammer parts

hammers to choose from, you'll find one just seems to fit your hand and work style better than other hammers, and over time it becomes a companion you always pick up first.

Don't buy cheap hammers. A quality hammer has a forged head with a crowned or slightly curved face. Cheaper hammers are made with cast-iron heads, and the face is usually flat. The metal on the head will also be rough, not smooth. Cheaper hammers may even shatter and cause a serious injury. A crowned-face hammer can be used to drive finish nails down flush with the wood surface without denting the wood. The crowned head is also designed to present more surface to the nail with a normal arm swing, which helps drive nails straight without bending them. Hammer heads may be smooth or, for rough framing work, corrugated, which prevents the head from slipping off the nails in hard driving chores. Claw hammers are available with a variety of handle materials, including wood, steel, and fiberglass (or graphite). All three materials are excellent, but there are differences. Wood has a more natural feel and is the most economical. Fiberglass and especially graphite handles offer less vibration for day-long use, and the handle is usually wrapped with soft foam or rubber—another plus for extended use.

Nailing hammers are available in sizes from 10 to 32 ounces. They may feature curved- or straight-claw styles.

Handles may be straight or hatchet-style and made of wood, fiberglass, or metal with molded-over materials for comfort.

The Stanley contractor graded jacketed hammers feature a jacketed graphite handle with a special ribbed grip and a patent-pending head-to-handle assembly. Steel handles provide more power for large chores. The Craftsman solid-steel hammer features a patented wooden plug for shock absorption and a foam exterior. Most claw hammers feature a straight handle, but the California Framer hammers from Vaughn feature a hatchet-style handle. Their BlueMax model also has an innovative magnetic nail holding slot capable of holding 16d and 20d nails. These are great for starting nails in places you can't reach with both hands. In addition, some hammers feature unusual head materials and designs. For instance, the Vaughan Ti-Tech Titanium hammer combines the speed driving power of titanium with the versatility of interchangeable steel caps. The lightweight titanium body swings faster for greater power at the point of impact with less stress and arm fatigue. The steel caps can be changed from milled face for rough framing to smooth face for finish work.

Many hammers feature antivibration design handles for day-long usage with fewer fatigue and joint problems.

The Vaughn Ti-Tech hammer features a titanium body with interchangeable steel caps.

Maintenance

Some hammer heads are held in place with one or more steel wedges. If the head becomes loose, you can often tighten it back in place by driving the wedge tighter. The first step is to hold the hammer upside down and rap sharply on the butt end of the handle. This will drive the head tighter. Then reseat the wedge by tapping in place.

The face of a hammer is extremely important and the part that causes the most trouble to the inexperienced. If you seem to be bending more nails than usual, look at the face. It might be scratched or covered with wood resin or dried glue. Place a piece of fine sandpaper flat on a workbench, and polish the face of it. Never grind the face of a hammer.

Magnetic and Tack Hammers

These small and lightweight hammers are primarily used to drive upholstery tacks. They are commonly double-faced with one face having a magnet inset. By placing a tack against the magnet, you can reach in and drive the tack in hard-to-get places. These small flat-faced hammers are also commonly used for driving glazing points to hold glass in windows or picture frames. In fact, a special glazing hammer features a swiveling head with a flat face on three sides.

A hammer face may become pitted or covered with wood resin or dried glue. Lightly sand the face with a piece of fine sandpaper held on a flat surface to restore the face.

Other hammers include tack or magnetic hammers designed for driving tacks or brads. The specialty hammer shown is an antique in the author's collection and used to drive glazing points in windows or pictures frames.

Framing work requires heavy hammers that can drive larger nails with force. Many also feature longer, hatchet-style handles.

Mallets

Soft-faced hammers and mallets come in several sizes, shapes, and materials. They are available with rubber, hard plastic, and rawhide faces. The primary uses of these mallets are for wood chisels and carving chisels. They can also be used to tap in dowels, drive glued joints together for clamping, or for any other woodworking chores where you don't wish to mar the wood surface. Dead-blow hammers normally have nylon faces, and their heads are partially filled with steel shot to increase impact and reduce rebound.

Soft-faced hammers and mallets can be used to tap wood joints together when gluing them up or with wood and carving chisels.

Ball-Peen Hammers

These metalworking hammers are designed for riveting, center punching, and bending or shaping soft metals. They are available in sizes from 2 to 48 ounces. It's important to have a variety of sizes for different chores. One end of the head is round for riveting. The opposite end of the head is flat but has a beveled edge. Handles may be fiberglass or wood. Vaughn's exclusive hollow-core fiberglass handles provide great balance and more effective shock absorption than solid fiberglass handles. Two similar hammers include a machinist's riveting and a tinner's riveting. The machinist's riveting hammer has a round head with a flat striking face and a rounded cross-peen on the opposite end of the head. The tinner's features an octagon head with a flat striking face.

Hand-Drilling Hammers

These heavy, short-handled hammers are designed to use with star drills, masonry nails, steel chisels, and nail pullers. They provide lots of power and are available in sizes ranging up to three pounds.

Blacksmith and Double-Faced Hammers

Blacksmiths hammers feature a flat surface on one end of the head and a wedge shape for working metal on the opposite end of the head. They are available in sizes from two to three pounds. Double-faced hammers feature a flat face on either end of the head and are used for a variety of metal-working purposes, including blacksmithing. They range in head weights from two to four pounds, and both styles come with wood or fiberglass handles. A similar shaped hammer is the lineman's (farrier) or turning hammer.

Mauls

Last in the lineup are mauls and sledges. Mauls and sledges come in sizes from 1½ to 12 pounds and most feature wooden handles but fiberglass models are also available. These are used for everything from driving stakes for concrete forms to other heavy-duty chores.

A brick hammer.

Using A Hammer

Using a hammer to drive nails is simple. But then it's also not simple. Like any other skill, it takes practice, as well as proper technique. An old-time carney trick was to put your money down and see if you could drive a nail with one blow. A long-time carpenter, my dad could drive an 8d nail with a single blow sometimes. That trick doesn't do most of us any good, but driving nails easily and properly is important not only to reduce fatigue and time on the job, but also for a good, solid, and smooth construction. Bent nails don't hold framing pieces properly, and hammer tracks just don't work on fine furniture. One summer, while working with some kids on a church project, I taught a youngster the simple trick of **following** the nail when he began his first nail-driving chore. By the end of the day, he was bending fewer nails and having a great time.

HAMMER SAFETY

The first rule of safety is to always use the hammer for its intended use. Do not use claw hammers, brick hammers, or hatchets on hardened metal objects, such as cold chisels, punches, star drills, drift pins, masonry nails, pry bars, nail pullers, hitch pins, or clevises. Always use a hammer of the correct size for the chore, and make sure to strike the surface squarely. Do not create glancing blows. Do not strike a hammer or hatchet against another hatchet or hammer. And, the most important rule, always wear safety glasses or goggles when using hammers. Never use a hammer that has the following faults: loose handles or rubber grips, chipped or spalled face, broken or cracked claws, cracks in the eye section, mushroom heads, worn handles due to overstrikes, or cracked handles.

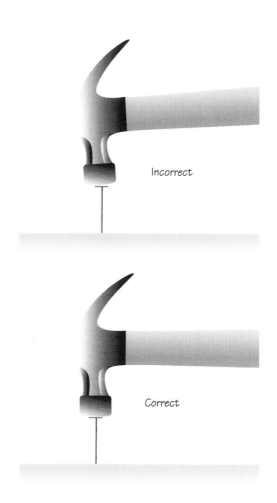

Using a hammer correctly means hitting the nail with the hammer face parallel to the nail head. It's not as easy as it might seem.

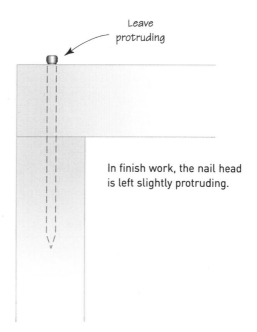

In finish work, the nail head is left slightly protruding.

Grasp the hammer handle near its end but where you have a balanced feel. Position the nail in place with your other hand, and tap it lightly with the hammer face to start it. Then lift and swing the hammer from the shoulder with a good arc of the arm. Let the hammer do the work. The most common mistake beginners make is choking up or grasping the hammer too tightly and too closely to the head. When you use a hammer correctly, you can get by with a lighter head, and the swing and leverage does the work rather than brute strength.

One trick my dad used in his cabinet building shop was to drill a hole in the end of his finishing hammer handle and melt a bit of beeswax into it. He then tipped a nail in the wax for driving in difficult woods. When driving nails in hardwoods and the ends of some softwoods, you may have to predrill nail holes to prevent splitting out the wood.

The first step in hammering is the proper grip. The hammer should be grasped near the rear of the handle to provide the most leverage. Placing the thumb on the top edge of the handle provides not only more leverage, but also better control. Place the nail in the desired position, place the hammer head down on the nail head, hold it squarely in place, and give the nail a light tap to set it in place. Remove your fingers from the nail and drive the nail in place. It's best to use several light to moderate blows rather than trying to drive with fewer blows. This allows the wood to separate better for easier nail penetration and helps to prevent bending the nail. With the correct size hammer to match the nail size and chore,

the hammer weight and swing will do the most work without having to create a strong down force with your arm. The latter doesn't allow for control and is fatiguing, and over time it can cause problems, such as tendonitis, a common problem many old-timer carpenters suffer from. If driving nails in hardwoods, always predrill through the top board, or through the top and into the lower board, to a depth of about two-thirds of the nail's length. Also, if driving near the end of a board for finish work, even softwoods should be predrilled. For finish work, the nail should only be driven until the bulbous end of the nail is still above the wood surface. Then drive the nail slightly below the wood surface with a nail set. Nail sets come in different sizes. Choose a nail set that is slightly smaller than the nail head. On most finish work, nails should be driven about six inches apart.

Nails may be surface nailed or edge nailed. Nails may be driven straight in or, many times in framing chores, at an angle called **toe-nailing.** In the latter technique, the starting piece must be blocked or held in place to prevent it shifting as the nail is started. For best holding power, the piece should be toe-nailed on both sides.

If the nail bends over, remove it by pulling it with the claw. To prevent marring a finish, place a piece of wood under the claw. A large block of wood under a straight claw can be used to pull even the most stubborn nail. Another method of removing long nails or those with damaged heads is to hook the nail with the claw and turn the hammer sideways. Then rehook, turn, and repeat until the nail is removed.

Use a nail set to drive the nail below the wood surface. Fill the indentation with wood putty.

It's best to predrill finish nail holes in hardwoods and at the ends of all stock.

Nails

A discussion of hammers wouldn't be complete without covering nails, the primary use of woodworking hammers. Nails are available in a wide variety of sizes and styles. They are measured by the **penny** (abbreviated "d") and sold in bulk by the pound or in boxes off the rack. Nails are sized according to their length and the gauge of wire it is created from. An eight penny (8d) nail is, for example, 2½" long, while a 10d nail is 3" long. The most commonly used nails are 6, 8, 10, and 16d. Choosing the proper nails is as important as choosing the proper hammer. The four most commonly used nails are multipurpose and include common and box nails with flat heads, and casing and finish nails with narrow heads that can be sunk below the wood surface and concealed. Although of the same general shape, common nails are thicker than box nails. Casing nails, although of the same length as finish nails, are slightly thicker. The first step in choosing a nail is one that will hold without undue splitting, but length is also important. When surface nailing, the length of the nail should be $\frac{3}{16}$" less than the total thickness of the combined pieces. When edge nailing, the nail length should be three times the thickness of the top or first piece of material.

A wide variety of specialty nails are also available, including drywall, roofing, underfloor, spiral-grooved, coated, and so forth. Nails for use in exterior projects often have a special zinc coating and are called galvanized nails. These prevent corrosion from rust on siding and trim.

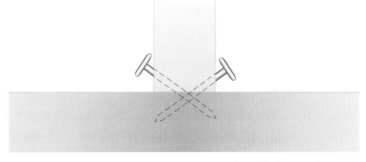

Nails can be driven straight in or at an angle called toenailing.

To pull a stubborn nail, place a block of wood under the claw for more leverage.

If the nail head is damaged or the nail is bent, place the nail in the claw and turn the hammer sideways. Repeat until the nail is removed.

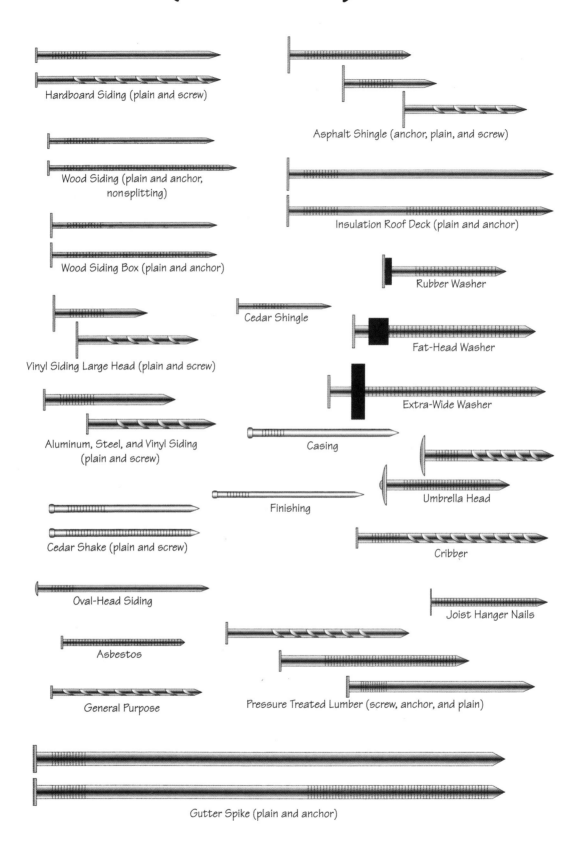

Exterior Nails (Zinc Coated)

Hardboard Siding (plain and screw)

Asphalt Shingle (anchor, plain, and screw)

Wood Siding (plain and anchor, nonsplitting)

Insulation Roof Deck (plain and anchor)

Wood Siding Box (plain and anchor)

Rubber Washer

Vinyl Siding Large Head (plain and screw)

Cedar Shingle

Fat-Head Washer

Aluminum, Steel, and Vinyl Siding (plain and screw)

Extra-Wide Washer

Casing

Finishing

Umbrella Head

Cedar Shake (plain and screw)

Cribber

Oval-Head Siding

Joist Hanger Nails

Asbestos

General Purpose

Pressure Treated Lumber (screw, anchor, and plain)

Gutter Spike (plain and anchor)

HAND TOOLS

Interior and Other Nails

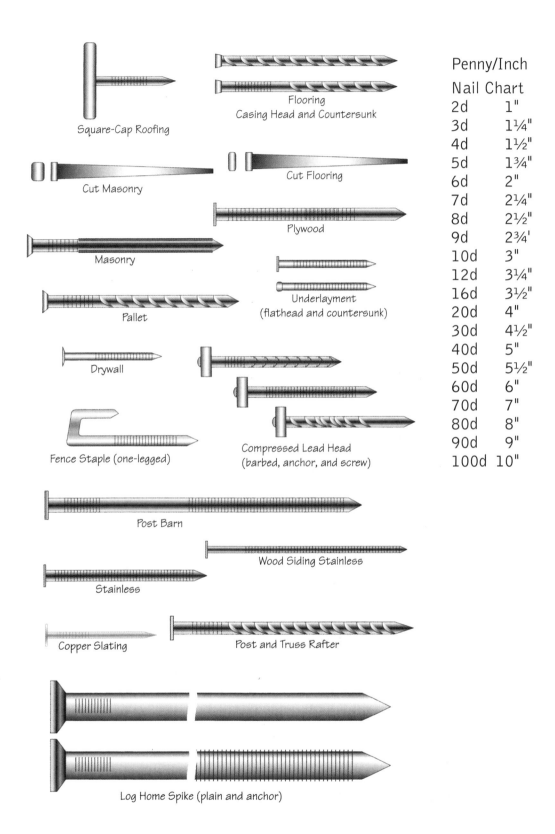

Square-Cap Roofing

Flooring
Casing Head and Countersunk

Cut Masonry

Cut Flooring

Plywood

Masonry

Underlayment
(flathead and countersunk)

Pallet

Drywall

Fence Staple (one-legged)

Compressed Lead Head
(barbed, anchor, and screw)

Post Barn

Wood Siding Stainless

Stainless

Copper Slating

Post and Truss Rafter

Log Home Spike (plain and anchor)

Penny/Inch
Nail Chart

2d	1"
3d	1¼"
4d	1½"
5d	1¾"
6d	2"
7d	2¼"
8d	2½"
9d	2¾'
10d	3"
12d	3¼"
16d	3½"
20d	4"
30d	4½"
40d	5"
50d	5½"
60d	6"
70d	7"
80d	8"
90d	9"
100d	10"

HANDSAWS

Not too many years ago, a carpenter's toolbox held a variety of handsaws. Cordless portable circular and jig saws have taken over much of the sawing chores, but handsaws are still valuable for many jobs. For the "purist" woodworker, handsaws are still extremely important.

Types of Handsaws

Today woodworking handsaws are available in a variety of shapes, including traditional push/pull and Japanese pull, as well as in coping, jab, and other styles.

Traditional push/pull handsaws include crosscut, rip, toolbox, backed or miter saws, and dovetail saws. Handsaws are available in different lengths, ranging from 16" to 26". Saws are also available with different tooth spacing, designated as **teeth per inch.** The fewer the teeth, the faster the saw cuts but creates a coarser cut.

Crosscut saws designed for rough carpentry work usually have 6 to 8 teeth per inch. A standard crosscut saw is used for 90 percent of woodworking chores. Rip saws have even fewer teeth per inch, normally 5½. Fine-toothed saws, such as miter and backed saws or saws used for fine woodworking, may have 10 to 12 or more teeth per inch. Crosscut saws are designed for cutting across the grain with the saw cutting on the push stroke. The teeth on a crosscut saw are filed with a bevel angle, and they act like tiny skew chisels to cut away the material. On the pull stroke, the teeth first score the wood like points of two parallel knife blades as the saw is drawn across the grain. Then on the push stroke, the

Handsaws are available in different grades of cutting coarseness defined by teeth per inch. A standard crosscut saw has 6 to 8 teeth per inch.

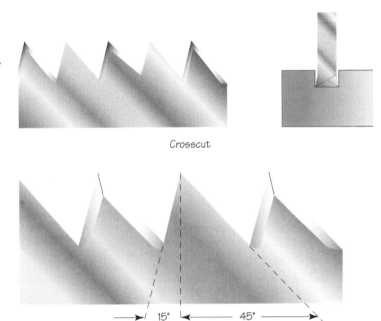

Crosscut

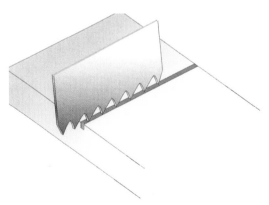

Crosscut saws are designed for cutting across the grain. The teeth are filed to a bevel edge, and the teeth first score the wood like two parallel knife blades and then clean out between as the stroke is continued.

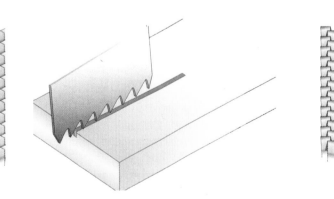

A ripping saw is designed to cut with the grain. They are designed to cut like vertical chisels.

edges of the teeth begin paring the groove as it is formed and clear the sawdust from the kerf.

The rip saw is designed for cutting with the grain and cuts on the push stroke. The front face of rip saw teeth have an angle of 8°; the back angle is 52°. Rip teeth are filed straight across the face and give the appearance of a series of chisel edges. Rip saw teeth cut like vertical chisels. First on one side of the blade, small pieces of wood are cut loose across the grain and pushed out. Then on the other side, the tooth following plows out a similar particle. Both rip and crosscut saws have the teeth set or alternately bent to the left and right. The bending of the teeth makes the cut, or **kerf,** wider than the thickness of the blade. For even greater clearance, the best quality saws are taper ground, or thinner at the point and back than at the butt and teeth.

Crosscut saws are normally set evenly about one-fourth the thickness of the blade. Rip saws are set approximately one-third of their thickness. Handles may be wood, usually beech, however, some modern saws utilize a plastic handle with an over-mold, a soft area for easier handling.

The blades of most traditional handsaws have a slightly concave edge for better balance.

The toolbox saw is a small saw with a fairly stiff back. The coarse teeth are designed to cut on both the push and pull strokes. Toolbox saws are designed to fit in a toolbox and are very handy for cutting areas you can't get to with a power saw.

Backed or miter saws are similar to standard crosscut saws, except they have a stiffener along the back edge and a deep blade. Miter saws run to 30" and

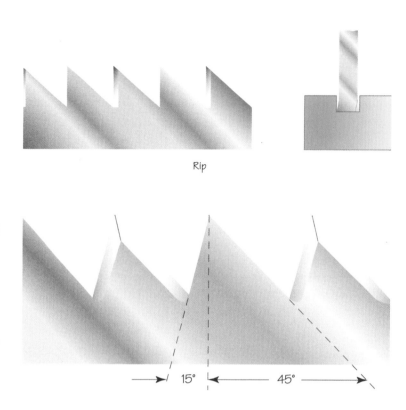

Rip

15°   45°

Toolbox saws are short, relatively coarse cutting saws to be carried in a toolbox for those chores not suited to a power saw.

are commonly used in miter boxes. They may come with the box or separately. You can also build your own miter box fairly easily. With these saws and a miter box, you can make extremely accurate cuts for millwork and wood joints. Backed saws are typically a bit shorter and are used by holding the saw teeth horizontally over the work rather than at an angle, as with cross-cut and rip saws. Both backed and miter saws are extremely fine-toothed.

A bench hook can be used with both backed and miter saws for making more accurate cuts. A dovetail saw is similar to backed and miter saws but usually smaller. The dovetail saw can also be used for cutting veneer, but a veneer saw works better for this chore.

Japanese saws are designed to cut on the pull stroke rather than the push stroke. For this reason, they have thinner, more flexible blades. They're great for making extremely fine cuts in furniture and other woodworking construction. Some models have a double blade, one coarse and a finer-toothed blade on the opposite side.

Handsaws are also available for cutting curved shapes. An old-time tool was the bow saw. We think of these as being used mostly for heavy-duty sawing, but old-time bow saws also were used for finer work. The coping or fret saw is a somewhat more modern version of the old bow saw and also smaller, so it's easier to use. Another type of saw is the jab or keyhole saw. These saws were initially used to cut the straight part of a keyhole in doors or drawers. Some jab-type saws are available with coarse teeth for rough cutting of Sheetrock and paneling.

Backed or miter saws have a stiffener along the back and are commonly fine toothed, or 10 to 12 teeth per inch. These saws are designed for making smooth cuts on molding and other stock.

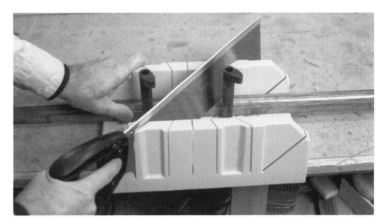

Miter saws are often used in a miter box for cutting molding. The Stanley miter box has a variety of angle guides plus holding pins.

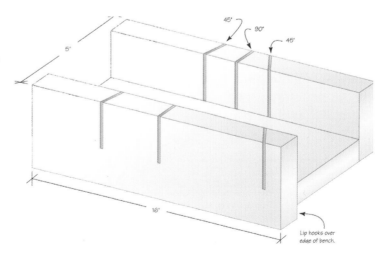

How to Use Saws

Like any tool, skill is involved in the use of handsaws. They are, however, relatively easy to learn to use if you take your time and learn the proper holding and stroke methods. Practice on scrap wood until you learn the procedures. In many instances, hand sawing is done with the board supported on a sturdy sawhorse or pair of sawhorses. You can build your own sawhorses quite easily. You may wish to have a couple of sawhorses of different heights for different chores. Other sawing chores, such as dovetails and furniture joints, are often cut with the work in a vise or on a workbench.

The first step is to mark the cut line. Use a combination square, carpenter's, or layout square to make a square line for a right angle cut. Use a combination square for 45° cuts. When first learning to cut with a handsaw, you may wish to mark cut lines on the edges of the stock in addition to the top mark.

Place the stock to be cut with the off or waste side overhanging the end of the sawhorse or sawhorses. Do not place the stock across a pair of sawhorses and cut between them. The cut will bind the saw. Position the saw with about a third of the blade protruding past the board edge and at a fairly low angle. The blade should be positioned on the waste side of the marked cutting line. If you're right-handed, grasp the edge of the stock next to the saw blade with your left hand. Raise your thumb and position it against the saw blade to help guide it. This position is used only to start the saw perpendicular to the workpiece. Once the cut is started, bring your thumb back into position on the stock. Hold the saw handle with your right hand and with your forefinger alongside the handle and pointing along the saw. Draw the saw backward a few times to start the cut. Lift the saw slightly each time on the return stroke until the cut, or kerf, is established. Once you have about a half to an inch of cut started, raise the handle of the saw so the

A shop-made bench hook can be used for accurate cutting with miter or backed saws.

A dovetail saw is similar to miter saws but smaller and used for hand cutting dovetails.

Japanese saws are designed to cut on the pull stroke and have thin, flexible blades. They're primarily used for creating fine furniture and cabinetry.

Coping or fret saws are used for making curved cuts in stock. For fretwork, first bore a hole and insert the blade. A support piece holding the piece to be cut is a great aid.

saw is at about a 45° angle to the stock and use long, steady, and smooth forward strokes to make the cut. You should never have to force the saw. Use smooth, steady strokes and allow the saw teeth to do the work. On the downward or push stroke, apply only light pressure to keep the blade in position. Try to use most of the saw blade so you don't prematurely dull the center portion of the blade. The hardest part for beginners to learn is to maintain a 90° cut to the stock. This takes practice, but by following the lines marked on the side of the stock in addition to the top line, it's easier to do. Always look directly down on the top of the blade. If the saw blade bends to work out-of-square, bend it slightly to bring it back square. If the saw leaves the line, twisting the handle slightly can bring it back on line. As you complete the end of the cut, reach around and support the off end of the overhanging stock. Use light, short strokes at the end to prevent splitting the wood.

A rip saw is used in much the same manner, except the angle is steeper, usually about 60°. Start at the very tip of the saw blade to make the beginning cuts, and use long, even strokes. If ripping long stock, place it over two sawhorses with the starting end protruding past one sawhorse. Make the cut until you get close to the sawhorse. Then move the stock back and make the cut between the sawhorses.

When using a miter or backsaw in a miter box, align the cut line with the slots in the box. Hold the workpiece tightly against the back of the box. Holding the saw handle slightly upward, start the cut slowly and carefully with a back or pull stroke. Once the cut is started, lower the saw gradually until it is level and continue making the cut. Make sure you hold the saw firmly to make straight and accurate cuts. You can also hold stock firmly on a workbench using a bench hook. If you are cutting long stock, two hooks, one on each end of the bench, can be helpful. Hold the stock

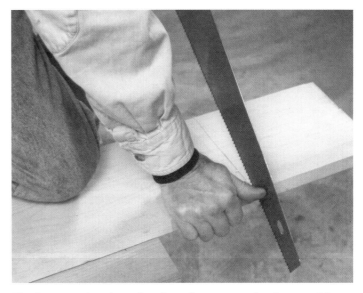

The first step in using a handsaw for crosscutting is to position the stock on sawhorses at a comfortable knee height with the off end overhanging one sawhorse. Then mark the cut line across the stock with a square. Hold the saw with about a third of the blade protruding past the board edge at a fairly low angle. Right-handed persons should grasp the edge of the stock with the left hand. Position the thumb against the saw blade to help guide it, and keep it perpendicular to the workpiece.

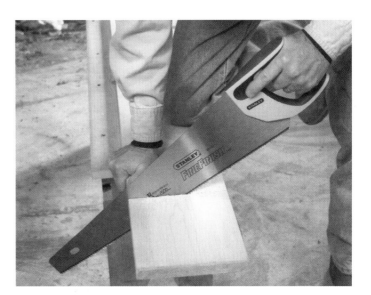

Hold the saw handle with your right hand with your forefinger extended alongside the handle. Note the Stanley saw shown has a molded-in feature to hold your finger in place. Draw the saw backward a few times to begin the cut. Lift the saw slightly between backstrokes.

firmly against the bench hook and make the cuts square and straight.

A coping saw can be used to make irregular cuts or to cut cove molding. The coping saw blade is easily removed, so it can do fret work. For the latter, first bore a starting hole through the stock, remove one end of the saw blade, insert the blade through the hole, and reinstall the blade. If making sharp turns in cuts, the blade can be loosened and turned at different angles as required. A support jig or saddle can help in using a coping saw for these types of cuts. The support jig has a notch cut in it and is clamped to a workbench or in a vise. The stock is placed on the jig and turned to allow cutting the contours.

Cutting cope joints on molding is another coping saw chore, and it's easy to guess where the name came from. The molding to be cut is laid down flat and a piece of matching molding positioned at a 90° angle down on it. The molding profile is marked on the piece to be cut and then the coping saw used to cut the contour. This is an especially effective way of fitting molding into corners that may not be perfectly square where a miter joint might not fit as precisely.

Compass, jab, and keyhole saws are all used to make fairly straight cuts, after a starter hole has been bored.

Saw Maintenance

The most important maintenance chore with saws is preventing rust. Keep the saw blades well-oiled with light machine oil or an occasional dusting spray with rust preventive and wipe down. A rusty saw is hard to use. Remove the rust with rust preventive and No.0000 steel wool. When used with some woods, saw blades may gum-up from resins, with resin on the blade and in the teeth. Remove the resin with lacquer thinner and a cloth. (Do this outside or in a well-ventilated area.) Finish on handles can also eventually wear. Refinish or recoat with linseed oil. The screws holding the handle on the blade may eventually work loose, requiring retightening.

The major problem with handsaws is dulling of the teeth or losing the set of the teeth. Your best bet is to take the saw to an expert and allow them to resharpen and reset the teeth. It takes a bit of expertise and special equipment to do this. If you do decide to tackle the chore, you'll need an adjustable file guide, saw blade jointer, and a plier-type tooth setter. You'll need triangular taper files of different sizes for the different size teeth as per the following chart.

Special vises are also made to clamp the blades for sharpening, but you can use a 1x3 of hardwood on

Once the cut is started, bring your thumb back into position on the stock. Use long, steady strokes with the saw held at about a 45° angle to the stock to continue the cut. As you reach the end of the cut, reach around with your left hand and support the cut-off stock.

POINTS PER INCH

4½, 5 — 7" regular

6, 7 — 7" slim

8, 9, 10 — 6" extra slim

11, 12 — 5" extra slim

13, 14 — 5" double extra slim

15, 16 — 4" double extra slim

either side of the blade, clamping them and the blade in a bench vise.

If the blade is fairly new, you may only need to touch up the teeth with the file. Make sure to file in the direction of the tooth set. If the teeth are well-worn, uneven in size and shape, and with little set, the saw will have to be completely redone which involves: 1. jointing; 2. reshaping; 3. setting; 4. resharpening.

A saw jointer has a small file set in its top edge and rides on the saw teeth. Moving the jointer back and forth across the teeth dresses the teeth down to a uniform height. To reshape, the file is held in a file guide set at 90° to the blade. By filing straight across, the teeth are reshaped to bring the teeth edges to the proper angles with gullets of uniform depth.

The teeth are then reset. The setter bends the teeth alternately outwards the same distance. This creates a saw kerf that is slightly thicker than the blade thickness. The first step is to adjust the setter to match the teeth per inch of the blade. This is done by rotating the anvil on the setter. The set depth should not exceed half the height of the tooth. Adjust the gauge screw so the setter will slide easily on the saw and then starting at the tip of the saw, bend every other tooth in the direction of the original set. Turn the saw around to set the alternating teeth on the opposite side.

The last step is to resharpen the teeth. With the saw in the vise, set the filing guide to the correct angle. This is 60 to 75° for crosscut and 90° for rip saws. Beginning at the tip of the saw, place the file on the left of the first tooth that is facing you. Push the file across the tooth, lift it slightly and pull it back for the return stroke. The file will cut the bevel on the tooth facing you and the bevel on the back of the next tooth. File until the jointed flat spots are reduced to half size. Move the file to the next alternating tooth and repeat until you file all teeth in that direction. Always shift the blade so it's held firmly in the vise. When you reach the handle end and all teeth in that direction are filed, turn the saw around in the vise, reset the filing guide to the same but opposite angle and sharpen the teeth set in the opposite direction.

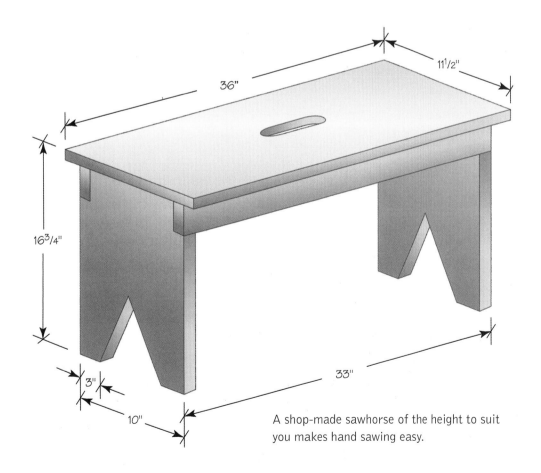

A shop-made sawhorse of the height to suit you makes hand sawing easy.

MEASURING, MARKING, AND LAYOUT TOOLS

Not as glamorous as other tools, measuring and marking tools, however, are some of the most important tools in your shop, toolbox, or kitchen tool drawer. Regardless of whether building furniture, kitchen cabinets, installing tile, or wallpapering, accurate measurements are extremely important. These days a wide range of traditional and modern measuring and marking tools are available.

My dad's major rule on measuring for kitchen cabinets in his custom shop was whoever measured for the cabinets did the layout of the cabinets, and they used the same ruler for both. It saved a lot of headaches, especially when fitting cabinets between two walls. It's not only important to use the correct tools for specific jobs, but to use them properly, as well.

Rulers, Tape and Folding

The most common measuring tools are tapes. These come in a wide variety of lengths and widths, from W to 1". Lengths start at 6' and can run up to 300'. The tapes are most often steel in the smaller lengths, but may be fiberglass or "soft" tape on the 300' sizes. Most carpenters' tapes have stud marks at 16" and 24". I also prefer the tapes with increments marked on one side, for instance, $\frac{1}{8}$", $\frac{1}{4}$", and so forth. Tapes are available in the traditional standard model, as well as tapes that lock in position, with or without a push button, and return automatically. The latter are extremely useful when laying out a building wall. With the tape locked in place over the plate, it's easy to mark stud locations. Magnetic hook tapes allow you to fasten the hook end to metal and pull the tape open, great for laying out metal studs.

If you've ever tried to extend a tape along the top of a rafter or floor joist for a measurement, you know one of the frustrations of building. The Black & Decker 15' powered tape measure does this effortlessly. The battery-powered tape extends automatically at the push of a button, allowing you to measure a distance without having a second helper hold the end in awkward places. It also leaves one hand free for marking.

Tapes are also available for specialized chores, including masonry and building layout. The latter are available in long lengths for laying out foundations and slabs. Wheel tapes are available for measuring long distances, for instance laying piping, building curbing, and surveying. McFeeley's carries a number of unusual tapes, including peel-and-stick measuring tapes you can affix to a cut-off saw, workbench, or on special purpose jigs. They also carry the Flatback Cabinetmaker's tape that lies flat for measuring. A story tape is available that provides a story pole on your hip. The matte finish blade has an area designed for pencil marks and recording notes right on the tape.

Measuring tools have been some of the most important craftsman tools from the time mankind began settling and building. These days a blend of traditional and modern measuring tools is available. Tapes and other means of measuring distances are the first order of business. Tape measures are available in a wide range of lengths with different markings for different chores.

The smaller measuring tapes often provide precise increments of measure, such as $\frac{1}{8}$".

A good contractor's tape, along with a framing square, make laying out building plates for stud walls quick and easy. The tapes are marked with 16" and 24" stud locations.

A carpenter's folding wooden ruler is a tradition, and better choices include a slide-out extension that enables you to determine inside measurements. Some also conveniently measure with the beginning one inch on either end. Metal shop rules are handy for any number of things, from accurate measurement of dovetail and mortise and tenon joints and other precision work. With a smooth, straight edge, they can also be used for checking the flatness of planes, wood surfaces, table tops, and setting jointer blades in place.

Woodworker's calipers are also extremely handy, especially for taking inside measurements. These are wooden-bodied tools with a fixed and sliding jaw. The latter has measurement graduations marked on it.

Tips on Using

Make sure the hook on the tape is solidly attached. A loose hook on the end can lead to inaccuracies, as can a bent or twisted tape. Always make sure the tape is parallel to the area to be measured and there are no sags.

The use of a laser line, and the resulting tools, has completely changed many of today's carpentry and contractor chores. The Black & Decker Marksman,

100' and 300' tapes are available for laying out larger building projects.

If you've ever tried to extend a tape over a distance for a one-person measurement, you'll appreciate the Black & Decker powered tape measure. Just push the button for tape extension.

distance measurer with 3-in-1 sensor utilizes a laser line to measure distances. Simply point the instrument to the distance to be determined and press a button. The instrument can also be used to measure and calculate the area of a room. A 3-in-1 stud sensor is built in that can detect studs, metal, or live AC wires.

Levels and Plumb Bobs

Gravity is used for determining some measurements. The term "level" means any straight line that is horizontal to the surface of a body of still water. "Plumb" refers to a line that is at a right angle to a level surface. The traditional plumb bob is one of the most important carpenter and contractor tools. Plumb bobs with string lines are commonly used to establish a plumb line for installing wallpaper, setting posts, establishing foundation corners and other chores. Most quality plumb bobs are made of solid, noncorrosive brass, although some may be coated with a corrosion-resistant finish. To use a plumb bob, attach it to a string and attach the string directly over the area to be plumbed. Make sure the plumb bob is allowed to swing free. Wait until it is motionless before marking plumb. Some chalk line boxes also have a pointed end for establishing plumb. Once the box is hanging plumb, simply hold the chalk line against the surface and snap the plumb line.

Levels utilize a vial with a bubble and again gravity to establish either plumb or level. The principle of the spirit level is the air bubble in a liquid-filled glass tube will rise to the highest point. Alcohol or ether is generally used because it will not freeze at ordinary temperatures. The glass tube is slightly curved, filled with alcohol, and sealed. When the tube is held in the horizontal position, the air bubble rises to the highest point.

Levels are available in several lengths, ranging from just a few inches to several feet. The smaller torpedo models are used for close work in tight places, while 16- and 24-inch levels are quite often used for masonry purposes. Three- and four-foot levels are best for framing and other contractor chores. Levels are also available in a variety of materials, including wood, wood with brass trim, brass, plastic, and aluminum. Levels may have one plumb vial and one level vial, or two of each so you can use either side of the level. Most also have a 45° vial.

If you need to measure long distances, say for curbs, asphalt, and other projects, a wheeled tape, such as the Lufkin model shown, is the answer.

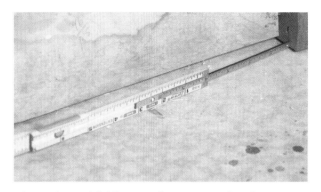

The traditional folding wooden carpenter's ruler is a must for cabinetmakers. Those with a slide extension, such as the Lufkin Red End shown, allow for precise inside measurements.

Hi-tech takes over with the Black & Decker distance measurer. It provides immediate push-button distance measures and computes square footage.

IRWIN Industrial Tools has a line of Strait-Line, box-beam levels with a number of innovations professionals and serious how-to folks will appreciate. The levels have precision machined vials from a solid block of acrylic, and they will not break, fog, fade, or develop a static charge. They are also suspended in the frame with a patented vial mounting system, rather than glued in place. The patented system allows for quick and easy in-field calibration for the utmost in accuracy.

The Craftsman SmartTool Plus has an angle sensor powered by a 9-volt battery that reads angles by degrees, percent of slope, or pitch in digital format. The level can also be set to beep at preset angles. This makes it easy to set sloped footings for patios and other chores. The Hi-Level, Direct Read Level, available from McFeelys, allows you to read the angle on a mechanical scale inside the vial.

To use a level, place it on the top or side of the object you wish to level or plumb. Take a reading to determine level or plumb. If the bubble is not between the lines of the vial but off to one side, lift that side away from the surface to view the approximate angle that the object is off level or plumb. Keep in mind what appears level over a distance of a couple of feet may be off one or two degrees on a longer span. If you have more than one level, a good rule to follow is to use the longest one that will fit the job. Some of the longer levels have extension in them to increase the length up to 10 feet. You can make an extension if you need a longer level. Choose a 2x4 of white pine or some other relatively stable, lightweight wood, measure it, let it set for about a week, then measure it again. If it seems stable, plane two opposite edges smooth and parallel. Use a pair of calipers to ensure the edges are parallel. Find the center end-for-end and mark for a hand hole. Taper the ends to lighten the weight and coat all surfaces with varnish to keep out moisture. To use, simply position the level on the extension board.

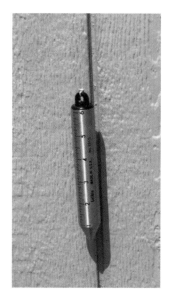

Plumb bobs go back as far as buildings have been constructed, and the Lufkin brass models are a long-time tradition. Use them to locate the exact corners of buildings or foundation walls.

Levels are equally important, and come in a wide variety of sizes, shapes, and materials.

The Black & Decker Gecko Grip level not only is easy to hold in place against a wall, but also has a removable 9" torpedo level along with a stud sensor.

If you need to level long distances, a shop-made, straight-edge level board can be helpful.

The new Craftsman Laser Trac 360° Rotary Laser replaces traditional chalk lines and levels and can project a level line on all walls or surfaces in a room at the same time. It features three rotary, or spinning, speeds (slow, medium, and fast) for optimum visibility. Line-segment settings are also available where only a line segment is needed. Uses include installing drop ceilings, taping prior to painting, wallpapering, installing chair rails or wainscoting, laying out tile, or leveling and setting countertops, cabinets, trim and millwork, plumbing decks, plumbing framing, and many more.

For outside work, as well as some inside chores, however, a traditional chalk line is necessary. The IRWIN Strait-Line SL6X chalk reel has a high-speed retrieve, which framers and other professionals will appreciate because it allows them to do their jobs faster. Designed with a helical gear system, it retrieves line up to six times faster than other standard reels. It also features a high-performance line two times stronger than other chalk lines. The twisted line, made of polyester and nylon blend materials, absorbs and holds chalk well.

A string level can be used for a rough lay-out of foundations, concrete block walls, concrete floors, and so forth. A string level is extremely useful in laying stone walls and other masonry chores.

Maintenance

Whether you own one or several, levels should be stored in a safe place where they won't be knocked down or dropped. Try to avoid leaving them in places with extreme temperatures, such as in the hot sun or near a heating unit. Treated with care, a good level will last several lifetimes.

The Craftsman SmartTool Plus is a digital level that shows angles by degrees, making it easy to set posts or set a slope as desired.

The IRWIN Strait-Line Level not only has all the features of a top-line level, but also the capability of in-field calibration, should that ever be needed.

The Craftsman Laser Trac, 360° Rotary Laser provides the capability of leveling four walls at a time or for chores, such as setting countertops, millwork, plumbing deck supports, and so forth. (Photo Courtesy of Craftsman)

Layout Tools

Squares are extremely important homeowner, contractor, and woodworking tools, and they are also available in a wide variety of sizes and types. Large squares for framers and builders are sometimes called "2-ft" squares and include both a carpenter and a framing square. The latter has rafter tables printed on it. Both, however, can be used for all framing chores from laying out rafters to marking stud locations and squaring boards for cutting. Traditional squares were made of steel; modem versions are often made of aluminum for lighter weight. These squares are also extremely handy for squaring furniture and cabinet projects during construction.

Holding the square with the manufacturer's logo up reveals the **face** of the square. The opposite side is called the **back.** The short arm of the square is called the **tongue;** the long arm is called the **blade.** A number of dimensional imprints and information is stamped on the square, allowing for a variety of chores. This is normally $\frac{1}{16}$" and $\frac{1}{8}$" graduations on the face of the square and $\frac{1}{16}$", $\frac{1}{10}$" and $1\frac{1}{2}$" graduations on the back of the square. On the face of the tongue are $\frac{1}{16}$" and $\frac{1}{8}$" graduations, while $\frac{1}{10}$" and $1\frac{1}{2}$" spacing are on the back of the tongue, plus a short $\frac{1}{100}$" scale. In addition there are 1" markings, rafter tables, brace measurements, an octagon scale, and a board measurement or **essex** table. A carpenter's or framing square holds a lot of information. Many feel a higher knowledge of mathematics is required to use a framing square, but it's actually the opposite; a square allows precise measurements fairly easily. A complete instruction manual comes with each square.

The rafter tables allow you to determine the lengths of common, hip, and valley rafters per-foot-run and also give the side cuts. Building rafters are denoted by pitch or fractions determined by the run, or distance, from building edge to centerline, and by rise, or the height from building wall to the top of the roof. For instance a 6/12 pitch roof means for every

You will also need a chalk line and the IRWIN Strait-Line chalk reel, which features a high-speed retrieve.

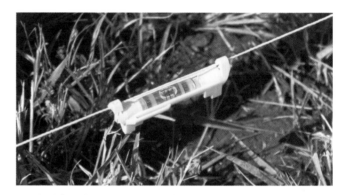

For building lay-out or laying block or stone walls, you'll need a string level and string.

Squares are extremely important, and the traditional framing square can be used for a wide variety of chores, from laying out rafters and stair stringers to marking cut-offs.

12" of run, the roof rises 6". The framing square is used to lay out the rafter, and it's basically fairly simple. With a 6/12 pitch, position the square on the end of the rafter board and locate 6" on the tongue (the rise) and 12" on the blade (the run). Measure from these points on the square, the distance should be approximately 13½". Multiply this by the run of the building, for instance 10'. This would be 135". Add 12" for an overhang and you have a final figure of 147", or the length of the rafter. To lay out the rafter, place the square at the end of the rafter board with the tongue on the left and facing away from you, the 6" on the outside edge of the tongue and the 12" mark on the blade should be on the upper edge of the board. Mark along the backside of the tongue to mark for the plumb cut at the ridge line. Measuring from the top of this mark to the opposite end of the board, mark the length of the rafter. This will be less one half the thickness of the ridge board. Then, holding the square in the same manner as before, mark down the side of the tongue. This denotes the plumb cut at the inside of the house wall for the notch called a bird's mouth. This notch seats the rafter on the wall plate. Add the overhang length and mark it with the square held in the same manner. Hold the square in place on the plumb line of the bird's mouth. Mark across the bottom edge of the blade. The depth of the bird's mouth is the wall thickness. Determine that and make a mark. Then move the square to that mark and mark down the bottom side of the tongue to create the horizontal line of the notch.

The C.H. Hanson Pivot Square makes it even easier to lay out rafters. The quality tool comes with a belt pouch that has a divider for the square, an instruction manual, and a carpenter's pencil. To use, start with the ridge board plumb cut. Simply set the adjustable angle blade to the desired pitch and mark for the cut. Using the same angle, mark the line-length of the rafter, as well as the plumb cut for the bird's mouth. Then hold the square in place with the base along the plumb cut line and mark the level line of the bird's mouth. Turn the square back in place for the plumb cut to complete the bird's mouth and to mark the tail cut.

A less common use of the framing square is as a protractor. If you draw a line from the 12" mark on the tongue to any point on the blade you are creating a particular angle. For instance, drawing a line from 12" on

The Hanson Pivot Square makes laying out rafters and determining angles quick and easy.

The Modified Square is a newer version of squares and offers a wide variety of uses.

The Stanley QuickSquare is a multipurpose layout tool that can be used as a saw guide, for angle measurements, and as a protractor.

HAND TOOLS

the tongue to 12" on the blade creates a 45° angle or a square with four sides. You can lay out any number of polygons using the technique. The secret is knowing the angles that create the number of sides required. For instance the angle for a polygon with 9 sides is measured at 12" on the tongue and $4\frac{3}{8}$ " on the blade. It's also important to remember that 30° from the horizontal line is 60° from the vertical line.

The A-Square, available from McFeely's, is a supersized square with an accurate 3-4-5 triangle that makes it easy to establish a right angle for many different construction chores, from laying out buildings to laying tile.

The Modified Square is a rather unusual square that will make stair and rafter layouts. It will also do other chores, such as finding the center of a circle.

One of the handiest squares for builders is the Quick Square Layout tool from Stanley. Small enough to fit in a tool pouch, the Quick Square has all the features of a framing square, miter square, and try square. It makes quick work of marking board cut-offs.

Another handy square I've used is a drywall square. Not only does the large four-foot square make quick work of marking drywall, it can also be used to mark plywood, paneling, and other large sheets for precise cuts with a portable circular saw.

Woodworking Bench Tools

Several woodworking layout tools are important for woodworkers and those building furniture and cabinetry. These are called **bench** tools because they're primarily used around or on the workbench or work table. The try square is a smaller square with one leg metal and the other leg often wood. It can be used to mark boards for cut-off, but is most commonly used for precise cabinet and furniture work, such as for marking for hinges, mortise and tenon joints, as well as dovetails. It is also used to assure square right angles of stock. This is an invaluable square for the serious furniture builder. The combination square features a metal blade, and a metal body with a 90° and 45° angle that slides on the blade. It also has a small level vial built into the body. This is one of the most versatile squares, used by both framers and woodworkers. Some combination squares come with an auxiliary body that has two 45° angles. This allows you to locate the center of round stock. It can also be set to use as a marking gauge. The sliding T-bevel square allows you to mark precise angles by adjusting the blade, on the body. An updated version is the Bosch digital angle finder. This high-tech digital tool allows you to set precise angles or measure existing angles, all with a digital display.

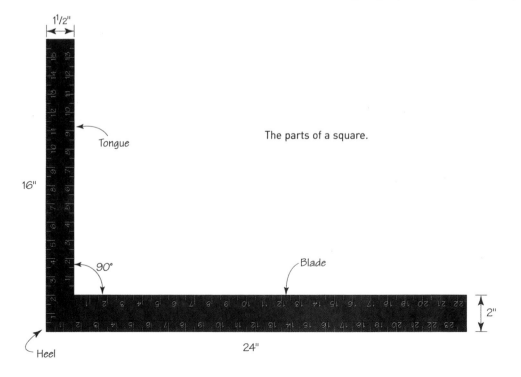

The parts of a square.

A marking gauge is used for scribing any number of layout chores, including locating mortise and tenons, rabbets, and finger joints. The head of the gauge is held against the edge of the stock and the tiny knife or wheel marks the layout. The best ones have a graduated beam and a marking cutter that is removable for sharpening. The Veritas Micro-Adjust Wheel Marking Gauge utilizes a wheel cutter that cuts the wood fibers rather than tear them and provides extreme accuracy. The Veritas Saddle Square allows you to transfer a line from one surface to another perpendicular surface by providing a 90° angle to allow scribing two perpendicular surfaces at one time. Their Dovetail Saddle Markers allow you to quickly and easily scribe dovetails. For marking precision cuts, such as furniture dovetails, a marking knife, such as that from WoodCraft Supply, is better than a pencil. You can make your own marking knife, or you can simply use an X-Acto craft knife.

Three other important bench tools include a steel rule, winding sticks, and a dovetail template. The steel rule has two uses, of course the most obvious is measuring, but the second, which is just as important, is checking for flatness. Position the rule on the surface edge down with a bright light from the back side. Any light coming through indicates unevenness in the surface. A rule is useless unless straight in the case of a rule or square in the case of a square. Check a rule by marking against the edge, then turning the rule over and repeating. To check a square, mark across a board, then flop the square over and check to see if the marks are the same. Winding sticks are two strips of well-seasoned wood of the same measurement. They are placed on opposite ends of a piece of stock and sighted across against a bright light. Any twist in the stock is easily discerned. In addition to purchased dovetail markers, you can make up your own from either metal or wood.

Last but not least in measuring tools is a good set of inside and outside calipers. These can be used for measuring wood turnings, mortise and tenon joints, precise stock dimensions, and any number of metalworking chores. An excellent choice is the Avenger 6-inch Digital Caliper. It has an oversized display for easy-to-read measurements in both inches and millimeters and inside and outside jaws.

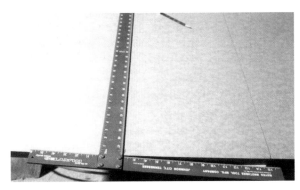

A large Sheetrock square can also be used to mark for cuts on plywood and other sheet goods.

The Bosch digital angle finder makes quick work of determining angles and for marking angles.

POLYGON CUT ANGLES

No. of Sides	Tongue Dimension	Blade Dimension
3	12"	$20\frac{7}{8}$"
4	12"	12"
5	12"	$8\frac{25}{32}$"
6	12"	$6\frac{15}{16}$"
7	12"	$5\frac{25}{32}$"
8	12"	$3\frac{31}{32}$"
9	12"	$4\frac{3}{8}$"
10	12"	$3\frac{7}{8}$"
11	12"	$3\frac{17}{32}$"
12	12"	$3\frac{7}{32}$"
14	12"	$2\frac{3}{4}$"
16	12"	$2\frac{13}{32}$"
18	12"	$2\frac{1}{8}$"
20	12"	$1\frac{29}{32}$"

A small try-square is often used at the workbench for marking furniture and cabinet joints and cuts.

If you need to make an angle, a sliding T-bevel square can be set to any angle.

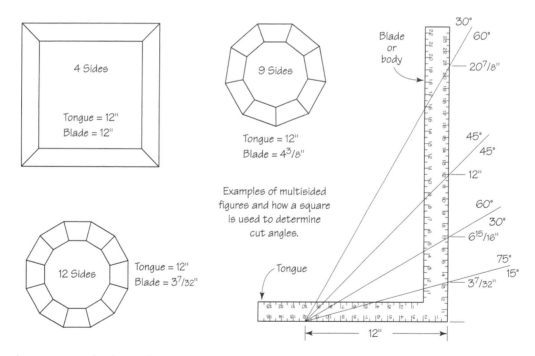

4 Sides

Tongue = 12"
Blade = 12"

9 Sides

Tongue = 12"
Blade = 4$^3/_8$"

Examples of multisided figures and how a square is used to determine cut angles.

12 Sides

Tongue = 12"
Blade = 3$^7/_{32}$"

Blade or body

30°
60°
20$^7/_8$"

45°
45°
12"

60°
30°
6$^{15}/_{16}$"

75°
15°
3$^7/_{32}$"

Tongue

12"

A square can also be used as a protractor.

A combination square can be used as a 90 and 45° marking gauge or the sliding tongue can be set to mark a specific width.

Both wood and digital calipers are extremely important.

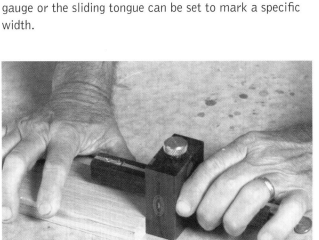

A marking gauge is used for building fine furniture and cabinetry, providing layout marks for joints, such as mortise and tenon.

Dovetail joints are also very important for many fine furniture projects. A dovetail gauge, such as the one shown from Woodcraft Supply, is extremely handy.

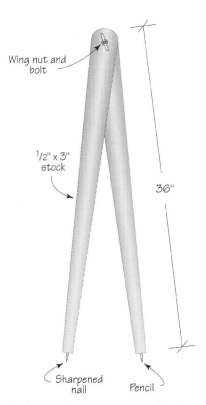

Wing nut and bolt

1/2" x 3" stock

36"

Sharpened nail

Pencil

A shop-made compass can also be invaluable.

How To Layout Rafters with a Framing Square

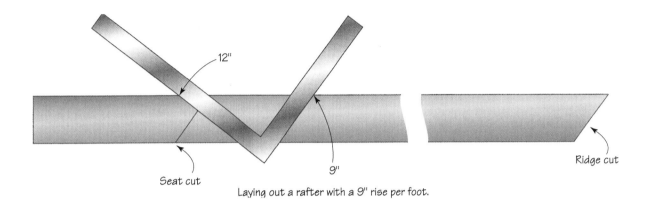

Laying out a rafter with a 9" rise per foot.

Seat cut

12"

9"

Ridge cut

Two Methods Can Be Used To Layout A Rafter. The First Is Mathematical.

Rafters can also be laid out using the step-off method. A rafter square is used to step-off the rafter by using the square to represent the rise and run of the roof. Use the scale on the small blade, called the tongue, to represent the roof's rise, and the scale on the large blade, called the body, to represent the run. The rafter shown is for a $^{12}/_6$ pitch roof, and has a total run of 12'3", and an overhang of 1'8". Position the rafter on a pair of sawhorses and locate the 12" mark on the body of the square on the edge of the rafter board. Locate the rise, or 6" mark on the tongue, and position it on the same edge. Draw a line along the back of the tongue. This is the plumb cut for the centerline of the ridge. Holding the square in the same position, make a mark 3" on the body and slide the rafter in place to mark off the odd unit. Then step-off 12" increments until the building line is reached. Reverse the square to mark the bird's mouth cut, overhang, and tail cut. Then return to the top of the rafter to make the plumb cut correct for the thickness of the ridge. The mark should be made one-half of the ridge plate thickness.

Rafters Can Also be Laid Out Using the "Step-Off" Method.

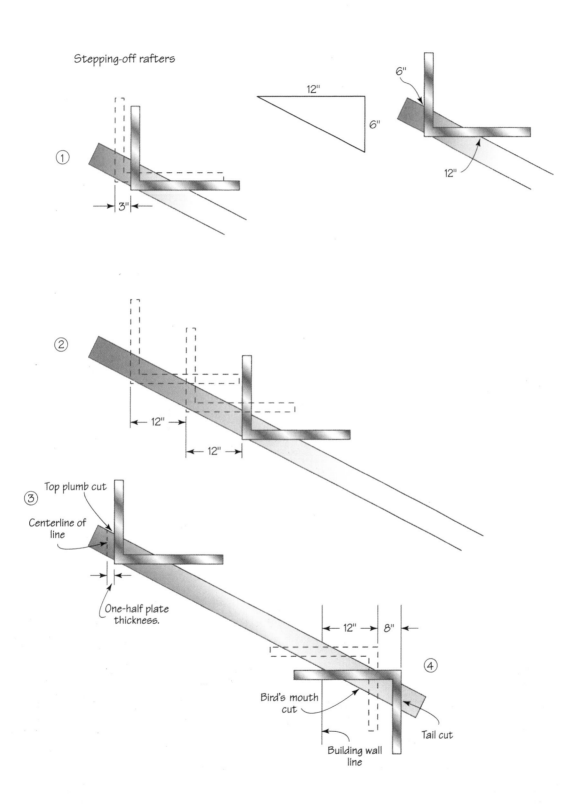

Stepping-off rafters

① 3"

12"

6"

6"

12"

② 12" 12"

③ Top plumb cut

Centerline of line

One-half plate thickness.

④ 12" 8"

Bird's mouth cut

Building wall line

Tail cut

CHISELS AND GOUGES

A chisel was the cause of my first workshop accident. At age six or seven, I slipped into my dad's woodworking shop and was using his chisel with the blade pointing up toward me. The chisel slipped and slammed up into the bottom of my nose, resulting in a hefty cut and lots of blood. Mom fainted, Dad gave me a really hard talking to, and then they both decided, although officially under the age limit, I should be enrolled in dad's 4-H woodworking classes.

Indeed, a chisel can create a nasty cut, but chisels and gouges are also some of the most important woodworking tools. Quality tools will last a lifetime, and several will hone to a razor edge and stay sharp a long time. This means they are safer than inexpensive chisels, which will dull quickly and require extra effort to use, so your work will not be as accurate.

Chisel Types

Several different types of chisel handle designs are available. Socket chisels have a blade that ends in a socket, which is fitted into a wood or plastic handle with a steel cap. Quality heavy-duty chisels have a one-piece blade and tang that extends through the handle of plastic or wood, and usually have a steel cap. Thus, the force of the hammer blow is directed right through to the blade. These chisels are commonly used for heavy-duty chores that require a lot of pounding, for instance in cutting away wood flooring. Some heavy-duty floor chisels are all steel. Tang chisels and gouges have a V-pointed tang forced into a wooden or plastic handle. These chisels and gouges are designed for hand work only and should not be struck with a hammer or mallet.

In addition to different handles, chisels are available in several different blade styles. Some special-chore chisels include paring, firmer, butt, and mortise. A paring chisel is used without a hammer.

It is pushed with one hand and guided with the other to pare off thin shavings of wood. The blade is normally fairly short, thin, and ground on just one edge. Firmer chisels have long blades with cutting edges ground like a knife with both edges beveled. They are commonly used with a mallet or hammer for mortises and other similar work. Butt chisels are the most common and are general purpose tools with a short blade of about three to four inches long. They usually have a sturdy handle and are used with a hammer or mallet. The blade on mortise chisels is somewhat longer and they also have a heavy-duty handle for use with a hammer or mallet. Both butt and mortise chisels are also commonly called beveled-edge chisels because one edge of the blade has a bevel while the back edge is straight. This allows cutting a mortise or recess with straight sides. The sides of the chisel blade are also beveled, and this allows you to cut in dovetails or into undercut corners.

Chisels are available with two handle types: socket chisels have a blade that ends in a socket, which is fitted into a wood or plastic handle. A steel cap may also be added. These chisels can be used with a mallet or hammer. Steel shank end cap chisels can be used with hammer or mallet for heavy cutting chores.

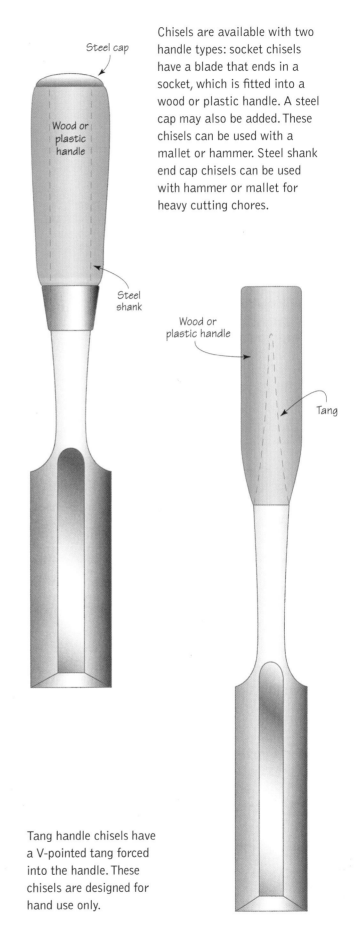

Steel cap

Wood or plastic handle

Steel shank

Wood or plastic handle

Tang

Tang handle chisels have a V-pointed tang forced into the handle. These chisels are designed for hand use only.

Specialty chisels include drawer lock chisels, which are shaped like an offset screwdriver and are used to cut in confined places, such as for drawer locks. Other specialty chisels include corner, slick, mill, and framing.

Chisels also come in different blade widths, but ¼", ½", ¾", 1" and 2" are the most common. A set of six different sizes will handle all your woodworking chores.

Uses

Before using chisels, check their condition. The chisel should have a sharp, properly ground cutting edge not only to do a better job, but also to accomplish the work safer and quicker. If doing heavy-duty work, safety goggles or glasses are suggested. Always make sure the workpiece is securely braced or clamped. Do not push or drive a chisel blade toward yourself, including your hand. Or, as in my early accident, push toward your head. When at all possible, cut with the grain. Cutting across the grain will cause splintering or rough cuts. Cutting with the grain creates a smoother finish cut. Also, don't cut directly down to the line with your first cuts. Make light, paring cuts to create a smooth cut and not go past the layout line.

Chisels and gouges can be used in two ways: one is by pushing with the heel of one hand while the tool is guided with the fingers of the opposite hand.

This method is used when only a small amount of material is to be removed and the finish cut must be smooth. A skilled craftsman can chamfer an edge or cut a shallow mortise that appears to be molded in place and there will be no need for sanding.

A second method of using chisels and gouges is with a hammer or mallet. Force is necessary when making vertical marking cuts for deep mortises and when removing large chunks of wood. Square or round tenons also require the use of a hammer or mallet. The flat edge of the chisel is held against the cut line, with the bevel on the waste

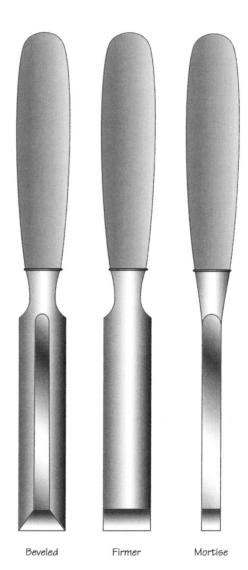

Chisels also have several different blade styles and come in different widths.

Beveled   Firmer   Mortise

Chisels are used in one of two methods, a hammer or mallet is used when making deep cuts for mortises and when removing large portions of wood.

side of the line. Keep turning the stock as you make the cuts, making sure the chisel is cutting in the right direction. Watch for grain run-outs. This occurs when you take too deep a cut and the cut follows the grain of the wood rather than your layout lines. Start any deep cuts with a saw or drill, and then finish with the chisel.

Where possible, cuts should be made with the grain of the wood. Cutting is easier and the finish will be smoother; generally the chisel will tend to ride up and out of the stock. When you cut against the grain, the finish will be rough and there is a tendency for the chisel to dig deeper. Against the grain, take shallower **bites** and more of them.

Two basic cuts are used for almost all chisel work, the **paring** and **chop** cuts. If cutting a recess, for instance for a door hinge, the first step is to mark the outline of the recess with a marking gauge. Then, using the widest chisel you have, or one that will reach the width of the hinge, use vertical chop cuts from the door edge down to the depth of the recess along and to the lines marked by the marking gauge. The back or straight edge of the chisel should be against the lines to create a straight, vertical cut. The second cut is a series of vertical chop cuts against the grain and down to the depth line. The third cut is from the side to remove the waste material between the chop cuts. The back, flat side of the chisel is held down against the side line of the recess. Finally the chisel is turned with the bevel side down and the bottom of the recess smoothed with paring cuts. The same tactic is used to cut a recess in the center of the stock or to pare down the edge of a board.

Some table and furniture legs have stopped chamfers on them, and these can also easily be cut with a sharp bevel chisel. The first step is to lay out the chamfer. Use a marking gauge to mark the edges of the cut of the chamfer on two sides of the stock.

Mark for the stopped end of the chamfer. With the chisel held at a 45° angle to the edge of the stock and with the flat side down, make the

When only a small amount of material is to be removed, or when creating a finish cut, chisels are used by the hands alone. Push the handle with the heel of the hand guiding the blade with the opposite hand.

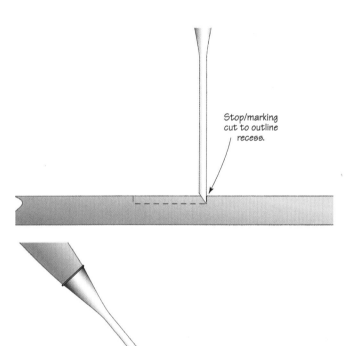

Stop/marking cut to outline recess.

Digs in if bevel is up.

A bevel chisel can be used with the bevel up or down depending on the cut. With the bevel up, the chisel digs deeper.

stopped cut. Then make chop cuts the length of the leg and down to the chamfer marks on both sides. Turn the chisel with the beveled side down, and remove the material between the vertical chop cuts. Again, use a paring cut to smooth the chamfer. A small block plane can also be used to make the final smoothing cuts on the chamfer.

Chisels can also be used to make mortise and tenon joints. Make the mortise first. Mark the outline of the mortise using a marking gauge, and then mark the centerline of the mortise. Use a drill to bore overlapping holes on the centerline with a bit the same diameter as the mortise width. This is best done with a drill press, but can also be done by hand. If boring by hand, bore two holes, one in each end of the mortise. Then remove all waste material between the holes and around the edges of the mortise with a chisel using chop cuts.

To create the tenon, score all outlines of the tenon with a marking gauge. Saw down to the scored lines on four sides at the back of the tenon with a miter or tenon saw. Then use a chisel to remove the outer waste pieces. Smooth up the tenon with paring cuts and try fitting the tenon as you go to achieve a secure, smooth fit.

Gouges

Gouges are chisels with curved or V-shaped edges. These are most commonly used for woodcarving and decorative furniture work. Gouges come in an almost infinite range of sizes and shapes. The curved blade chisels, called **sweeps,** graduate from almost flat to deep U-curves in a wide range of sizes. The smaller gouges are called **veiners,** while the larger ones with quick turns are called **fluters.** Gouges with a slight curve or almost flat curve are called **flats.** V-shaped gouges are called **parting** tools and, again, are available in a variety of angles and sizes. The angles are described as acute, medium, or obtuse. Gouges also come with different end

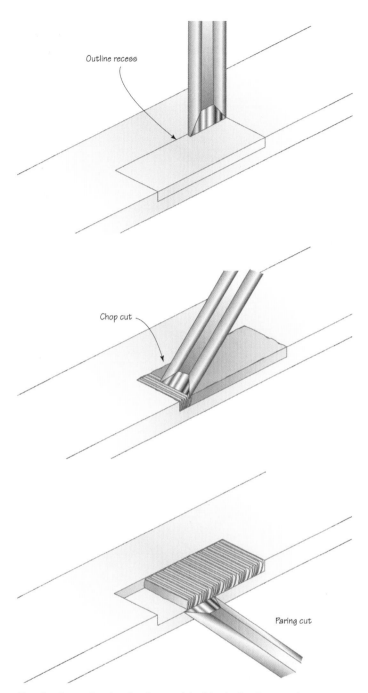

Two basic methods of using a chisel include chop and paring cuts.

shapes, either **skews** or **firmers**, either **oblique** or **square** on their ends. And the shanks may be **straight, offset,** or **fishtail** shaped. The latter allows you to work with greater clearance of the cutting edge. Handle shapes also vary. Gouges may be used with wood mallets or by hand, depending on the chore.

Gouges used for wood carving are handled in much the same manner as for chisels with some exceptions. In many instances, the carving will be a low relief. The first step is to transfer the design of the carving to the stock. Use a small veining gouge to outline the design, cutting on the outside or background side of the carving. Choose a gouge that comes the closest to fitting the design, and carefully follow the outline, tapping the chisel with a mallet. Watch the grain carefully as you make cuts. When cutting across or diagonally with the grain, it's easy to chip or break out sections of the design.

Maintenance

Chisel and gouge handles should be kept smooth and in good working shape. The blades should be kept well-oiled and rust free. The most important job is maintaining a sharp edge. In the case of a chipped or damaged blade, the first step is to grind the blade to the correct angle. Chisel blades should be ground flat and at the correct angle, or slightly hollow-ground. They should not be ground with a rounded cutting edge. Use a light touch on the grinding wheel and keep the blade moving so you don't allow the edge to overheat, which will soften the edge.

Once the chisel has been reshaped, hone it to razor sharpness. A number of tools and sharpening devices can be used with chisels to maintain the proper angle during sharpening, honing, and whetting.

Do not store chisels loosely in a drawer. They roll around, bang together, and the cutting edges become dull. Keep chisels and gouges handy and upright in a holder on the workbench.

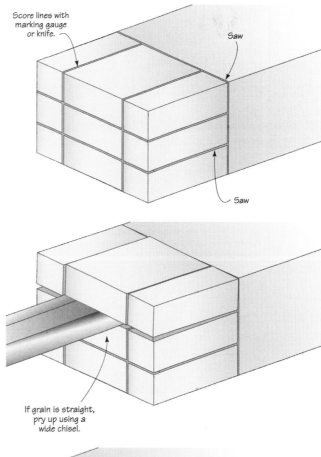

Score lines with marking gauge or knife.

Saw

Saw

If grain is straight, pry up using a wide chisel.

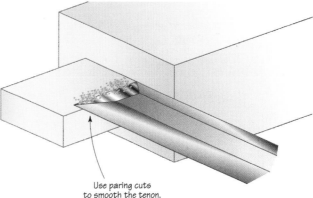

Use paring cuts to smooth the tenon.

Two basic methods of using a chisel include chop and paring cuts.

Gouges are basically chisels with curved or V-shaped edges.

Choose gouges with shapes to closely match the cuts, and be careful when cutting across or diagonally across the grain to prevent tear-outs.

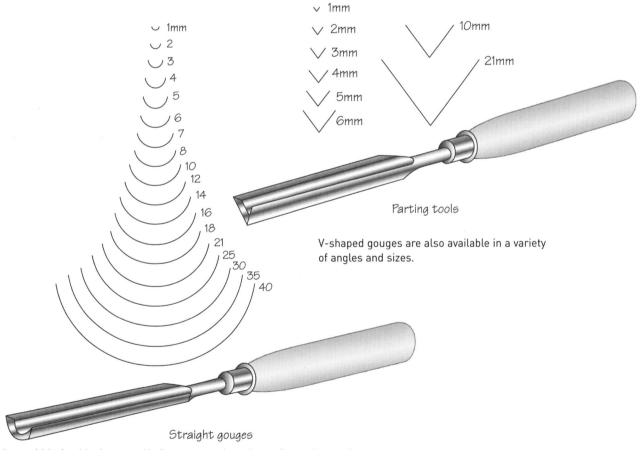

∪ 1mm
∪ 2
∪ 3
∪ 4
∪ 5
∪ 6
∪ 7
∪ 8
10
12
14
16
18
21
25
30
35
40

ⱽ 1mm
ⱽ 2mm
ⱽ 3mm
ⱽ 4mm
ⱽ 5mm
ⱽ 6mm
10mm
21mm

Parting tools

V-shaped gouges are also available in a variety of angles and sizes.

Straight gouges

Curved blade chisels are called sweeps and graduate from almost flat to deep U-curves in a wide range of sizes.

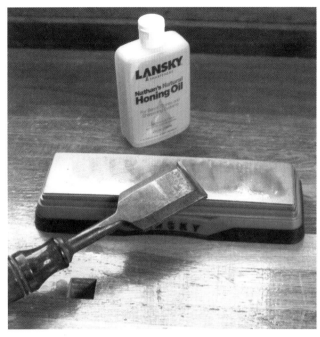

Keep cheisels sharp, regularly honing them between jobs.

Damaged blades can be ground on a grinding wheel, then honed using a tool, such as the Delta Sharpening Center.

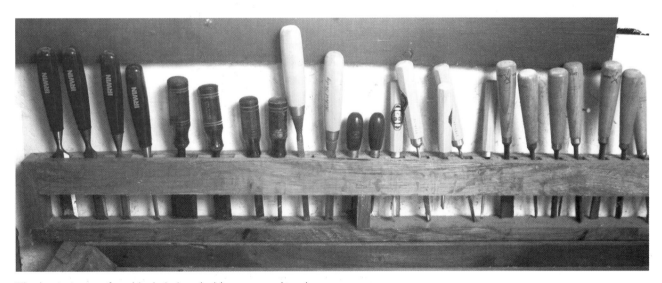

The best storage for chisels is in a holder on your bench.

HAND PLANES

Hand planes are the epitome of fine woodworking. Serious woodworkers use them; serious collectors collect them. I'm both. I began with some of my dad's old planes and enjoy looking for antique and unusual planes. But even the antique planes have to be in working order, because I like to use them as well as collect them. Planes come in a wide variety of sizes, styles, and for specific woodworking purposes. Planes are available made entirely of metal or made of wood with metal blades. Blades are available for the ultimate woodworkers to make their own planes, as the old-timers often did. Planes can range in price from about $25 for new, less expensive models to planes costing several hundred dollars.

Types of Hand Planes

The primary use of planes is for surfacing or smoothing wood surfaces. Wood can be smoothed with other means as well, including power planing, hand sanding, and the use of scrapers. But in the hands of an expert, hand planes will produce the smoothest finish. Planes consist of three basic parts; the blade or iron, as it's more correctly called; the body, either wood or cast iron. Beech is a popular material for wood bodies because it's extremely stable. The third basic part is a device to hold the blade in place. On wooden planes, this is a simple wedge; on metal planes, a lever cap. Both wood and metal planes have advantages and disadvantages. Wood planes slide more easily across the wood surface, but their sole, or bottom, sometimes isn't true.

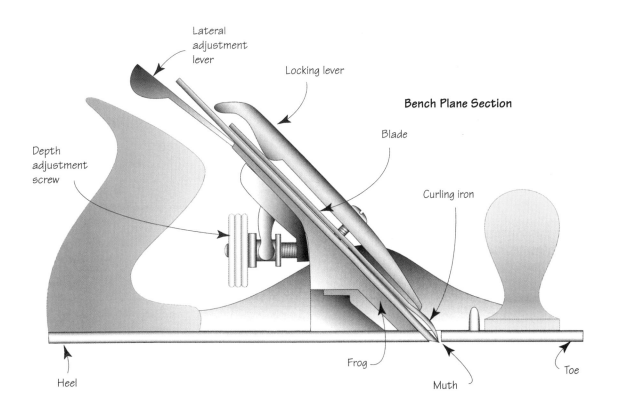

Bench Plane Section

Lateral adjustment lever

Locking lever

Blade

Curling iron

Depth adjustment screw

Frog

Muth

Toe

Heel

Metal planes have become more common these days, although quality wooden planes are still available and popular with many woodworkers. Metal bench planes consist of several parts: the body, consisting of the sole, which has a heel, toe, and mouth; rear and front handle (except for block planes); a depth of cut adjusting screw; lateral adjusting lever; cap and lever cap screw; frog and frog adjusting screw; and blade and curling iron, also sometimes called a plane-iron cap. Metal or adjustable wooden planes may appear complicated, but they're actually fairly simple to adjust and operate.

Although there are several styles, the four basic bench planes include: block plane, jack plane, smoothing plane, and fore plane. This is primarily based on the length of the sole, although each of the types may have a variety of sole lengths.

Other names may be used for some of the styles. Try planes, jointer, and bench planes are names used interchangeably.

One old-fashioned plane, the roughing or **scrub** plane, is no longer found.

This plane featured heavy-duty rounded corner blades and was used primarily for cleaning and truing rough lumber.

Planes may be **high** or **low** angle. This is determined by the angle the blade sits in relation to the sole. Low-angle planes are good for working end grain, across the grain, or gnarly, highly figured wood.

High-angle planes are the most common and cut faster, but can be difficult to use on figured wood.

Block planes are fairly small, usually around 6" in length. They are designed to be used with one hand and quite often used for end-grain work, cutting chamfers on edges and working other **small** areas. A block plane does not produce as smooth a surface on larger stock. A bull-nose block plane has the blade positioned right at the front edge and can be used for smoothing in tight places or up against another surface.

Jack planes are the most common and normally run from 14 to 16" in length.

Although there are a variety of styles, four basic planes include (from left to right) the fore plane, jack plane, smoothing plane, and block plane.

Block planes, such as this E.C.E. Primus Plane, are small and used with one hand for end-grain work, beveling edges, and other small chores.

Block planes can also be used to create chamfers on edges.

The Woodcraft Supply bull-nose block plane allows you to get into tight corners and cut right to the edge.

Fore or trying planes are the longest. They can be used for leveling of stock or jointing edges to be joined.
The plane shown is an antique plane from the author's collection.

Smoothing planes, such as the E.C.E. Primus plane shown, can provide the ultimate in smoothing a wood surface, even surpassing sandpaper. The quality plane shown is very easy to adjust and use.

Kind of a jack-of-all-trades, jack planes can be used for almost any purpose, making them a good all-around choice for the single-plane owner. The longest planes are the fore plane or trying plane. These run from 18" to 24" long and are also sometimes called **jointer** planes. As you can guess, one of the main uses is for planing the edges of stock for edge jointing. With their long soles, they can take the place of a powered jointer. The long soles also make them good for rough-shaping, dimensioning, or leveling stock.

Smoothing planes are also sometimes called **bench** planes. Smoothing planes range from 9" to 10" in length and their primary use is to provide a final smooth surface. Smoothing planes can provide a smoother surface than sanding.

Block planes are commonly used for squaring the edges of stock. By clamping a couple of boards on either side of the edge, you can create a wider surface to hold the plane level. Another trick is to tap the edge of a try square down on the wood edge with a soft mallet. This reveals any areas out of square and provides a method of marking a right-angled edge.

If planing end grain, a small scrap block clamped to the edge can prevent splitting out the end. Block planes are also the choice for cutting chamfers on wood edges. Use a try square to mark a line to plane to on the adjoining surfaces.

A variety of planes are also available for doing specific wood shaping chores. The antique rabbet plane shown is also from the author's collection. It was obviously a well-loved tool and is used for cutting a rabbet on the edge of stock.

A modern version of the rabbit plane is adjustable.

Shaping or Specialty Planes

A number of specialty planes are also available for shaping wood. One of the traditional old-time planes is the Stanley molding plane. It has blades of different shapes that are inserted and used to create moldings on edges. Although they are no longer being made, the old Stanley planes are still around but are rare and the cost is high. Single-blade molding planes are fairly common in flea markets and they can still be used to hand cut moldings. Regardless of separate blades or a fixed blade, molding planes are actually the reverse of the shape you desire to cut. They consist of rounding (convex) and hollowing (concave) as per the shape of their soles, not the finished shape to be cut. Grooving planes include the various routers, such as an inletting plane for routing hinge recesses; both wooden and metal router planes for routing of all types; and round or gutter planes for hollowing concave moldings. The combination plane can be used for plowing, rabbeting, grooving, molding beeds, ogees, reeds, hollow, and rounds. It often comes with twenty-four various sizes and shapes.

Flea market planes will probably require sharpening or even reshaping the blades, but the blades are usually simply held in place with a wedge. Molding planes should be used with light cuts, progressively deepening the cut as you go until you reach the full profile.

A router plane has a footed blade that allows it to be used to rout grooves or dadoes. Router planes are available with wooden or metal bodies. These planes are somewhat difficult to work unless the blade is kept absolutely sharp and only light cuts are made, lowering the blade as you go. On wooden-bodied planes, the blade is tapped downward; on metal planes, a screw adjustment is available. (It's also a good idea to outline the area to be routed and then use a chisel to further deepen the area.) The rabbet or shoulder plane is used to cut rabbets or shoulders.

The plough plane, also from the author's collection, can be used to cut rabbets, grooves and matching tongue, and groove joints.

The Woodcraft Supply rounding plane is used to cut a rounded edge on a stock. A good example is a table edge.

A hollowing plane, such as that shown from Woodcraft Supply, does just the opposite, cutting a concave or hollowed surface.

A chamfer plane has an L-shape with a blade centered to cut chamfers on edges. A newer version is the Slickplane. It has two carbide-tipped blades and can put a $\frac{1}{16}$" radius on sharp corners faster than a router. It comes with either a radius or chamfer blade from Grizzly. Hollow and rounding planes are used to cut either concave or convex surfaces. A circular plane has a flexible steel sole and is used for planing concave surfaces, such as chair bottoms.

A molding plane, such as this antique, was once used to create molding and millwork, edge tables, and so forth.

Adjusting and Tuning Planes

Planes have a number of controls, depending on their construction and style. Many wooden planes have only a wooden wedge to hold the blade in place, and the blade angle is not changeable. The blade is positioned for the depth of cut and the wedge tapped in place to hold the blade. Metal planes, and some wooden-body planes, have a turn screw for adjusting the depth of cut. The amount of wood to be removed with each stroke is important. A blade set to cut too deep may take off a lot of wood, but also takes a lot of force. Set it too shallow and little material is removed, requiring more strokes. Most metal planes also have a curling iron, sometimes called an iron cap, and are held together by a screw. The curling iron not only adds stiffness to the blade, but also causes the shavings to curl up and out, rather than clogging the mouth. Position the curling iron so it leaves about $\frac{1}{16}$ of an inch or less of the blade exposed, and then fasten the blade and iron together. Position the blade and iron assembly in the plane body against the frog, making sure the cap is snug enough to hold the adjustments but allows for easy adjustments. Turn the adjustment screw just enough to make the cutting edge project from the mouth of the base.

If the edge projects too much, the iron is hard to work; too little and you won't get an even shaving. One method of adjusting for depth is to place a

Properly adjusting a plane is very important.

The blade, or iron, should be set to the proper depth. In most instances, this is done by turning the depth adjustment screw.

piece of thin cardboard or stiff paper on a flat, smooth surface. Place the plane on the cardboard and adjust the plane blade so it barely touches the smooth surface. This will cut a shaving approximately the thickness of the paper. Once the depth has been adjusted, use the lever cap to make sure the blade is locked square in the housing. The blade must be absolutely parallel with the front edge of the mouth. In most instances, the plane will be set at the factory for general purpose work. You can, however, adjust the front to widen the mouth for coarse cutting or tighten the mouth for finer work.

Set the blade parallel with the front edge of the mouth by using the lever and lever cap.

Planes with a curling iron should have the blade protruding about 1/i6" past the curling iron

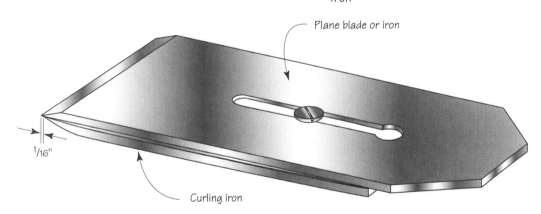

Plane blade or iron

1/16"

Curling iron

Setting a blade in a wooden scrub plane

The blade must also be absolutely parallel with the front edge of the mouth.

Incorrect - too high

Correct

Planing Techniques

If at all possible, always plane with the grain of the wood or with the grain slanting in the direction of the stroke. Make a fine test cut, and if the plane digs in and is set to the correct depth, you are planing against the grain. Make your first few strokes at an angle across the wood surface. This creates a **shearing** cut and is much faster and easier to do than a cut made parallel to the wood surface. After roughing or leveling, make your final cuts parallel to the direction of the grain.

Begin your stroke with the blade off the end of the surface and downward pressure applied to the front knob or handle. Once the entire plane is situated on the work, apply equal pressure to back and front handles or knobs. As the plane reaches off the opposite end, apply more pressure to the back handle. This prevents an arched edge caused by the plane rocking up at the beginning and down on the end of the stroke.

When planing end grain, hold the plane at an angle to provide a shear cut.

To smooth a wide board, begin with the scrub or jack plane and dimension the board to suit. A pair of winding sticks can be used to check for any high or low spots. These are simply straight sticks that are placed on the surface. With a back light behind them, it's easy to see any problems. After dimensioning the surface, use the smoothing plane to create the final glass-smooth surface. When planing an edge, a shooting board on the bench can make the chore easier and more precise.

When using specialty planes, such as molding fillister planes, make shallow cuts until you reach the full-depth cut.

First cuts should be made at a slight angle across the wood surface. Note the chalk marks. This allows you to see what has been planed.

Begin the stroke with the blade off the end of the surface, and apply downward pressure to the front knob or handle as you make the planing stroke. Then apply more pressure to the back handle as you complete the stroke.

When planing end grain, hold the plane at a slight angle to create a shear cut.

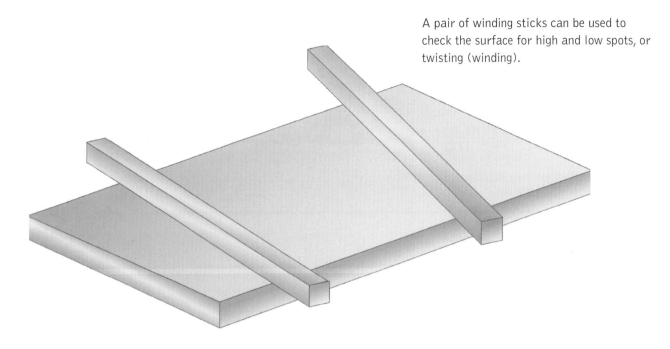

A pair of winding sticks can be used to check the surface for high and low spots, or twisting (winding).

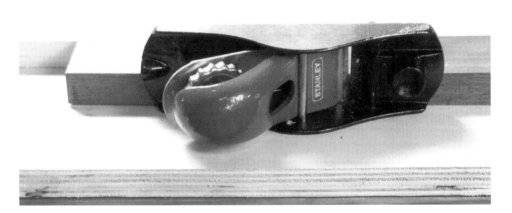

A shooting board can be used to hold stock for edge planing.

When using specialty planes, take light, shallow cuts, progressing deeper until you reach full depth.

Maintaining and Sharpening

Maintain your planes in good shape by applying an occasional coat of light oil to the bed and adjustments. Use steel wool if necessary to keep the bottom and the bed rust-free. A bit of linseed oil can be used to keep old-time wooden planes in good shape. Always carefully inspect the workpiece to make sure there are no embedded nails or screws, gravel, or grit. When you are through using or when storing planes, lay them on their sides to protect the blades. After you complete a plane stroke, lift it from the work surface to carry it back to the next starting place.

Make sure you keep the blade sharp and the edge ground at the correct angle. Unless the blade has been badly mistreated, honing is usually all that's needed. But first, you must remove the iron or blade. On wooden planes with the blade held with a wedge, removal of the plane iron is easy. Merely remove the wooden holding wedge, and then pull out the iron. To remove a plane iron from a metal plane, first lift the locking lever. (See the drawing on page 53.) Next, lift out the plane iron and cap. They are connected by a cap screw, which can be removed using a large screwdriver or, with some planes, the end of the lever cap.

A blade can be hand-honed using a good bench stone. Woodcraft Supply has a chisel and plane blade-sharpening guide that helps to maintain a consistent angle. Stanley also has an excellent plane-honing guide.

If the blade is damaged and has deep nicks, you will first have to grind it back into shape. Plane irons, depending on the type, are ground to an angle between 20° and 40°. Planes specifically for use with softwoods can be ground to 20°. A general-purpose iron for use with both hardwoods and softwoods should have a bevel of 25°, or a bevel width of about 2½ times the thickness the blade. However, this bevel will not plane without

The Delta Sharpening Center has a dry wheel for grinding and reshaping blades, and a wet wheel for honing.

chattering on difficult or gnarly hardwoods. For hardwood use exclusively, the bevel should be at 30° or just under twice the thickness of the blade. An angle of 35° is often ground on scrub and molding plane irons. Heavy-duty scrub planes will have the edge ground from 40° to 45° to provide adequate back clearance.

It's important to keep a flat bevel. A concave bevel, such as is often caused by grinding on a round wheel, creates a weak edge. A rounded bevel on the other hand, prevents the edge from biting in properly. Also, the edge of the blade may be ground in different shapes, depending on the use of the plane. A jack plane typically has a rounded extension of about $\frac{1}{64}$" and a scrub plane a rounded extension of about $\frac{3}{16}$", rounding back to the corners. A smoothing or try plane may have straight or curved corners.

If you must use a grinding wheel to reshape the edge, use a grinding wheel with an angle rest, and keep the metal moving, grinding just a little at a time to prevent overheating or bluing the edge and drawing the temper. When the blade has been properly ground, turn the blade over to remove the slight **burr** left on the back. Once the edge has been ground, it will have to be honed again.

The Delta Sharpening Center is the perfect tool for sharpening both chisels and plane blades. It can also be used with an accessory to sharpen power planer blades. The tool has a dry wheel with an angle guide that can be used to grind the edge on the plane blades. This makes it much easier to achieve a more precise angle than hand holding to a grinding wheel. To use the dry wheel with the tool and chisel holder, first remove the dry wheel tool rest and eye shield. Rotate the wheel guard to the rear and tighten the holding screw. Remove the tool rest and mounting post from the wet-wheel side of the machine and insert into the tool rest assembly in the dry side. Adjust the tool holder to the proper angle.

After the blade has been ground, the wet hone on top is then used to hone the blades. The wet hone has a water reservoir that keeps a steady supply of water applied to the hone. Again, the tool rest keeps the blade at the correct angle for honing.

Specialty plane blades require a bit more work. These will usually have to be ground and honed using different techniques to match the blade profile. A Dremel tool and appropriate grinding bits and wheels can often be used for curved shaped blades, such as molding planes.

Make sure you keep plane blades sharp. They can be honed by hand using the Stanley honing stone and guide.

Other Surfacing Tools

Other related tools I've used include a draw knife, a spokeshave, and inshave. The drawknife can be used for rounding and shaping and, as its name suggests, it is drawn rather than pushed across the surface. It is an excellent tool for rough carving the edges of stock that is to be turned on a lathe. A spokeshave is also valuable. Its blade is adjustable and can be used for planing curved edges, either pushed or pulled. As its name implies, in the old days it was used for shaping wooden spokes for wheels. The inshave looks like a drawknife but has a curved blade. It is used for such chores as sculpting chair seats or scooping out bowls.

Another type of surfacing tool is a **scratch-stock**. This is a shop-made tool that allows you to duplicate beads and other shapes. The edge of a metal blank is shaped using files or a hand grinder with the cutter held between two wooden pieces with bolts and nuts. To use, position the fence portion of the wooden holder against the side of the stock, adjust the cutter, and tighten the bolts. Pull the tool along in a series of light strokes to **scratch** the shape.

A set of cabinet scrapers can also be invaluable for the serious woodworker, furniture maker, or cabinetmaker. These thin metal blades are pulled across the surface. If properly sharpened, they produce a finer, smoother finish than sanding because the wood fibers are shaved off rather than abraded. To sharpen, file the edge square, then burnish a hook angle on one surface of the edge.

A drawknife is another surfacing tool that can be valuable to furniture makers and woodworkers.

A spokeshave or inshave are other wood surfacing tools that may find their way into your shop.

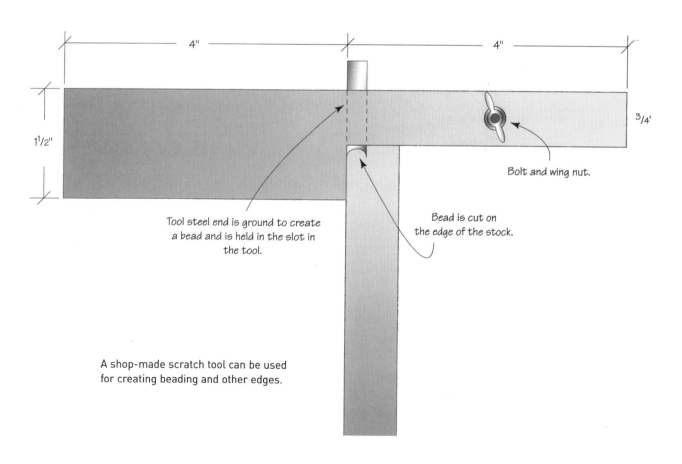

4"

4"

1¹/₂"

³/₄'

Bolt and wing nut.

Tool steel end is ground to create
a bead and is held in the slot in
the tool.

Bead is cut on
the edge of the stock.

A shop-made scratch tool can be used
for creating beading and other edges.

OTHER HAND TOOLS

In addition to the tools previously mentioned, a number of other hand tools are also necessary. In some cases of purists woodworkers, these tools may be preferred over power tools. These include: drills and bits, rasps and files, clamps, pliers, and screwdrivers.

Drills and Bits

The creation of cordless drills has allowed drilling holes anywhere you desire without the necessity of a cord. In days past, however, large holes were bored with a brace and bit. Small holes were bored with a hand drill or push drill. A brace with auger bits can still be valuable for those out-of-the-way chores, such as hanging a gate in the back forty. A quality brace and set of auger bits, or a hand drill with a good set of twist bits, will last a lifetime. A brace with an expansive bit will allow you to drill holes up to five inches in diameter in wood. I've used a brace and bit, as well as a hand auger, for working with post and beam construction. Buy a quality brace with a reversible ratchet above the chuck. This lets you back out a stuck bit or bore a hole in a restricted location, using a partial twist each way. Buy good bits or drills, take care of the tools, and they'll be ready whenever you

In days past, holes were bored with hand drills, and a brace with bits is still a good toolbox tool to have on hand.

OTHER HAND TOOLS

Auger bits are available in a variety of diameters and lengths.

Twist   Auger

In addition to auger bits, twist drill bits are used in hand and breast drills.

need them. Hand-drilling bits include auger, expansive, forstner, and spur, along with fluted bits for use with push drills. Auger bits have a square shank and a screw point that pulls the bit into the wood as you turn it.

To use a brace and bit, fit the square shank of the bit into the brace and turn the chuck to tighten and hold the bit in place. Hold the bit perpendicular to the workpiece or at the angle you desire and slowly turn the handle, holding the rotating palm handle in your opposite hand. On thick wood, you will occasionally need to turn the bit back out to clear away the chips. To use an expansive bit, loosen the set screw, move the adjustable blade to one-half the diameter of the hole to be bored, and reset the screw.

My first tool set was a Stanley tool box with a number of tools, including a hand drill. Hand drills have a handle, or in days past, a flat U-handle top. The latter is called a **breast** drill because it is positioned against the breast to create pressure for boring. Twist drill bits are commonly used with a hand drill and it can be used to bore holes in wood or metal.

A push drill is handy for drilling small holes, such as for starting screws or nails, hanging picture frames, and other chores. These tools utilize small bits with straight flutes cut in them. A variety of bits are stored inside the handle. To use, simply push and then let up. As you push, the drill bit turns one direction, when you let up it turns back the opposite.

Files and Rasps

Both files and rasps have their place in the wood shop. The file is one of the oldest tools known to history.

One biblical reference to files is, "They had a file for the mattocks, and for the coulters and for the axes and to sharpen the goads."(1 Samuel XIII: 21). Today there are literally thousands of different files and file cuts. There is practically a file for any job from filing metal on car bodies, cleaning spark plugs, sharpening saw blades, or shaping wood. Files, however, are standardized by three things: their length, their kind or name, and their cut.

The length of a file is always measured between its heel (part of the file where the tang begins) and the point or end opposite. The name denotes whether it is a flat, mill, half-round, chainsaw, crosscut, machinist, Swiss pattern maker's, or rasp. The cut of the file is determined by the coarseness or character of its teeth. The teeth could be single cut, double cut, rasp cut, coarse, bastard, or smooth cut. To get the most out of a file, you should use the right one for a particular job.

A mill file is used for sharpening saw blades, lawn-mower blades, and in general smoothing and finishing metal. Configurations include: crosscut, chainsaw, triangular, and so forth. Machinist's files are double cut and used for almost any kind of metal work. Their finish is rougher than a mill file and they cut faster. Machinist's files come in many sizes and shapes.

Files can be used for such chores as smoothing plastic laminate edges.

Wood rasps are important wood shaping tools that can be used for smoothing or roughing out carvings.

Swiss pattern files are delicately shaped and used in precision work by jewelers, model makers, and gunsmiths. Curved-tooth files are specialty files used almost exclusively by the auto body repair field. Wood rasps are extremely important tools for cabinetmakers, boat builders, furniture builders, and wood sculptors. They remove material fast, but require a follow up with finishing files or sandpaper.

Files should be cleaned occasionally using a good file brush. If not cleaned between uses, particles from the last job may scratch a soft surface.

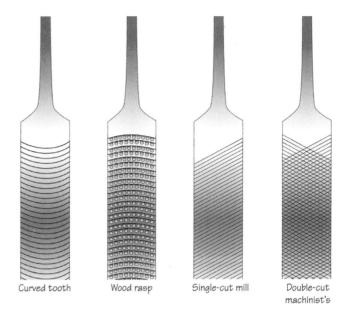

Curved tooth   Wood rasp   Single-cut mill   Double-cut machinist's

Clamps

Clamps are a very important part of the woodworker's tool collection. Almost all wood joints require glue and clamps are required to hold the parts together until the glue sets. I've been collecting clamps for years, and yet it still seems I don't have enough for my clamping chores. Clamps are available in a number of different styles, each designed for specific gluing problems. The five basic woodworkers clamps include: C-clamps (also called a carriagemaker's clamps); spring clamps; hand clamps (wood screws); bar or pipe clamps; and web or band clamps. Other types with more specialty uses include: miter clamp, veneer press, and workbench hold-downs. You can also make up some specialty clamps in your shop for specific chores. In most instances it's a good idea to buy clamps in pairs. You will almost always need two clamps of similar style or size for most clamping chores. Buy quality clamps, adding them to your collection as you need them.

Clamps are a necessary tool for any woodworking shop, and a variety of clamps are often needed.

C-Clamps

As the name suggests, C-clamps have a c-shaped body with a bolt through the base. C-clamps are available in a wide range of sizes and they will do a wide variety of clamping chores. Use scrap wood as jaw pads since the small clamp pads can mar wood quite easily. Several different styles of C-clamps are available, including wide-jaw, deep-throat, and so forth. Another similar type of clamp is the edge clamp. It is shaped similar to a C-clamp but has three screws. The edge clamp is used for such jobs as clamping trim or edging to the edge of a table or counter top.

Hand Wood Screw Clamps

Hand wood screw clamps are the classics of woodworking. They consist of two blocks of wood connected by two parallel bolts. The jaws should be parallel to the workpieces being clamped, although the clamps can also be used at an angle for oddly shaped clamping projects. The simplest way to operate the clamp is to grasp both handles and flip the clamp over. This method keeps the jaws parallel, which is important in clamping two flat surfaces together. The ability to close the jaws at angles, however, is also an advantage of this type of clamp as you can clamp tapered or irregularly shaped objects by adjusting the clamps to fit the shape. Occasionally wipe the wood with linseed oil and use a spray lubricant on the metal screws to assure they are easy working.

Bar or Pipe Clamps

Bar clamps are available in several different styles and lots of sizes. One end is fixed; the other clamping pad is movable on the bar. Some bar clamps utilize a solid steel bar, while others have machined aluminum bars. The latter are lighter in weight and easier to handle, but the sliding pad must fit into notches in the bar, and this makes them somewhat more difficult to align. Pipe clamps have clamp fixtures you simply attach to a section of plumbing pipe. One end of the pipe must be threaded. Pipe clamps are economical and you can make them up in any length needed, even extra long clamps. Rockier also has a pipe extender that allows you to fasten two shorter clamps into one long clamp. These days, a number of one-handed bar clamps are available. The Irwin Quick-Gri-XP one-handed bar clamp is a good example. A lever allows for instant opening of the clamp with one hand. Squeezing the handle tightens the clamp. When

Hand wood screw clamps are a workshop tradition. They can be used to clamp even or oddly shaped workpieces.

Bar or pipe clamps are commonly used to glue narrow stock together to create wider stock.

One-handed grip clamps are quick and easy to use.

clamping up wide stock, it's a good idea to use two clamps on top and two on the bottom. On sections over 4 or 5 feet long, use three clamps on each side. When tightening the clamps, make sure the feet of the clamps rest on a solid, smooth surface and that the wood sections are down solid against the clamp bars in all places to avoid warping or twisting. A deep-bar clamp combines the best of both the C-clamp and bar clamp. It will reach places the bar clamp won't.

Spring clamps are small, lightweight tools used for lightweight clamping tasks. They are operated simply by squeezing the handles. Buy several different size pairs. You'll find them extremely handy and versatile.

Band or web clamps are great for those jobs that require pressure around an object, such as a drum table, hexagonal flower box, irregular chair legs, and others. Band clamps consist of a long nylon strap pulled through a metal clamp that has a screw for tightening. When you use band clamps, be careful not to get glue on them, or they will be hard to pull free and the dried glue may scratch later jobs.

One special type of clamp is the picture-frame clamp. Two styles are available, one a 45° platform that holds one corner of the frame. It can be fastened to your workbench and used for gluing frames while driving brads. The other type has four 90° corner braces threaded on a steel cable. The frame is

positioned on a worktable and the braces placed at each corner of the frame. When the cable is drawn up, all four corners are held in place.

When you need to clamp something to the top of your workbench, use a bench hold-down clamp. This device slips over the head of a **drop-down** bolt in the benchtop.

When using any kind of clamp, place leather or hardwood pads between the clamp and the wood surface. Always wipe up excess glue right away and go slow with the clamping to avoid breaking or cracking the pieces to be joined. Clamps exert tremendous pressure, so apply only enough to get the job done. Check squareness and alignment as you draw up the clamps.

Clamps are quality tools that will last a lifetime if taken care of. Wipe them with a good rust preventive oil and remove any glue after each job.

Pliers

Pliers are basic tools that have unlimited uses. Many are designed to perform one specific function. These tools range in size from tiny electronics pliers no larger than tweezers to heavy-duty types that weigh more than a pound. Slip-joint pliers are the most common type. They adjust to two different openings by sliding the handles in the slot. The purpose of the slot is to retain leverage when changing from large to small objects. Another type

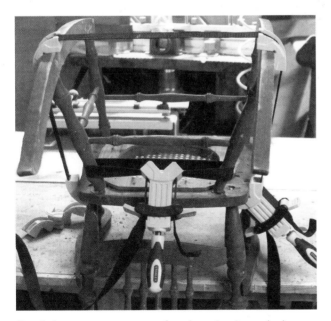

Band clamps are necessary for clamping irregularly shaped projects, such as chairs, stools, and so forth.

A benchtop hold-down is another important clamp that can be used to hold stock for carving and other chores.

of slip-joint pliers is the arc-joint. The jaws are serrated and the handles quite long for extra leverage. One type, called water-pump pliers, has smooth jaws. The jaws can be adjusted to several different openings and are positioned so they remain almost parallel at all times. These pliers are commonly used around the house for turning pipe and installing sink traps and fittings.

Lineman's pliers are an all-purpose electrician's tool. They have cutting edges on the side and a serrated nose for grasping and twisting wires. The grips are vinyl- or rubber-coated for safety.

Stripping pliers are used primarily for stripping insulation from electrical wires. They have cutters for wires sizes 12 to 24 gauge. Most also have side cutters and a serrated nose for gripping wire.

Cutting pliers come in many sizes, but in two main types. One type is diagonal and is used for cutting wire, light sheet metal, and so forth. End cutters, which are usually larger and stronger, are used to cut nails, heavy wire, and even small bolts. They are designed to cut flush to the surface and are sometimes called nippers.

Long-nose pliers also come in different shapes. One type, called chain pliers, has side cutters and serrated

jaws. Needlenose pliers usually don't have the cutter and the jaws are sometimes smooth or serrated only at the end. One special shape is the **bent nose** pliers. These are usually bent at 90°, although other shapes may be employed for special uses.

Lock-grip pliers can be squeezed shut on an object and locked in place. The jaws are deeply serrated for a tight grip and most models have a tripping lever, as well as a screw adjustment for depth.

Store pliers in a rack and keep them clean and well-oiled. Make sure the handles on electrical pliers aren't nicked or cut. If they are, dip the handles in a rubber solution to recoat them.

Screwdrivers

You will also need an assortment of screwdrivers, although many driving chores these days are done with drill/drivers or impact drivers. Long-handled, short-handled, flat blade, and Phillips drivers are all necessary. Keep screwdrivers in several sizes and match the head size to the chore. A head that is too small or too large can damage the screw slot or slots.

A variety of pliers is necessary.

As is a variety of screwdrivers.

A tool belt provides a means of holding and carrying tools at the job site.

Tool Belt

If you're working on a job site, a tool belt can be helpful for organizing and carrying tools. A wide variety of sizes and types are available. Make sure you get a belt that fits you and holds and organizes the specific tools you'll be using.

Build and Fill a Carpenter's Box

In days past, most carpentry and trim or finish work was done with hand tools, and carpenters carried their tools to the site in a handmade wooden box. My dad, a finish carpenter who specialized in trim work and cabinetry, had several boxes with a variety of tools, one box for his planes alone. These days, a great deal of carpentry and trim work is done with power tools, but a toolbox of selected hand tools is still invaluable. A toolbox also makes a great organized place to safely store your tools in the shop, as well as tote them to the job. The box shown is a compilation of several boxes I've built, some from teaching 4-H woodworking, as well as some ideas from a few of dad's boxes. The box

shown is made of white pine to keep the weight down. If it's to be a workshop box, you might prefer to make it of a finer hardwood. The box shown is also fairly simple to build, but you could use hand-cut dovetail joints and other construction as a showcase for your work. The box is sized to hold a framing or carpenter's square, as well as a two-foot level and a variety of tools.

The first step in construction is to enlarge the squared drawing and create a pattern for the ends. Using a saber saw or band saw, cut the ends to shape. Note the sides are notched into the ends. Sand the cut edges smooth. Cut the top divider piece to width and length. Note it is ³⁄₁₆" less the width of the end pieces. Fasten it in place between the two ends with screws or finish nails. The divider fits flush with the front of the toolbox, leaving an open space in the back to allow for a framing square to slide down into. Cut the bottom and fasten in place with screws or finish nails. Then cut the back piece and fasten it in place. Cut the upper front piece and fasten in place. The top divider piece has holding strips for several tools. This includes a strip fastened to the back edge, then a second strip set slightly over the thickness of a level to hold a two-foot level. An Irwin Dovetail/Jamb saw is held in place in the front

In days past, tradesmen carried their tools to the job site in handmade wooden boxes. A carpenter's toolbox is still a great way of toting a number of tools. The box shown holds a variety of hand tools, plus a small cordless drill/driver.

with a holding strip. This little saw is great for trimming jambs and other tight places. Install a pair of 1½" x 1½" blocks between the last holding strip for the level, and the inside edge of the jamb saw support strip. These have slots cut in their top edges to hold a pair of hand saws upright. The handle is a piece of 1x1, ripped from a 2x4 with its edges rounded with a router. Install with glue and screws through each end into the handle ends.

Bore holes in the back top edge to hold screwdrivers, nail sets, punches, and other tools. Additional tool holders are built into the ends of the box. One end has a ¾" piece with holes bored in it to hold paddle bits and pencils. The opposite end has a chisel holder for wood chisels. This is constructed of ½" thick materials. Cut the front piece and lay it on a work table and then cut ½" x ½" spacers to go between the chisels. Position the chisels in place and glue the spacers to the back side of the front board and between the chisels with hot-melt glue. Add a ½" bottom to the holder, then fasten the holder to the toolbox end with screws or finish nails. Spaces between the saws and level holding strip can hold a number of other tools, including

measuring tools, a stud finder, and so forth.

The drawer front overlaps the end tool holders and the toolbox bottom. Cut the ¾" drawer front to size, but it has a dado to hold the bottom, so ¾" x ¾" end blocks are fastened to the ends to conceal the dado. Cut the ½" drawer side pieces to size. The drawer bottom is cut from ¼" hardboard and held in place in the front and sides with dadoes. These are cut using a tablesaw with the blade set ¼" high. Make a cut, move the fence slightly, make another cut, and continue moving and cutting until you have a dado slightly over ¼" wide.

Fasten the sides to the front with glue and finish nails. Cut the back and fasten between the sides with glue and finish nails. Install the bottom in the dadoes. Use a carpenter's square to make sure the drawer is square, and then fasten the bottom down on the bottom edges of the back with small flat-head nails. The drawer is held in place with a pair of wooden turn buttons. Set the finish nails below the wood surface; fill with wood putty and sand smooth. Finish the toolbox as desired. I left mine unfinished to age naturally. Now comes the fun of filling your new carpenter's box.

A drawer in the bottom of the box holds a small plastic divided box with nails, wood putty and additional tools. The top divider has holding strips for a level and saws, as well as a slot in the back to hold a carpenter's square.

inches (millimeters)

REFERENCE	QUANTITY	PART	STOCK	THICKNESS	[mm]	WIDTH	[mm]	LENGTH	[mm]
A	2	ends	pine	¾	[19]	10	[254]	14½	[368]
B	1	top divider	pine	¾	[19]	8⁵⁄₁₆	[211]	24¼	[616]
C	1	bottom	pine	¾	[19]	8½	[216]	24¼	[616]
D	1	back	pine	¾	[19]	7½	[191]	25¾	[654]
E	1	front	pine	¾	[19]	3	[76]	25¾	[654]
F	1	handle	pine	1	[25]	1	[25]	24¼	[616]
G	1	paddle-bit holder	pine	¾	[19]	4	[102]	9¼	[235]
H	1	chisel holder front	pine	½	[13]	4	[102]	9¼	[235]
I	5	chisel holder dividers	pine	½	[13]	½	[13]	4	[102]
J	1	chisel holder end block	pine	½	[13]	2	[51]	4	[102]
K	1	drawer front	pine	¾	[19]	4½	[114]	26	[660]
L	2	drawer front end blocks	pine	¾	[19]	¾	[19]	4½	[114]
M	2	drawer sides	pine	½	[13]	3½	[89]	7¾	[197]
N	1	drawer back	pine	½	[13]	3½	[89]	22⅞	[581]
O	1	drawer bottom	hardboard	¼	[19]	3¾	[95]	23⅜	[594]
P	2	drawer turn bottons	pine	½	[13]	½	[13]	3	[76]

TOOLS TO TOTE

carpenter's or framing square

try square

sliding T-bevel

2 hammers (12- and 16-ounce)

nail set

2 handsaws

pull saw

coping saw

two-foot level

tape measure

folding rule

2 planes (block and bench)

chisels

utility knife

pliers

screwdrivers

stud finder

drill bits

cordless drill/driver with bits and driver assortment

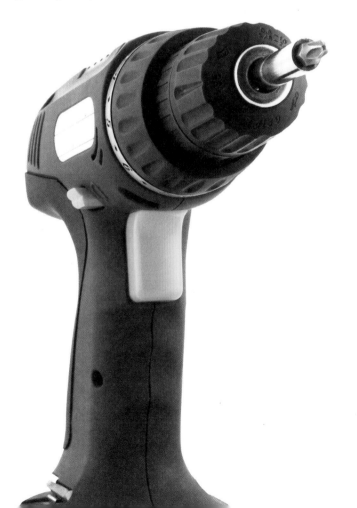

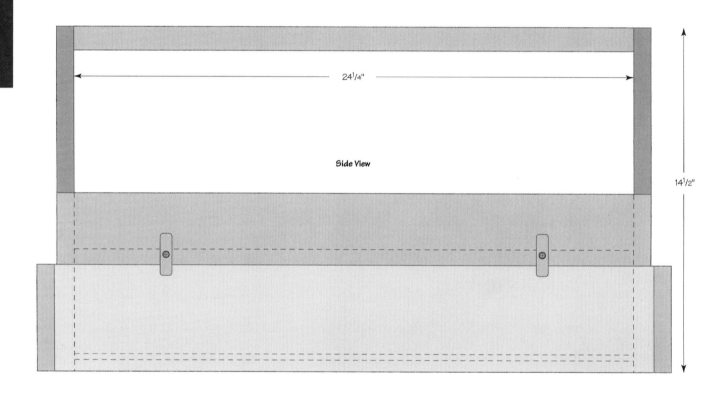

24^1/4"

Side View

14^1/2"

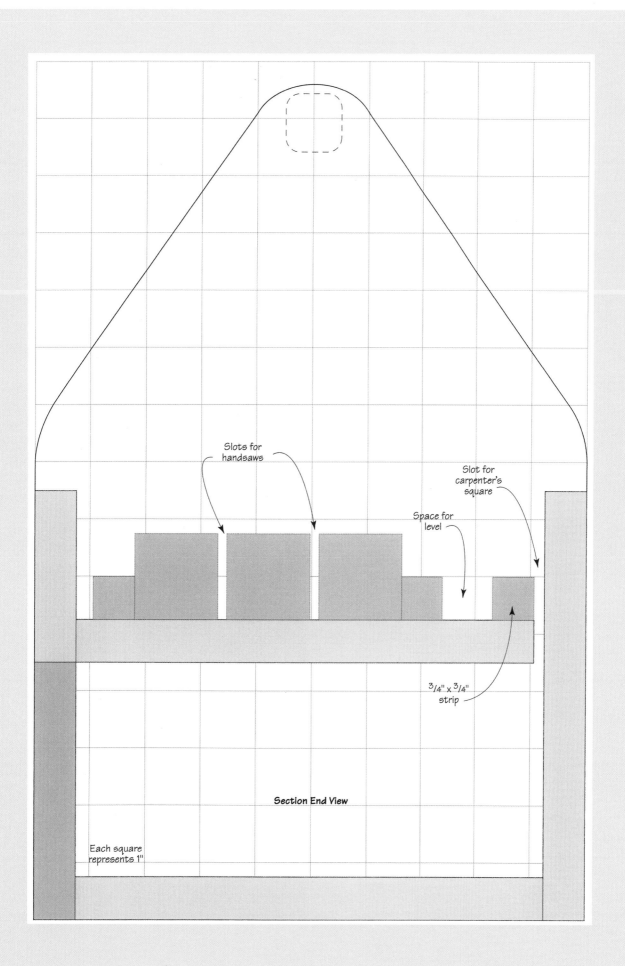

Slots for
handsaws

Slot for
carpenter's
square

Space for
level

$^3/4$" x $^3/4$"
strip

Section End View

Each square
represents 1"

2

PORTABLE ELECTRIC TOOLS

PORTABLE ELECTRIC TOOLS have become "essential" to woodworkers, builders, and homeowners. Many of us rely almost entirely on these modern-day wonders. Today a wide range of portable electric power tools are available to do just about any job you can imagine and probably some you can't. Portable electric tools are available corded or cordless. The first tools were corded, and a number of corded tools are still available. These are primarily the choice of contractors and those who need bigger capacity tools that can be used all day without changing batteries. New battery technology, however, has made a big difference in these choices, even for contractors. With today's batteries, one in use and one on the charger, you're set to go all day without the tethering cord. For years NiCad was THE battery technology, but lithium-ion battery technology, previously utilized in cell phones and laptops, has been one of the biggest innovations in portable electric tools. These batteries provide longer run time and more power with less weight than former technologies, allowing tool makers to provide unique innovations for ultra-compact tools with mind-boggling power. For instance, a 36-volt lithium-ion battery offers twice the voltage capacity of an 18-volt NiCad battery, but weighs nearly the same. Run time has also increased, as well as shelf life between battery charges. And you can recharge at any time without the memory effect.

DRILLS, DRILL/DRIVERS, AND IMPACT DRIVERS

One of the largest categories of portable power tools is drills, drill/drivers, and impact drivers. A wide range of sizes, prices, and models are available from a number of manufacturers. With today's drills and drill/drivers, along with a wide variety of accessories, almost any chore can be done, including mashing potatoes.

Portable electric drills have been a main tool for woodworking and cabinet shops, contractors, and do-it-yourselfers for years. The first power drills were quite simple, bulky, and heavy but a definite improvement over hand drills. Made of metal, they were also somewhat dangerous, and electrical shock was always a possibility on the work site. As the product developed, double-insulation was a major step. Then came variable speed, allowing for better control in drilling operations. The next major step was a clutch that allowed for changing the torque, producing screwdriving capability and drill/drivers. A reverse feature developed at the same time. Then came cordless tool models, and in fact, drill/drivers were the first cordless tools. Working in a cabinet shop installing doors and drawers by the hour, I really appreciated when these new tools came about.

What to Look For

Both corded and cordless have some of the same features. Variable speed is extremely common and this makes it easy to start a hole or fastener slow and then speed up as needed. Speed ranges vary from 0—800 rpm, up to 0—2,800 rpm. And reversing is also important for backing out heavy bits or removing fasteners. A dual range switch is also found on many drills and allows you to switch between high speeds for drilling and low range, high torque for fastening chores. These days, drill and drill/driver chucks are available in two sizes and two types. The sizes denote the largest bit diameter the chuck will hold, and drills are commonly sold with ⅜" or ½" chucks. The latter are more common on the larger, more powerful corded models. Chucks may be keyed or keyless. The latter have become increasingly popular on both corded and cordless models, although some of the larger corded models still feature a keyed chuck because you can apply more torque to tighten the bit in place. Another feature that can be helpful at times is a movable side handle.

Drills and drill/drivers are both available in both corded and cordless models.

Drill and drill/drivers are available in a wide range of sizes, powers, and shapes.

This swing-out handle can be positioned as needed to provide more pressure on the drill or to hold the drill steadier. Drills are also available in a variety of shapes, including the popular pistol and T-handle. The latter is commonly used with cordless models and is more balanced. Another popular feature is an over-molded handle for comfort.

Drills and drill/drivers are available both corded and cordless. Cordless models are the most popular and will handle just about any chore. With today's powerful batteries and cordless drills, it would seem there is no need for corded models. For heavy duty chores, however, it's hard to beat a corded drill. They provide more power and on the larger chores you don't have to worry about running out of battery power. Corded drills are measured by amps and range from 5 up to 7.5 amps. In most instances, you'll be using these for big jobs, so a ½" drill with 7.5 amps is the best choice.

Cordless drills and drill/drivers are denoted by volts and range from 12 to 36 volts. Dedicated screwdrivers or drivers range from 9 up to 12 volts. The higher the voltage of the drill/driver, the heavier and larger the drill/driver is in size. The 24- and 36-volt models are definitely bulky and hefty. You certainly don't want to heft them all day installing hardware on cabinets.

Keyless chuck

Torque adjustment ring

Two-speed gear train

Direction of rotation reversing switch

Switch trigger

Battery pack

Both corded and cordless models share some of the same features.

A 12-volt model will do most cabinet and woodworking chores, with an 18-volt probably the best all-around choice. For the bigger chores, however, the 24- and 36-volt models are hard to beat. These models are extremely powerful. You better hold on tight if boring large holes in tough wood, as I discovered boring fence hardware holes in hedge posts. Some companies also offer the larger models with hammer/drill capacity.

In addition to the features shared by corded models, cordless drills also have a clutch. This allows you to change the torque from light-duty drilling to heavy-duty driving chores. Most have settings ranging up to the number 24, the highest torque. A drilling position is also located on the collar. To change simply turn the collar on the drill head.

Adjustable screw guns, such as the Black & Decker Rota-Driver are available so you can get into tight spots.

Cordless drill/drivers are the most popular, and the smaller models are best for woodworking, cabinetry, and around the home.

The more powerful models are best for heavy-duty chores.

For those heavy-duty chores, such as extended boring in concrete or even concrete demolition, hammer/drills, such as the Rigid 1/2", 24-volt Lithium-Ion model shown, are the best choice.

DRILLS AND DRIVERS

Dedicated Drivers

Another category is the dedicated drivers. A wide variety of these are available, ranging from the tiny hand drivers to Sheetrock drivers, to stand-up, deck-screw drivers. Homeowners appreciate the little drivers, and they are available in a wide range of sizes. They are also available with pistol, straight, and changeable handle designs, allowing you to do driving chores in a wide variety of situations, including tight spots.

Using

Drills and drill/drivers are so common and simple to operate, little is needed in the way of instruction. Insert the bit or driver into the chuck and tighten in place with either the chuck key or by hand in the case of keyless chucks. Select the range for drilling or fastening, and select the desired torque range. Select forward or reverse by pushing the switch on the handle sideways. Position the bit in place and start slow, increasing the speed as needed for the chore. If the chuck ratchets before the desired result is achieved, increase the collar setting and continue tightening the screw. Repeat until you reach the correct setting, and then use this setting for the remaining screws. Hammer drills have a switch that lets you select between straight drilling and hammer drilling.

Other dedicated drivers include stand-up, deck-screw drivers, such as the Milwaukee Sharp-Fire. These make it easy to install decks, roof decking, and other chores.

Dedicated drivers are also extremely handy, especially the small kind that can be kept handy in the kitchen.

Hammer Drills

Another category is the heavy-duty hammer drills. Anchoring items to concrete or masonry often requires boring a hole, inserting an anchor of some sort, then bolting or screwing the item in place. Good examples include porch piers, step railings, and safety hand bars. The flashing around chimneys is another example.

What to Look For

Three different types of tools can be used for boring holes: a standard rotary drill, a rotary percussion hammer drill, and a rotary hammer. The different tools have different uses. If drilling just a few holes, they can usually be bored with an ordinary rotary drill and a masonry bit. With these drills, the penetration is directly dependent on the amount of pressure applied and the rpm. As the hardness of the material, as well as the size of the hole, increases, more pressure is required. Then a variable speed drill is needed. The drill should be run fairly low, around 350 to 750 rpm. Frequently removing the bit from the hole to clear out the cuttings will help prevent the bit from overheating.

Impact drivers are the "hottest" fastening tools and well-appreciated by both serious do-it-yourselfers and contractors. The Bosch 10.8V Litheon battery powered IMPACTOR provides tots of power in a tiny package. These tools utilize a hammer and anvil to create impacts, while at the same time turning the fastener.

Impact drivers and square-head screws make deck projects easy.

The drilling chore is done much quicker and easier with a rotary percussion hammer drill. This type of drill has the same basic three-jaw chuck as a rotary drill. The drill also has an electro-mechanical hammering system. This consists of a gear assembly providing an impact to the chuck. These impacts may range from 20,000 to over 50,000 blows per minute (BPM). Penetration is determined by the rate of the rotary percussion hammer providing impact energy, as well as the pressure applied to the bit and the rpm. With these types of tools, the harder you push, the harder the impact, but also the more wear-and-tear on the unit. This is the most common type of hammer drill in use by homeowners. Most of these drills are also available as combination, rotary drill/drivers, and hammer drills with the modes switch selected. With the appropriate bit, they can also be used for drilling other materials, such as wood or metal. Hammer drills are primarily designed to be used for masonry work with some light concrete work, and they are adequate for most homeowner chores. They're faster than rotary drills but slower than the rotary hammers.

Rotary hammers are used for larger chores and are designed primarily for concrete work, although they can be used for softer masonry materials.

Rotary hammers have an electro-hammer system with a free-floating percussion piston. The impact force is much greater than that of a rotary percussion hammer drill. The tool supplies the impact without additional pressure needed from the operator. In fact, applying pressure reduces the impact. If you have a number of holes to bore in concrete, these dedicated models are the best choice. They are a bit pricier than hammer drills and also lack the versatility of hammer drills. If you don't wish to purchase a rotary hammer for one-time use, they can often be rented. The chucks in these units are designed to accept special bits for additional strength. Older models utilized a splined bit. The most common systems these days, utilized throughout the industry, were designed by Bosch and include: the SDS-Plus and SDX-Max Systems. The former is the most common system. Both hammer drills and rotary hammers are designed to bore at specific optimum drill hole ranges. Also available for demolition purposes are the combo-models that have both rotary hammer and demolition modes. Hammer drills are available in both the corded and the more convenient cordless models. Some are dedicated hammer drills; some are rotary drill/drivers with a selective hammer action.

The PT5100 rotary hammer petrol drill is ideal for use where the use of electricity is not advisable for safety reasons or for use in remote locations, saving the need for generators and cordless tools.

Drill Bits and Accessories

If you work long enough, you'll discover you really can't have too many drill bits. They're needed for numerous around-the-home, shop, and contractor chores. Bits are available for drilling just about any material available, including wood, the various metals, concrete, stone, tile, and even glass. As you can guess, a wide variety of bits and tools for drilling are available for use with portable drills and drill presses. These include standard twist drill bits, auger bits, spade bits, Forstner bits, expansion bits, step-drill bits, hole saws, pilot-hole and screw bits, and plug cutters.

Twist Drill Bits

Twist drill bits are some of the most common shop tools. They're available in a wide range of sizes, point, and twist shapes and are not only available in standard industrial-grade steel, but also in "exotic" materials, including titanium coated, black oxide, and cobalt.

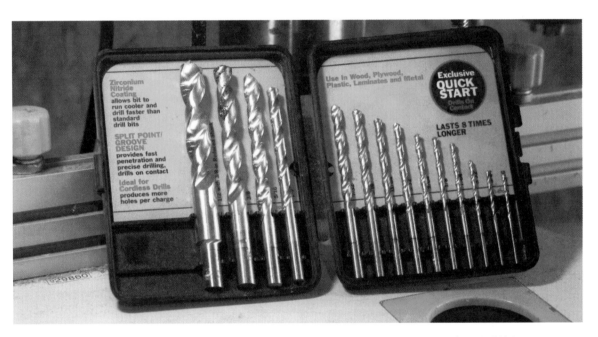

Drill bits are the most common tool accessory, a $740 million North American market. Drill bits are available in a wide variety of types, sizes, and materials for specific metal- and wood-boring chores.

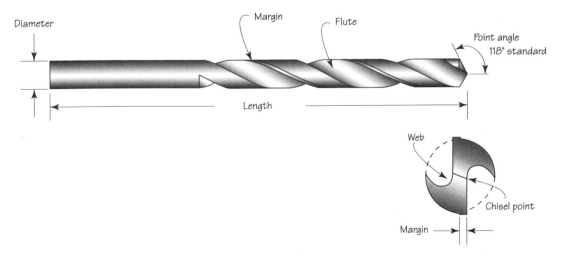

Twist drill bits are the most common and are available in a variety of sizes, materials, and shapes. Shown is a typical drill bit configuration.

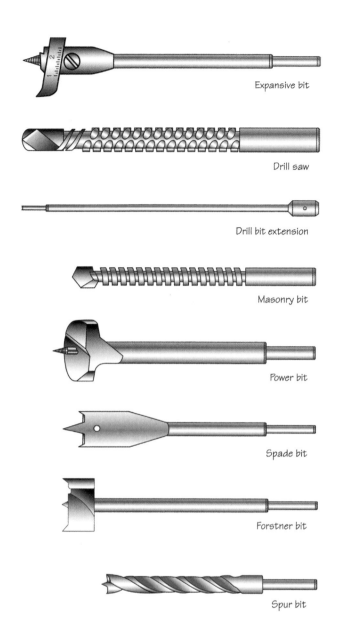

Expansive bit

Drill saw

Drill bit extension

Masonry bit

Power bit

Spade bit

Forstner bit

Spur bit

Drill bits are available in a variety of styles for different materials.

Buy good quality bits. Inexpensive bits are a frustration and can be dangerous, causing you to push or exert force when drilling.

Drill bit sizes are found in four categories: fractional sizes, wire gauge sizes, letter sizes, and metric. Fractional sizes begin at $\frac{1}{64}$" and run up to over 4". The smaller bits increase in size by $\frac{1}{64}$", the mid-size bits by $\frac{1}{32}$" and the larger bits by $\frac{1}{16}$". Wire gauge numbers run from #1 through #80, with #80 being the smallest. All sizes are less than $\frac{1}{4}$" and begin at 0.0135 inch (#80) up to 0.2280 inch (#1). The numbers correspond to standard wire sizes. These bits are used where exact hole dimensions are required, such as when tapping threads in holes. Letter-size bits begin the next size up from #1 wire gauge. They begin at 0.2340 inch (A) and run to 0.4062 inch (Z). The largest size is smaller than $\frac{7}{16}$". Again, these are used where precise hole sizes are needed. Metric bits are available in millimeters. One millimeter (mm) is equal to 0.394".

Twist drills are commonly sold in a standard length, called **jobber** lengths, the length varying according to the bit diameter. These will handle most of the jobs you'll tackle, but at times a longer length may be needed. In this case, extensions are available for $\frac{1}{4}$" size bit shanks. With many hex-heads available these days, an extension will fit most bit sizes, but they are designed primarily for woodworking, not metal chores.

The next step in twist drill school is the point angle. Typically 118° is the most common angle. But these drills require a starting dimple in metal with a center punch, otherwise the bit will walk or skate away from the hole location. Bits with a 135° point will start their own hole in metal and, of course, can be used on many other materials. Brad-point bits provide even more precise starting in both metal and wood. Woodcraft Supply carries extra-long, 10" brad-point bits, handy for many furniture construction chores.

The helix and flute angles are also important, and again, there's more variety to choose from, depending on the job. The Bosch Speed Helix design has an aggressive flute structure engineered to remove material faster. The 135° split point eliminates walking, making the bit more efficient with up to three times faster penetration than bits designed with Standard Helix. Quicker penetration also means less energy on the part of the drill turning the bit, as well as the user pressing down, which translates into more battery life for a cordless drill/driver and less fatigue on the part of the user.

Twist drill bits are made of a variety of materials, with carbon steel the softest. High speed steel (HSS) bits are also available. Exotic materials include black oxide, titanium, and cobalt. Each is designed for a specific purpose and Bosch has designs in these bits, as well. Their High-Speed Steel Black Oxide bits are all-purpose for heavy-duty drilling in wood, plastic, carbon, and alloy steels, aluminum, and soft cast iron.

Titanium is designed for repetitive heavy-duty drilling in wood, plastic, common stainless steels, carbon and alloy steels and soft cast iron. The Bosch titanium drill bit line offers the industry's toughest titanium bits. By coating each bit with high-speed steel-titanium nitride, Bosch not only made the surface of the bit harder, in excess of 80 HRC (Hardness Rockwell), but also dramatically reduced the amount of heat and friction created between the bit and the workpiece. As a result, the bit will last up to six times longer than standard black oxide bits and drill through more materials.

Bits are available in decimal and metric sizes with round or hexagonal shanks.

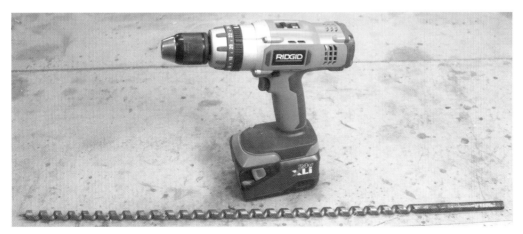

Auger bits are longer than most other bits and are used for boring holes to run wiring or plumbing.

Spade bits are used where rapid drilling of tough materials is needed. The new Bosch RapidFeed spade bits have a patent-pending tip similar to the screw tip of an auger bit and an increased cutting angle.

Forstner bits are used where precise holes are required.

Zirconium coated bits, such as the Craftsman bit sets, are coated with zirconium nitride for extra strength and feature a split-point and groove design that breaks up chips for faster penetration and more precise drilling. The point design eliminates walking.

Cobalt bits will drill extremely hard materials, including hardened stainless steel, cast iron, and titanium, but can also be used for wood and plastics. The Bosch cobalt drill bits feature a special alloy that allows the bits to heat up to 1,100° F., allowing each to last in extremely abrasive materials that would normally destroy any other bit. Further advancing the efficiency, Bosch also increased the overall bit hardness up to 68 HRC, perfect for penetrating tough or abrasive materials. A 135° split point starts drilling on contact by eliminating walking. And finally, a thicker web design increases the overall rigidity to prevent the bit from snapping in hard materials.

Auger Bits

Auger bits solve the problem of boring deep holes and fairly large holes, such as through several studs to run wiring or plumbing. Auger bits are typically 7" in length and will cut through three 2x4s. For even deeper holes, ship augers, with lengths of up to 17", are available.

Spade Bits

Another alternative to boring quick and large holes in studs and other projects is with spade bits. Sometimes called **paddle** bits because of their shape, these bits come in a variety of sizes and make quick work of boring rough-in holes. The RapidFeed spade bits from Bosch have a patent-pending tip similar to a screw tip on an auger bit. The RapidFeed design helps pull the bit through the wood. This allows the bit to cut up to three times faster than other spade bits. An increased cutting angle accommodates the increased speed of cut. Specially engineered cutting spurs on each edge actually scribe the outer edge of the hole before the cutting edge removes the material, creating a cleaner hole. An alternative to spade bits for boring these types of holes are the WoodEater bits from Vermont American. These bits will cut three times faster and last seven times longer than spade bits. The Milwaukee PathFinder bits are also great for these chores. They have a unique design with six different cutting edges, allowing the bit to cut forward, backward, and on all sides. This makes precise, clean holes in wood, composites, chipboard, plasterboard, and hard plastics.

Forstner Bits

Forstner bits are the best choice for boring precise holes in wood. These bits feature a precise diameter with a circular cutting edge protruding past a center cutting edge and a spur in the center to guide the bit. They are best used in drill presses for precise work, although they can be hand-held with less precision. They are not quite as fast a cutting bit as the spade and other fast-style bits. Woodcraft Supply offers a 16-bit set in a wooden box. Individual bits are also available. Rockier offers carbide Forstner bits in extra lengths for boring deeper holes. They also have an exclusive drill jig guide that helps position the bit precisely in place.

Expansive Bits

Expansive bits are wood boring bits that can be adjusted to "infinite" hole sizes. These bits are available in several sizes, ranging from to ⅝" to 1¾" and ⅞" to 3". They are available with tapered shanks for use in hand-held brace-and-bit sets or with hex shanks for use with power drills.

Step-Drill Bits

Step-drill bits allow you to drill multiple sizes of holes with just one bit by simply stopping the bit at the desired hole diameter. The IRWIN Unibit with SpeedPoint Tip Geometry allows faster starts and penetrates six times faster than former bits. The flute design reduces vibration and provides more control for precise round holes in mild steel, copper, brass, aluminum, plastic, acrylic, wood, and laminates. Unibit step drills are made of industrial grade high-speed steel. Laser marked sizes make for easy identification of hole sizes. Titanium nitride coating is available on several sizes to create less friction.

Pilot-Hole Bits

Pilot-hole bits allow you to drill screw holes and countersink or counterbore at the same time

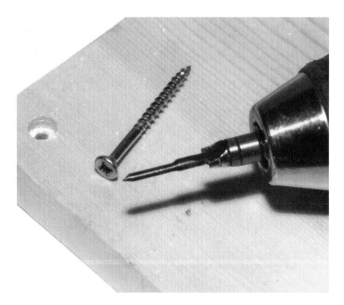

Pilot-hole bits allow you to drill pilot holes for screwing in hardwoods to prevent splitting. They may also be used as countersink or counterbore bits, depending on their style. One type, such as the Stanley shown, is solid and is made to match specific screw sizes.

Another type of pilot-hole bit allows you to adjust the bit length to match the screw length. The Craftsman Speed-Lok System countersink/pilot-hole bits are available with a fast change chuck. Insert the chuck in the drill bit. Use the countersink bit to drill the hole, flip the holder, and you can drive the screw.

in wood. These bits are the choice when fastening wood pieces, especially hardwoods that may split without drilling pilot holes. Pilot-hole bits are available in several sizes to match standard screw sizes. Some are one piece and must be matched to screw lengths, as well. Another version has an adjustable bit fitted into the bit body that can be adjusted to the screw length. Matching the pilot-bits are plug cutters that can be used to cut plugs of matching or contrasting woods to cover the screws.

Specialty Bits

Other specialty bits include the Vermont American glass and tile bits for smooth accurate drilling of ceramic tile, marble, china, mirrors, and glass. The spear-pointed tip reduces breakout. Countersinks are bits designed to countersink screws. If you do a lot of cabinet work, installing numerous hinges, self-centering hinge drilling Vix bits from Woodcraft Supply make precise and quick work of drilling holes for hinge screws. Although not actually drill bits, hole saws utilize a drill bit to center a circular saw to cut large holes in wood, metal, plastics, and other materials. Hammer drill masonry bits are available in several styles for rotary hammer drills or standard drills. Masonry bits with double flutes, such as from Vermont American, provide faster cleaning of materials. Also available from Vermont American are Tapcon concrete screw bits for drilling pilot holes for one-quarter-inch Tapcon concrete fasteners.

Quick Connector Systems

One of the biggest changes in drill bits is the introduction of hex-shank bits. This makes it easier to lock the bit in a drill or drill press and prevents slipping. The second major advance is the creation of quick connector systems that allow instant changing of bits and other accessories, such as drivers. These are available in a number of different sets and individually, as well. The Craftsman

Hole saws are available in several different sizes to bore large holes, such as when installing locks in doors.

Masonry bits are used for boring in concrete and other masonry.

Speed-Lok System comes in a 120-piece Master Drill and Driver Set that includes a quick connector, hex-shank twist drills, spade bits, masonry bits, pilot-hole bits, numerous drivers, and other accessories. Rockier offers their Insty-Driver System of cabinetmaker bits with self-centering bits, tapered drill bits, and countersinks. Bosch offers their Clic-Change Quick-Change Bit System in numerous twist, masonry, and other bits, as well as drivers. DeWalt's Rapid Load Quick Change sets also utilize a quick-change chuck.

Quick connector systems allow you to instantly change bits, drivers, and other accessories.

Masonry Bits

Carbide-tipped masonry bits are available for the various rotary drills, hammer drills, and rotary hammers, and the proper bits must be used with the different tools. These bits are not designed to be used to drill metal, wood, or other materials. It's important to choose the correct bit to fit the type of tool being used. Ordinary carbide-tipped masonry bits are fine for rotating drills. They are designed with fast spiral flutes for drilling in soft to medium masonry materials, such as brick or block. Deep-fluted bits are best used in concrete where the deep flutes help clean out the concrete chips and dust. Straight-shank rotary-hammer bits are designed to take the high impact loads created by a rotary percussion hammer drill and should be used in those.

Do not use worn bits as they may drill holes larger than will match up with the different anchoring systems. Make sure the bit is seated properly in the chuck and the chuck is working properly. If drilling in soft or damp material, frequently remove the bit and clean out the flutes to prevent overheating of the bit. Do not submerse the bit in water to cool it off. Carbide-tipped bits may shatter and the materials they are being used on may chip. Always wear proper eye protection and proper clothing.

A doweling jig allows you to use a drill bit to create strong dowel joints.

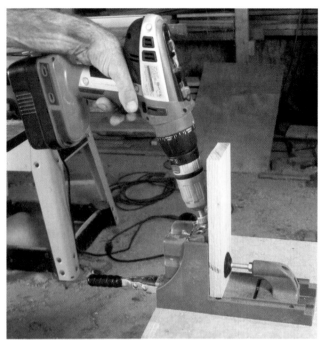

One popular joint is the pocket-hole using the Kreg system, a drill and bit. The system allows you to drill precise holes in wood joints and join the workpieces with countersunk screws.

Impact Drivers

A wide range of powerful fastening tools are available for a wide variety of fasteners. One of the fastest growing segments in power fasteners is impact drivers. I tested a Craftsman 14.4V EX impact driver when they first came out. My first job, constructing a deck for a church mission project, sold me on the tool. After the first hour, several other fellow construction workers had decided the tool was definitely on their Christmas list. Usage and popularity of impact drivers has steadily increased due to their size, fastening power, and nonreactionary torque. If you haven't tried one of these power fasteners, you owe yourself a test drive. They can deliver up to 2000 inch pounds (in. lbs.) of torque, allowing you to drive deck screws, and install windows and doors quick and easy, and even drive lag bolts into wood, fasten anchors into concrete, and other tough chores. And they do it with ease. There is negligible torque feel. In fact, most operate best with a light grip on the handle.

What to Look For

These tools are primarily cordless and, again, power is denoted by torque. But you may be surprised at the power of some of these tools. Almost all portable electric tool manufacturers now offer this popular tool. Following are some I've tested. Bosch Power Tools has a full line of impact drivers, starting with their innovative ultra-compact 10.8V Litheon IMPACTOR Fastening Driver. Merely 6" tall by 6½" long and weighing only 2.2 pounds, the little driver is less than half the size and weight of an 18V NiCad impact driver. A high performance motor and all metal gears produce 1,800 rpm and 3,000 BPM, creating 800 in. lbs. of torque with the hammer and anvil system. Compared to a standard 18V drill/driver (500 in. lbs.), the 10.8V unit is 60 percent more powerful and barely measures bigger than an average contractor's hand. It easily fits into your tool belt for a wide range of chores and is especially effective at driving self-tapping screws. The IMPACTOR comes standard with Litheon charger and two batteries. I don't understand why some companies sell impact drivers with only one battery. These are job-site tools, and no contractor or serious remodeler wants to wait for a single battery to recharge on the job. Of course, a second battery can be purchased separately. I have used this little tool day-in and day-out 7 or 8 hours a day driving screws for decks, siding, and sunroofs.

Moving up in size, the Bosch 14.4V Litheon IMPACTOR provides more power with 3,200 BPM for faster fastening. The 14.4V model produces 95.83 ft. lbs. of torque. This is the best all-around size for most fastening chores, and the tool also comes with a handy belt-loop holder. You can simply slide it onto your belt or tool pouch belt when not in use. It also comes with two batteries and an interchangeable bit with built in bit holder. An adjustable LED light increases visibility.

The MaxSelect impact driver from Ridgid features a compact design to allow for close quarters operation. It has an LED light for workplaces with inadequate lighting. The high torque motor delivers 1,490 in. lbs. of torque. One great feature is a variable speed switch that allows for slow, controlled starts and fast finishes. As I've discovered in testing units, this is one of the most appreciated features. The unit produces 3,300 BPM in 24-volt mode. It features a ¼" quick coupler, a single-ended impact bit, and comes with one battery.

The Heavy Duty 18V cordless impact driver kit from DeWalt produces 1,170 in. lbs. of maximum torque with 0–2,400 rpm and 0–3,000 BPM. It features a textured antislip comfort grip and an all metal transmission. The heavy-duty impacting mechanism directs torque to the fastener without kickback. It comes with two XRP batteries, a one hour charger, and a case.

As we move up in torque, Bosch has their 18V NiCad ½" High-Torque Impact Wrench (not driver). With a ½" square drive anvil for ½" sockets, this is the answer for the tougher jobsite chores. The tool turns

at 1,900 RPM to deliver 2,100 BPM and the highest torque in its class at 350 ft. lbs. The tool's head-length is over an inch shorter than most competition, measuring only 9½" and it weighs 7.5 lbs. The new tool will drive a wide range of fasteners including: lag bolts, Tapcons, large wedge and sleeve anchors, high-strength friction grip bolts, structural bolts, hex bolts, CleveLoc nuts, high nuts, and more. The new jobsite tool is perfect for setting up temporary structural braces, anchoring pipe or equipment, or tightening down fasteners. The unit comes with two 18V BLUECORE NiCad batteries, a 30-minute charger, and a carrying case.

The IMPACT READY impact accessory set from De-Walt is designed especially for the impact-driver market, with performance in impact drivers up to 2000 in. lbs. of torque. The 38-piece accessory set includes two patented products. The innovative pivoting bit holder enables you to achieve accessibility to tight spots with 20° of flex, eliminating the need for most right-angle attachments. An auto-locking feature prevents accidental pivoting and allows normal straight use. The pivot holder has a 4" hex shank and is made of durable stainless steel construction with a built-in magnet. New double-ended bit tips provide two usable ends. These bit tips fit in all bit tip holders, drive guides, drywall guns, and drivers. The set includes the most commonly used 6-point thin-walled deep sockets, including ⅜", ⁷⁄₁₆", ½" and ⁹⁄₁₆" sizes. The set also includes nut setters, socket adapters, and screwdriving bits.

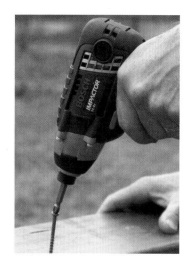

The Bosch 14.4 volt IMPACTOR has a belt-loop feature, allowing you to hang it on your tool belt.

DRILLS AND DRIVERS

PORTABLE ELECTRIC SAWS

Portable electric saws include circular saws, reciprocating saws, and saber or jigsaws. Each has its own preferred use. Some are versatile enough to use for several chores, others are more specialized. You may eventually want or need all three of these saws.

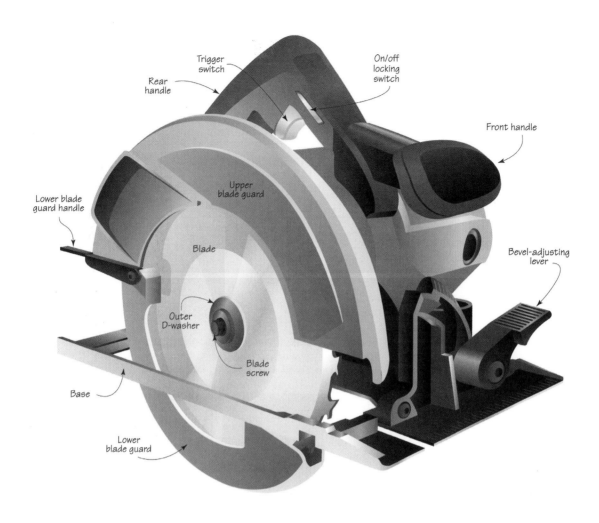

Trigger
switch

On/off
locking
switch

Rear
handle

Front handle

Lower blade
guard handle

Upper
blade guard

Blade

Bevel-adjusting
lever

Outer
D-washer

Blade
screw

Base

Lower
blade guard

Circular Saws

The Skil Corporation invented portable circular saws just after World War II, and the name **Skilsaw** became synonymous with the tools. The new saw allowed carpenters to cut through a framing 2x4 much faster than with a handsaw and thus helped fuel the booming home-construction business of the time. Portable circular saws have come a long way from their beginning, although they still operate in the same manner. Portable circular saws can be used for crosscutting, ripping (with a ripping guide), making bevel and miter or compound miter cuts, and can be used to create rabbet or dado joints. They can be used to cut large sheets of plywood, paneling, or other materials much easier than with a table or radial arm saw. And, fitted with the correct blades, they can be used to cut tile, fiberglass, concrete, and even metal.

What to Look For

Circular saws are sized by the blade diameter the saw accepts. The size ranges from small 4" trim saws up to big 15" framing saws. Circular saws are available as corded or cordless, with the latter becoming increasingly more powerful and popular. Corded saws are rated by horsepower and range from one-half up to almost four horsepower. A good all-around choice for most homeowner chores, and the most popular size available, is a 7½" saw with two to three horsepower. Cordless saws are rated by volts and range from 14 up to 36 volts. Another good choice for the homeowner is an 18-volt, 6½" saw. Remember, however, the deepest cut that can be made by a circular saw is just a bit less than half the diameter of the blade. This means a 6½" saw will easily cut through 1½" or 2" materials on a crosscut. The blade will cut through almost 3" of material, which will make a 45° bevel cut through 2x material. The larger the saw, the more power, but also the more weight. The smaller trim saws are best for interior framing, for cutting plywood, or for chores where deep bevel cutting is not required.

Circular saws are easy and comfortable to use with a number of great features. Black & Decker features a plastic window for easy viewing of the cut line in their cordless model. Skil's corded 7¼", 2.6 horsepower circular saw with Sight Light has a built-in light for a better view of the workpiece. The Craftsman Laser Trac model features a laser light showing where the blade intersects the workpiece. Milwaukee's corded Tilt-Lok Handle Saw has an eight-position, user-adjustable main handle for maximum comfort and control in a variety of situations. A number of DeWalt corded saws feature an electric brake. Porter Cable offers a 4½" trim saw, and a 7¼", 15-amp framer's saw with case.

Bosch has a line of lightweight corded circular saws, the CS10 and CS20, that will fit a lot of professional needs, especially framers. A rugged composite footplate answers the number one complaint about job site circular saws from contractors. The foot plate is not only extremely tough, but will also glide across even wet wood. Featuring lightweight magnesium upper and lower guards, the saws have 15-amp motors, offering great power to weight ratios. These saws are also the first to include depth detent systems, which helps improve accuracy of cuts. The saws will handle a maximum bevel of 56° for steep pitch cuts. A blower and patent-pending quadrant designed system quickly removes sawdust to ensure a clear line of sight. The CS20 offers other features I liked in testing. There's a rafter hook, the first ever on a lightweight circular saw. When you're in the rafters and need to store the saw for a moment, we've all used a lot of creative means, not all safe. Simply snap out the rafter hook and hook to the nearest framing member. The saw stays in place. But the most important feature is

Cordless circular saws have become increasingly popular and the larger volt models can easily handle framing materials.

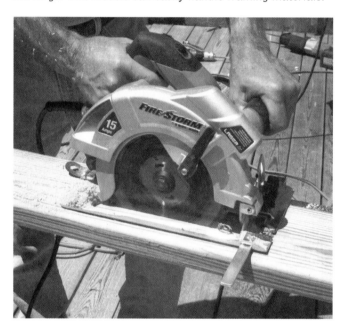

For day-long use, a corded saw may be preferred.

For those big chores, a worm-drive corded saw may be the best choice.

A rafter-hook, on this Bosch model, allows you to hang the saw in framing, a great help when installing rafters.

the direct connect system. Simply plug the extension power cord into the back of the saw. I can't begin to count the frustration of having to go back and unhook the end of a power tool cord that got caught on a decking, ladder, or framing job. That won't happen with this tool. The exclusive patent-pending 180° cord channel reduces cord stress while the cord lock mechanism secures the cord in position. The saw comes with a Bosch exclusive 24-tooth patented C3 Dynamite Carbide blade with blue antifriction coating.

I've tested the Bosch 24-volt cordless circular saw extensively and found it to be an excellent all-around circular saw without the inconvenience of a cord. Their 18V, 6½" circular saw has become even more popular with both do-it-your-selfers and contractors. The saw features rear depth adjustment to quickly match stock for more accurate cuts, 50° bevel that cut 2x materials and a 45° positive stop that accurately adjusts the bevel for the most common cut.

Contractors often rely on worm-driven corded circular saws for serious, heavy-duty framing chores. Most of these feature a rear handle for easier vertical sawing, and the Skilsaw Mag 77, a 7¼" saw I tested, has precision-machined, matched worm gear sets for durability. The saw features a left-side blade for a clear view of the cut line. The rear handle also makes it easier to see and follow the cut line. A second top grip provides extra support when needed. The saw features a high-tech magnesium frame that is lightweight, yet extremely sturdy. The saw also has a high-strength aluminum shoe that glides smoothly over the wood surface.

Milwaukee Electric Tool Corporation's V28 Li-Ion cordless tool system utilizes Milwaukee's exclusive V or Lithium-Ion battery technology. The tool line up includes the V28 6½ circular saw. The saw features a fast 4200 rpm for great cutting power, a fast-acting electric brake, and a high-strength aircraft aluminum shoe that provides for precise cutting and resists bending. One of the features I liked best in testing the saw are the tactile grips. They're comfortable and provide good control. The saw has a 50° bevel capacity, with depth of cut at 45° of 1⅝". A spindle lock makes it easy to change blades and the magnesium guard cuts down on weight. The saw weighs 7.1 pounds with the battery.

Accessories

Do you need to trim a door or cut large sheets of plywood without chipping while using a circular saw? The EZ Smart Guide System from Eurekazone is the answer. The system consists of a patent-pending modular, extruded aluminum guide. A zero-clearance insert saw shoe is a universal to fit all right-bladed saws, corded or cordless. The shoe is easily attached and, once attached, slides in the tracks of the guide to provide precise cutting. The antichip, antisplintering insert keeps materials, even plywood, from lifting and chipping. Self-aligning connectors allow you to fasten two 50" sections together for crosscutting or ripping a sheet of plywood. Smart Clamps fasten to the bottom of the guide and firmly hold the guide in place.

The Pro-Cut Portable Saw Guide from Bench Dog, Inc., fits all 8¼" and smaller right-blade circular saws. It provides a sturdy, easily aligned guide for crosscutting dimension lumber perfectly every time and reduces kickback commonly associated with cutting thick lumber. It will cut plastic siding, I-Beams, beadboard, and even delicate veneers and melamine-coated board with little or no tear out. The tool is an excellent measuring and marking tool. Align Pro-Cut to your tape measure and you're ready to cut, no need to draw a cut line. A built-in 6" hook rule makes marking framing lumber easy, and it can even be used to lay out 45° angles.

The most common use is crosscutting materials. Make sure the work is well-supported.

With a ripping guide inserted in the saw base, a circular saw can also be used for ripping chores.

Laser-guided saws make it easy to cut large sheets of paneling or plywood.

When cutting plywood, make sure the sheets are well-supported, and set the blade depth so the blade just barely penetrates below the plywood surface.

When crosscutting plywood, place support strips beneath the plywood. This prevents the cut-off piece from falling down and breaking off at the end of the cut.

Using Circular Saws

As with any power tool, safe usage of circular saws is extremely important. Make sure you follow all manufacturers' safety rules. Circular saws now feature a lockout button in addition to the switch and both must be pressed to start and run the saw. A spring-driven retracting blade guard covers the blade, except when pushed out of the way by the stock. Sometimes, when ripping or making angled cuts, the guard must be manually pushed up and out of the way. Circular saws have a finger tab that allows you to move the guard without getting your fingers close to the spinning blade. Always wear safety glasses when using a circular saw, as sawdust can be thrown into your eyes.

The most common use of the portable circular saw is crosscutting stock. The stock must be well-supported and preferably clamped or held on a sawhorse or work surface with the stock protruding well away from the edge of the support surface. In most instances, the line to be sawn is marked with a pencil while using a square or try square held against the stock edge. The base plate of the saw has a line indicator. Note that the saw base may be left or right. Position that indicator on the marked line with the saw motor on the supported side of the stock. Stand behind the stock and slightly to the supported side. Align the line indicator with the line, start the saw, and push the saw into the stock. Use a steady, even motion to complete the cut. Be careful at the end of the cut so you don't angle off the line. You can also make the cut more precise by holding a try square or the Stanley Quick Square against the edge of the stock with one hand and guiding the saw base plate against the square.

Ripping is another common circular saw use, and rip guides are standard with most saws. Rip guides are fastened in the saw's base plate with a thumb screw and adjusted to the width of the stock to be cut. The guide is then placed on the outside of the stock, the blade started, and the saw pushed into the stock. Guide the saw with the rip guide riding along the outside edge of the stock.

Miter cuts can be made by first marking the miter lines with either the 45° arm of the try square or with a bevel gauge. In this case, you will have to lift the blade guard at the start of the cut.

Bevel cuts are made by loosening the angle adjustment knob and turning the saw to the correct bevel or angle. Compound miter cuts are made by setting the correct angle and then cutting at a miter, as well. Again, you will have to lift the blade guard to begin the cut.

Controlling the depth of cut is important. The depth of cut is adjusted by raising or lowering the saw base. When cutting through heavy stock, make sure the blade is cutting at full depth. When cutting thin stock, and especially plywood which may splinter fairly easily, set the blade to just barely cut through the material.

Rabbets can be cut in the edges of the stock by setting the saw blade to the proper depth and using the ripping guide to guide the blade. First, clamp a thick board to the stock to create a surface for the base to ride on and make the edge cut. Then remove the guide board and turn the stock down flat. Again, use the miter gauge to make the second cut to create the rabbet.

Dadoes can be cut by using a square or straight edge clamped in place across the stock to guide the saw base. With the blade set to the correct dado depth, make the first outside cut. Then slide the square over to guide the saw for the second outside cut. You can then make the successive freehand cuts between the two outside cuts to complete the dado.

Plunge cutting or creating pocket cuts is also fairly easy with circular saws. Lay out the outline of the hole with a square and a pencil. Position the saw base front down on the wood surface with the blade directly over one cut line and at the rear of the cut to be made, but not touching the wood. Turn on the saw and, holding the blade guard up

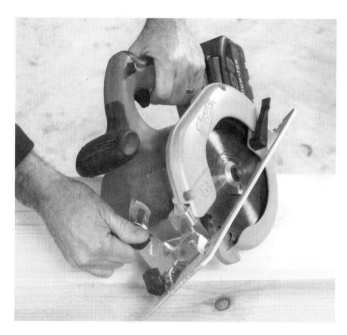

The saw base can be tilted, positioning the saw blade to make angled cuts. Compound miters can also be cut in this manner.

The depth cut can be adjusted to full depth or any depth between to cut through heavy or thin materials or to make rabbets and dadoes.

More accurate crosscuts can be made by using an accessory, such as the Bench Dog guide shown.

A circular saw can be used to make pocket cuts by starting the saw then lowering the blade into the cut line.

with the finger lever, slowly lower the saw into the stock until the base is flat on the wood surface. Continue the cut forward until you reach one corner. Repeat for the other cuts. Always turn the saw off and allow the blade to stop revolving before removing it from each cut. Do not try to back the saw out of the cut. Because a circular saw does not cut straight up and down, there will be a slight bit of stock left in all four corners. Finish cutting these with a handsaw or saber saw.

Cutting large sheets of plywood is easy with a circular saw if you follow a few tips. First, make sure the large sheets are well-supported. A pair of sawhorses is the initial start. Large, thin sheets, such as paneling, however, tend to sag. Use waste 2x4s between the sawhorses to support thin material. Snap a chalk line or use the Craftsman Accu-Rip circular saw guide to rip stock up to 24" in width. For crosscutting, set the saw blade to a depth just a little over the thickness of the plywood and cut across the waste 2x4s. Keep the 2x4s for future plywood cutting chores.

You can literally build a house with nothing more than a portable circular saw, hammer, measuring device, and square—many carpenters have done just that. Now you can even build that house without on-site electricity.

Choosing Blades

Circular saws are even more versatile, depending on the cutting blades used. A number of different woodworking blades are available for portable circular saws, including the standard, general purpose blades, rip, cut-off, as well as smooth trim/finish, and even aluminum/laminate blades. Of course, there are also metal and masonry cut-off blades.

Reciprocating and Other Power Saws

If macho-man Tim the Toolman had a favorite DIY tool, it was probably a reciprocating saw. You can really tear up a lot of stuff with one of these. Actually, they can provide some of the best controlled destruction. Reciprocating saws are great for cutting holes in places for remodeling. You can use them to cut out openings in walls for room additions or adding windows or doors. Or you can use them for installing items, such as built-in ironing boards. Floors can be cut to add heating and cooling ducts, to replace rotted floor boards, and other purposes. Rough cuts can be made to create decking and other 2x4 chores. Odd cuts can be made quickly in plywood for such things as roof decking for roof vents.

The reciprocating saw's versatility doesn't end there. Equipped with the right blade, they can cut plastic and metal. Cutting plastic plumbing pipe is one example. A metal pipe clamped in a vise can also be cut easily with a metal cutting blade. And pruning chores are a snap with cordless reciprocating saws.

Reciprocating saws are the tools of controlled destruction. They can be used for cutting holes in walls, floors, ceilings, and for any number of remodeling or contractor jobs.

With the correct blades, reciprocating saws can also be used to cut other materials, such as plastic, plumbing pipe, metals, etc.

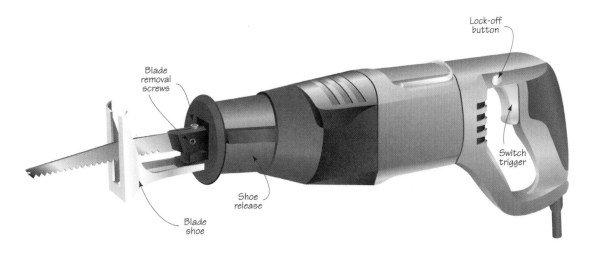

Blade removal screws

Lock-off button

Switch trigger

Shoe release

Blade shoe

With their fast, aggressive cutting, they leave a clean cut that heals better than the rough cut that manual pruning saws leave behind.

Reciprocating saws have been traditionally thought of as contractor and remodeler tools, but these days more and more homeowners are finding uses for them. There are some jobs no other tool can do. Top quality reciprocating saws are also now available cordless.

What to Look For

Reciprocating saws come with different size motors, ranging from 7.5 amps up to 11.8 amps. Of course, the more powerful saws are also heavier. Most of the saws these days feature quick-change blade clamps that allow for quick and easy changing of the blades. Some also come with dual action. The reciprocating action is used for metal, while an orbital action can be more effective in wood. It's also important to note the stroke length of the blade. Longer stroke lengths will cut more stock in a shorter time than will the shorter strokes lengths with less wear on the blade. In some instances, however, of cutting in small places, the shorter stroke lengths may be necessary. Almost all of the quality saws on the market feature variable speeds. This allows you to adjust the cutting speed to the material. It also makes it easier to start the saw. Begin with a slow speed to get the cut started in the right location, then speed up to complete the cut.

Quite often, reciprocating chores involve getting into tight spots. The Porter-Cable Tiger Claw

Variable Angle Saw combines two adjustable gear housings that allow the saw to be used in all kinds of cutting positions and conditions. The rear gear housing pivots 180° up and down with 13 positive stops for close-quarter cutting. When locked at 90°, the saw measures only 8½". The blade housing also rotates 360° with 12 positive stops. This allows you to configure the blade in any direction relative to the saw's body. This saw also features the Quick-Change blade clamp that allows you to change a blade in fewer than four seconds, no wrench required. The Porter-Cable Variable-Speed All-Purpose Tiger saw has both reciprocating and orbital actions.

The Milwaukee Hatchet reciprocating saw is a corded 7.5 amp model with an adjustable six-position pivoting handle that is built for use in tight spaces. At only 6.7 pounds, this Sawzall reciprocating saw is easily maneuvered in tight spaces, such as under counters and between studs and joists. The saw has a steel connecting rod and steel gear that strengthens the saw and provides longer life. The saw is counterbalanced for less vibration and smooth operation. The tool cuts at up to 3,000 strokes per minute (spm) with its variable speed trigger. The saw has an orbital action, which greatly enhances the speed of cut. The ¾" blade stroke length is ideal for close-quarter cutting.

DeWalt has a powerful 11.8 amp saw providing a 1¼" stroke length and a variable speed dial system that allows you to dial in the exact speed you need.

A counterbalance and rubber grips provide more control and less vibration.

The Craftsman 8.5 amp Professional Reciprocating Saw has counterweighted gearing to provide smooth operation with minimum vibration. Replaceable brushes help extend motor life. The saw has a 1⅛" blade stroke, tool-less blade changing, and an adjustable pivoting shoe that slides out for added control. The variable trigger allows no-load speeds from 0 to 2,600 spm. The ergonomically-designed rear handle features a two-finger trigger for added efficiency and control.

Black & Decker has designed a reciprocating saw just for the do-it-yourselfer. The saw is lightweight, weighing only 6.8 pounds, and is easy to maneuver in a variety of cutting conditions. A soft-grip rear handle and front boot adds comfort and reduces vibration. The 7.5 amp motor provides variable speeds from 0 to 2,400 spm. It also features Quick-Clamp tool-free blade changes.

Hitachi offers an 11 amp saw with a unique swing action that cuts through wood material twice as fast as a conventional orbital action saw. It has a 1¼" stroke, a dial-in maximum speed elector, variable speed control switch and a 1¾" keyless adjustable pivoting shoe.

To add even more versatility and a go-anywhere capability, reciprocating saws are also available as cordless models. This provides almost unlimited use on both wood and metal projects. Even with close-at-hand projects, you don't have a cord to mess with. The Black & Decker 18-volt Firestorm Cordless Cut Saw weighs only 6 pounds, 10 ounces and is easy to maneuver into a variety of cutting positions. It features a variable speed control trigger that controls the speed and a rotating shoe that fits tightly against cutting surfaces for accurate cuts. The 18-volt, high-capacity nickel cadmium battery delivers maximum power and run time. The 3,000 spm provide a fast cut and an electric brake stops the blade upon release of the trigger. The saw comes with a pruning attachment that stabilizes branches while they are being cut. The saw also comes in a soft bag for easy storage and portability. The

A pocket cut can be made with a reciprocating saw by angling the saw blade away from the work, turning on the saw, and carefully allowing the saw point to begin the cut.

Cordless reciprocating saws can also be used for tree pruning chores.

multipurpose bag has pockets for carrying. Cordless reciprocating saws can also be used for tree pruning chores.

The Craftsman 19.2 volt Cordless Reciprocating Saw has a powerful 900 series, 4-pole motor with 1.4 amp-hour battery that delivers plenty of sustained cutting power. The battery charges to full capacity in one hour. Variable speeds range from 0 to 2,500 spm. The saw has a 1³⁄₁₆" blade stroke with tool-less blade change. An adjustable pivot shoe facilitates plunge cuts. A soft overmolded front grip and rear handle add to operator comfort.

The Makita 18-volt MForce Reciprocating saw has tool-less blade changing, fast-stopping electric brake, tool-less shoe adjustment, and variable speed. The Bosch 18-volt model has dual cutting lengths, 1¼" and ¾" stroke lengths, and features tool-less changing and pushbutton foot adjustment.

The DeWalt 18-volt saw has a ⅞" stroke, 0 to 2,800 spm, and an electric brake that prevents blades from breaking when exiting a plunge cut. At 6.5 pounds, it's also extremely light. A pivoting shoe with an open top provides maximum visibility and reverses for upside-down cutting. You can cut fifty 2x4s, one hundred forty-four 1½" PVC pipes, or thirty 6" roof vents on one charge.

How to Use

To cut wood, first remove the battery pack, choose the correct blade for the chore, and install following manufacturer instructions. Make sure the blade is fully and firmly seated. Position the front of the saw shoe on the workpiece, aligning the cutting edge of the blade with the cut line on the workpiece. Grasp the rear handle with one hand and the front of the saw behind the shoe with the other. Turn on the saw and move it forward on the workpiece. Apply enough downward pressure to keep the saw steady. Apply just enough forward pressure to keep the saw cutting properly. Do not apply too much pressure in either direction or force the saw. This can be dangerous, break blades, and cause overheating of the motor.

A reciprocating saw is quite often used in a plunge cut mode to cut openings. This can sometimes be a bit tricky, so start slow and use extreme caution. You can easily break blades, damage the surface to be cut, and even sustain an injury. It is not recommended to plunge cut materials other than wood. Use only a 7 teeth-per-inch blade for this type of cut, and choose the shortest blade that will penetrate the work surface. Longer blades are harder to use to start the cut. Mark the line to be cut on the workpiece. Place the saw with the front edge of the shoe resting on the cut line, and tilt the saw upward, but do not allow the blade to come in contact with the workpiece. Make sure the blade is inside the cut. As the blade moves back and forth, it can actually start outside the cut. Start the saw and, using a high speed, slowly lower the blade into the workpiece until the blade cuts through the wood. Then continue raising the rear handle and lowering the blade into the workpiece until the shoe sits flat on the work surface. Move the saw forward to complete the cut.

Many kinds of metal can be cut with a reciprocating saw. Again, do not force and don't allow the blades to twist or bend. It's extremely important to match the blade to the metal and chore. If the blade chatters or vibrates excessively, use a finer-tooth metal-cutting blade. If the blade tends to heat up, use a slower speed. A coarse blade or slower speed can help prevent the blade teeth from becoming clogged with chips when cutting softer metals, such as aluminum. Cutting oil should be used when cutting metals to keep the blade cool, increase cutting action, and eliminate vibration and material tearing. Make sure to keep the exposed portion of the saw blade clean and free of metal chips by wiping frequently with an oily cloth. Make sure you dispose of the oil-soaked cloth properly to prevent a potential fire hazard. Clamp the workpiece solidly and saw close to the clamping point to prevent vibration of the workpiece. When cutting pipe, angle iron, or conduit, clamp the workpiece in a vice. When cutting thin sheet materials, a good tactic is to sandwich the material between hardboard or plywood and clamp the layers tightly. This will eliminate vibration and prevent tearing the material.

Saber Saws

Basically, a saber or jigsaw is designed for making curved cuts. The saber or jigsaw, however, is the most versatile of portable electric saws. With the right saw you can do just about anything you would do with a circular or reciprocating saw, although in some cases, maybe not as fast or efficiently. Again, the main purpose of the saw, however, is to make curved cuts, or interior cuts. In addition to scroll work, other chores include cutting countertops for sink cutouts and cutting woodwork and paneling for electrical outlets and fixtures. The saw excels at cutting concentric circles to build corner shelves, decorative wall plaques, baskets, intarsia, and pattern cutting for craft projects. It also is handy when working with trim such as half- or quarter-round molding and for cutting cope joints in trim. Not only can a jigsaw be used to cut wood, but with the right blade it's great for cutting plastic plumbing pipe and other plastics, including plastic laminates and many metals.

What to Look For

Jigsaws come either corded or cordless. It doesn't take much power to run a jigsaw blade, and a saw with two batteries will provide plenty of long-lasting power. If you are continually cutting through 2x framing materials, however, a corded model would be suggested. Corded models, for the most part, are also lighter in weight.

Corded models are graded by amps, with 3 being the lowest and 6 the highest. Corded models for heavy-duty work should have a 6-amp or greater motor. Cordless models are designated by battery power in volts. An 18- to 20-volt is fairly standard.

Short blade strokes of less than 1" do not allow for cutting through 1½" materials. Choose a saw with at least a 1" blade stroke. Variable speed is also important. You can use the higher speeds for cutting wood, the slower speeds for cutting

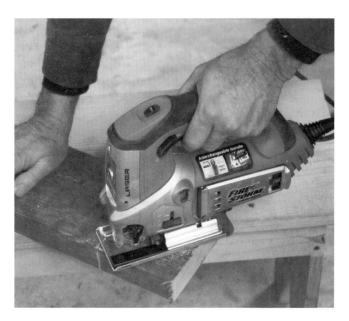

Jigsaws or saber saws are the most versatile of portable electric saws. They can be used to make straight cuts and round or irregular cuts in a wide variety of materials.

Jigsaws are available corded or cordless. If you do a lot of heavy-duty cutting, such as on framing, a corded model may be the best choice.

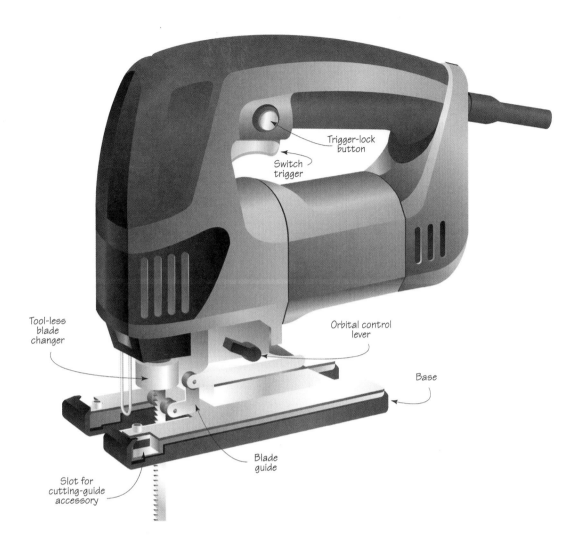

Trigger-lock button

Switch trigger

Tool-less blade changer

Orbital control lever

Base

Blade guide

Slot for cutting-guide accessory

plastic and metal. The latter cuts down on the heat generated and isn't as hard on the blade. Speed is sometimes controlled with a speed-control dial with a separate on-off switch. A trigger-controlled speed control, however, is easier to operate and provides more control. You can start slow and speed up or slow down as needed with the tip of your finger.

Jigsaws are available with orbital or straight (non-orbital) cutting action. This feature causes the blade top to pivot back and forth in addition to the up and down action. This increases the cutting speed, but creates a rougher cut. The amount of orbital action is usually available in degrees.

In the past, to change a blade, a set-screw was used to loosen the blade, using an Allen wrench or screwdriver, and changing a blade was a hassle. Tool-free blade changing has become increasingly popular. A variety of blade chucks are available.

The bases of jigsaws can be angled to create angle cuts, and the method of changing angles also varies. This can be done with an Allen wrench or other tool-use means or tool-free. Again, tool-free is the best choice.

Some saws have a scrolling feature so you can unlock the blade head, allowing the blade to swivel. In this case, the blade turns around a vertical axis, allowing you to make more intricate cuts. You guide the saw with one hand and the blade direction with the other. Or, in some cases, you can lock the blade at different angles for cutting in awkward places.

Some jigsaws come with dust collection ports. In other cases, add-on dust collecting is available. Either a collection port for a vacuum or a blower port is necessary to keep sawdust and chips out of the cutting line for ease of use.

Most of the better saws come with replaceable plastic base covers or inserts. When the base becomes scratched, you can easily swap it out and prevent scratching surfaces, such as plastic, veneers, or fine wood surfaces.

Some saws come equipped with a laser to guide the cut, but they're not very useful when making scrolled or curved cuts. LED lights, however, are a definite plus as they provide better visibility of the cut line.

A roller blade guard helps provide blade stability for precise cutting and an electric brake freezes the blade action when necessary. Anti-splinter inserts, usually available as an add-on but standard with some saws, can add to the ease of use and more precise cutting. A rip fence or guide-rule accessory provides a means of guiding the saw for straight cuts. Circular guides are also available as an option.

How to Use

Jigsaws are relatively easy to use and are an excellent starter tool for beginning woodworkers or youngsters. The design, pattern, or cut line is scribed or marked onto the work surface. The saw is held slightly away from the beginning of the cut line edge but down flat on the work surface. Turn on the saw, and slowly move the saw forward along the previously marked cut line. Make sure the saw base is held flush with the workpiece, or you may create a slanted cutting surface and break the blade. Always advance the saw slowly, especially when cutting curves or scrolling. Moving too quickly or forcing the blade can also create a slanted cut or break the blade. Some saws also allow you to flush cut by moving the base back so the blade protrudes slightly.

When bevel cutting, first remove the battery before making any adjustments. Using the method described in your owner's manual, tilt the blade to the bevel desired and then lock it in place.

Cutouts can be made in one of two methods. The first is to bore a starting hole or, in some

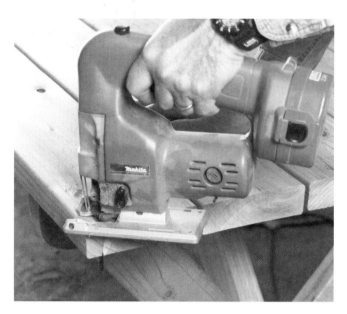

Cordless models have become more popular and will handle just about any homeowner or woodworking chore.

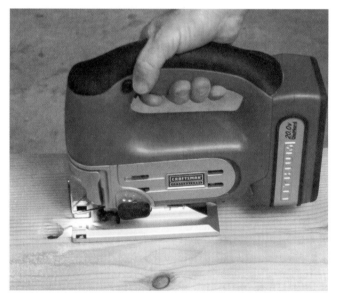

The features on the Craftsman Professional Model shown include: variable speed from 0 to 2300 spm, 1" strokes, four multi-position orbital-action settings, roller blade guard, tool-free blade and base adjustment, dust control, and integrated LED light.

instances, a starting hole in each corner. Insert the blade into the hole, start the saw, and begin the cut from inside the hole. I've also often used a jigsaw for cutting out window and door openings after sheet siding has been installed on a building using this method. Fasten the siding in place, bore holes from the inside of the building at each corner, use a straight edge to mark between the holes, and cut out the opening with a saber saw, cutting from the outside.

Another method is plunge cutting. With this method, you do not need to bore a starting hole. Tilt the saw up on the front edge of the saw base. The blade point should be positioned above the cut line on the workpiece surface. With firm pressure applied to the saw so the front edge of the base doesn't move, turn on the saw and slowly lower the back end. As the blade slices into the workpiece, slowly lower the back end until the base sits flat on the surface. Then continue the cut in the normal manner.

Metal cutting must be done with the appropriate metal-cutting blade. Always use a suitable coolant or cutting oil when cutting metal. If you don't, you will have significant blade wear. Another tactic is to lightly grease the underside of the work surface.

Blades

A wide variety of blade choices is available for jigsaws, including blades for cutting wood, ferrous and nonferrous metal, plastic, as well as mineral and composition materials. Blades are also available edged with tungsten carbide grit for cutting ceramic tile, slate, and other materials. A knife blade is available for cutting leather, rubber, insulating materials, ceiling tile, and wallboard. Woodcutting blades are commonly available in two styles: set tooth and hollow ground. Set-tooth blades have the teeth set or the teeth pointing alternately to each side. This creates a kerf for the blade to move through without binding. Hollow-ground blades do not have set, but the blade is tapered from the teeth to the sides to provide clearance. The number of teeth per inch (tpi) is also important. The more teeth per inch, the slower but smoother the cut. It's also important to use a blade with ample width when cutting wood thicker than ¼" or the blade may flex and wander.

For cuts beginning outside the workpiece edge, begin the cut by resting the saw base flat on the surface but with the blade not touching. Turn on the saw and move the blade into the cut line, then continue the cut.

Jigsaws can also be used to make bevel and compound cuts by adjusting the base.

Choosing The Proper Blade

STEP 1. Determine the type of blade shank that fits your saw. This may be either Ushank or Tshank.

STEP 2. Match the blade type to the job.

Blade types include:

BiMetal (BiM) — This is a highly flexible blade made of a tough combination of high-speed steel and high-carbon steel. It is suitable for the most demanding jobs where there is a high risk of breakage.

High-Speed Steel — These fully-hardened blades are ideal for cutting metal, aluminum, and nonferrous metal.

High-Carbon Steel — These softer steel blades are the choice for softer materials, such as wood, laminated particle board, and plastics.

STEP 3. Choose the correct tooth geometry for the type of cut desired.

Each material has a different density. It's important to match the material density with the proper blade geometry.

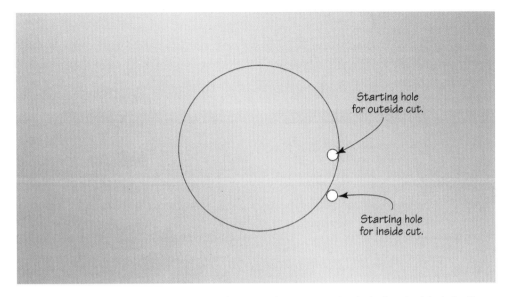

Cutouts can be made in two ways. The first is to bore a starting hole for the blade in the workpiece.

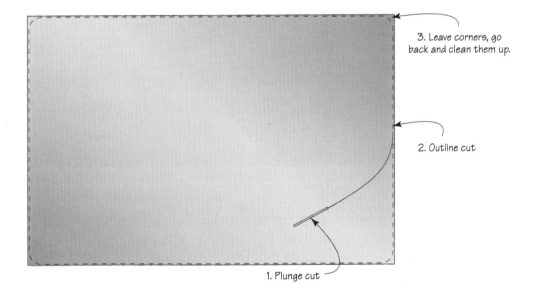

The second is to make a plunge cut. Tip the saw up on the front edge of its shoe, start saw, and slowly lower blade into the work. When the blade is fully into the work, make the cut. For a square cut, round off corners, then go back and remove the corner pieces.

ROUTERS

Routers are a way of life for some woodworkers. They blur the line between portable and bench tools, and the tasks they can perform are varied. They can be hand-held or held stationary in a router table. One of the more common router uses for the homeowner is edging plastic laminate or synthetic countertops. Routers can also be used to make molding and house trim, create picture-frame molding, and repair wood floors by cutting slots to remove damaged strips. With a hinge jig, routers can quickly rout hinge mortises for hanging interior and exterior doors, cut a decorative edge on furniture tops, and create raised panels for doors and drawers. With the appropriate jigs, routers can make finger, box, and dovetail joints and, using templates, rout signs in wood.

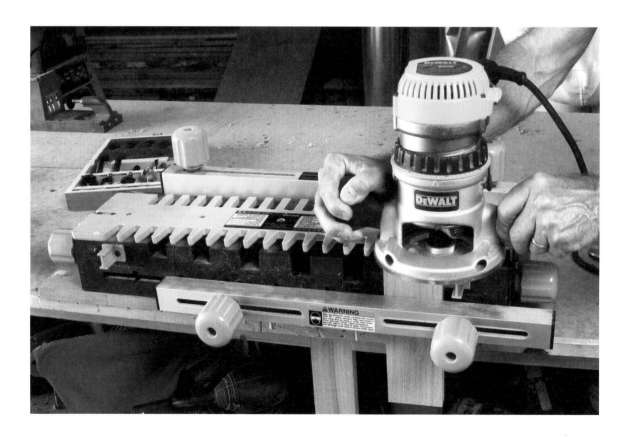

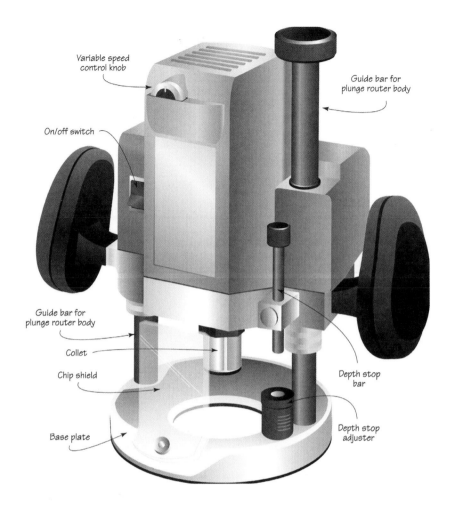

Variable speed
control knob

Guide bar for
plunge router body

On/off switch

Guide bar for
plunge router body

Collet

Chip shield

Base plate

Depth stop
bar

Depth stop
adjuster

WHAT TO LOOK FOR

Routers consist of a power head sliding up and down in an exterior housing, which sometimes has handles for holding the tool. The power head holds a bit in the bottom side. Dedicated routers range in size from 1¾ up to 3¼ horsepower. Routers may have one speed, several speeds, or variable speeds. The latter allows for more precise matching of the speed to the hardness of the wood. Some of the better routers also feature a soft-start, which reduces torque at the beginning of the start and provides longer tool life. Another feature to look for is a spindle lock. This allows for one-tool bit changing. A work light inside the base is also helpful.

Routers come with two base designs: fixed and plunge. Fixed-base routers have the cutter head firmly secured to the base with up and down movement governed by a locking dial. Fixed-base routers are used for edge work or in router tables. Fixed bases may consist of either a dual handle or a D-handle design or, in some cases, no handles. Some routers have the start-stop switch conveniently built into one of the handles. Others have the switch on top of the motor housing, which means you must remove your hand from one handle to use the switch.

Plunge routers have the head mounted on a spring-loaded column. The bit is started and then plunged down in the wood. This method is used for cutting surfaces, such as sign work, veining, carving, and others. The Freud 3¼-horsepower model has soft-start and electronic speed control for smooth cuts. Edge guide and template guide kits are handy accessories. DeWalt, Craftsman, Bosch, and Porter-Cable offer combo kits with both a fixed and plunge base and one cutterhead. DeWalt's kit comes in two sizes. One has a 1¾-horsepower, 24,500 rpm motor with an adjustable, tool-free motor cam lock that makes an easy base change from fixed to plunge. Another 2¼-horsepower kit has soft-start and variable speed. The plunge base features through-the-column dust collection. The Craftsman kit has a 2-horsepower motor and changes quickly from fixed to plunge without tools. The plunge base also has a dust collection attachment for a vacuum. The Porter-Cable kit has a 1¾-horsepower, variable-speed motor and comes with an edge guide. The Bosch models feature a 2¼-horsepower variable-speed motor with soft-start.

Traditionally, changing router bits has been neither fast nor easy. Conventional routers use a split collet and jam-nut arrangement to secure the cutting bit. To replace or change a bit, you must use one wrench to hold the spindle and another wrench to turn the chuck. Or use one wrench if the router has a spindle lock. In either case, it's awkward and time consuming. It's also impossible to get the bits set to the exact same depth if using them for matching cuts. The Craftsman QuikRout system is tool-free. The quick-change mechanism is designed for one-hand use. Bit installation is easy by placing it into the bit adapter then snapping it into the QuikRout system. Removing a bit requires only slight pressure on the quick-release collar. Each bit can be outfitted with its own adapter that, once installed, doesn't need adjusting. This allows for consistent repetitive cuts at the same depth without having to calibrate the router every time a bit is changed. With the ½" connector, changing between a ½" to a ¼" bit can be done in seconds. The system comes with the QuikRout connector, four bit adapters, and a convenient storage case. The Woodline USA Eliminator Chuck allows you to quickly change bits with a T-handle Allen wrench in seconds.

In addition to the basic router design, some spiral saw tools, such as the Roto Zip, also offer router bases and bits. Even little rotary tools, such as the Dremel, have an accessory router base that allows for miniature routing jobs. Dedicated laminate trimmers, similar to routers, are also available.

Routers are available in a variety of sizes, including the large model shown.

Routers are available with fixed or plunge bases. Some routers are available with both.

Small palm-style routers, often called laminate trimmers, have become increasingly popular.

Routers may have the on-off switch located on the motor or, in the case of the Porter-Cable model shown, on the handle.

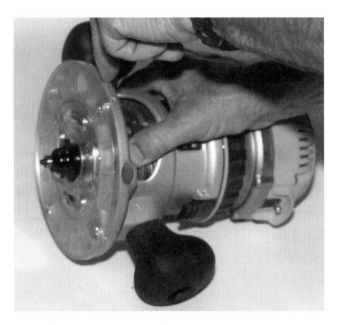

A spindle-lock makes changing bits easier.

Router Bits

A wide variety of routing bits are available. Some of the most common include straight bits in a variety of sizes, trimming bits, round nose (core box), dovetail, round-over, beading, round-over-beading combos, Roman ogee, cove and bead, chamfering, V-groove, pointed roundover, tongue and groove, lock miter, locking drawer glue joint, classical pattern, and multiform. The latter can create over 40 different moldings with just one bit. Slot cutters, door construction sets for stiles and rails, rabbeting bits, pattern-cutting bits, panel raising, key slot, hinge mortising, veining, radius-end cove, vertical panel-raising bits, rule-joint, plywood dado, and antique beading are other bits available. The No-Drip Edge bits from Grizzly allow you to create a rounded countertop edge on solid surface materials, such as CORIAN.

Some bits come with a spindle and cutters that can be interchanged for different cuts. Individual bits are available, as well as a wide variety of kits of the most popular shapes from many sources. Bits are available with ¼" or ½" diameter shanks. The ½" shank bits provide more support with less chatter, especially on the larger-size patterns. Purchase only top-quality bits that are carbide-tipped for long life. Woodcraft, Grizzly, and Freud offer antikickback router bits. The design of these industrial-quality carbide router bits limits the stock feed rate for safer routing operations. Some bits also come with a pilot or small roller on a bearing located below the bit cutter. These allow you to free-hand cut edges with the pilot following the shape of the edge, which can be straight or irregular. A guide bushing set allows you to match the cutter to a variety of templates. Templates can include such things as sign systems or hinge mortising guides. Or you

Types of Router Bits

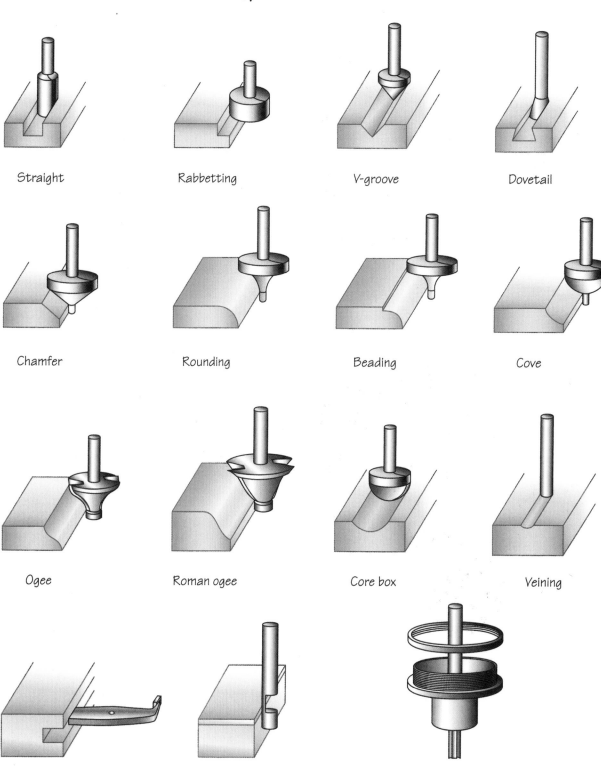

Straight

Rabbetting

V-groove

Dovetail

Chamfer

Rounding

Beading

Cove

Ogee

Roman ogee

Core box

Veining

Slotting

Laminate trimmer

Template guide

can make up your own templates for almost anything you can imagine.

Using Routers

Routers are fairly simple to use, but as with any power tool, proper and safe usage is important. Routers, which operate the bit at high speeds, throw a lot of wood chips and dust. Be sure to wear safety glasses or goggles. Routers are also somewhat loud, and hearing protection is advised. Before operating, make absolutely sure that the bit and/or any jigs or accessories are properly tightened and adjusted. Make sure all workpieces are clamped or secured to a solid work surface before beginning the routing job. Always use sharp cutters, dull cutters may cause the router to jump or kickback. Bits often become gummed with resin. To ensure accurate and smooth cuts, remove the gum with mineral spirits.

To insert a bit, first make sure the router is unplugged and the switch is off. Insert the round shank into the loosened collet as far as it will go, then pull it out about 1/16 of an inch. Using the wrench or wrenches provided, turn the collet nut clockwise while holding the spindle shaft with the second wrench or spindle lock. To adjust for the depth of cut, loosen the locking lever and turn the micrometer dial. Then relock the locking lever. Plunge routers have a depth stop, which can be set to stop the cutter at the desired depth.

With the router safely positioned flat on the work surface and the bit not contacting the wood, start the router and then move the bit into the wood. The direction of feed is extremely important for safe and successful routing. When routing edges, make the first cut across the end grain, and then cut with the grain. This will alleviate any splintering that may occur across the grain. Shape straight grain by moving left to right. Speed can run from 8,000 to 24,000 rpm. It's important to choose the proper router speed

Variable speed and soft-start are other features to look for.

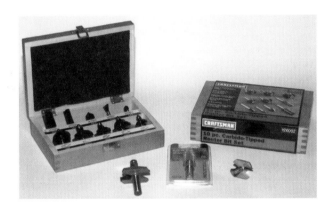

A wide variety of router bits are available for any number of routing techniques.

The most common use of a router is edge shaping.

for the project on routers that provide that option. The operating manual should provide a speed chart for the different woods and surfaces according to the model. It's important to keep the router moving while routing to prevent burn marks on the wood surface.

Routing is not only fun, it's addictive.

A router is not only a versatile shop tool, it can almost do magic, especially with a variety of accessories. Heavier routers are sometimes awkward to hold straight when edging stock. The TurnLock Offset Base from Milescraft creates a large stable base for edge work. Routers can also be used to create a wide variety of joints. When gluing up wide boards from narrow ones, edge joints can be created with a router using a variety of bit styles. These include tongue-and-groove, tongue-and-groove with V-edging for car siding, 90° V-groove male and female bits, and special glue-joint bits. Routers fitted with a slotting bit can also be used to cut rabbets for joining cabinet backs to sides, for cutting groove, slotting, and dadoes for joining drawer bottoms to drawers. Other joint bits include: drawer lock bits used to create glue joints for joining drawer sides and fronts; flute and bead bits for creating small boat planking; corner lock bits for 90° corner joints, such as in jewelry boxes; and corner lock miter bits. Another common joint is a dovetail joint, used for drawer construction, as well as furniture and small boxes. The Porter Cable 4200 Series dovetail jigs allow you to make all types of dovetail joints including: through dovetails, half-blind dovetails, rabbeted half-blind dovetails, and even box or finger joints. You will need a router base plate that accepts a guide bushing and guide bushings to fit the router-bit shank size. The TurnLock Router Base Plate fits most routers with a round base, is easy to install, and comes with two turn-in bushings. Additional

The TurnLock Offset Base from Milescraft provides a more stable hold when doing edge routing.

With a plunge router, such as the Firestrom shown, you can add even more magic. The bit is fed into the work surface to the depth needed by the action of the plunge base.

Plunge routing with a plunge router, a guide bushing, and handmade pattern is another popular routing technique.

You'll need a router base plate that accepts a guide bushing. The TurnLock Base Plate fits most routers and comes with turn-in bushings.

Dovetail joints are traditional and popular. They are precisely made using a dovetail jig, such as the Porter-Cable jig shown.

bushings are also available in a set ranging from 5⁄16" to 1". Creating dovetails is easy with the jig and router. A good choice in routers for the jig is the Porter-Cable Model 892 that not only features a soft-starting 12-amp motor, but quickly moves from fixed- to plunge- and spiral-down bases. The latter two are sold as accessories. A dual-position switch allows you to switch off power without letting go of the handles. And the fine depth settings with a finger micro knob allows for easy setting of the bit depth.

Plunge routing adds even more versatility, allowing you to surface plane, create fluting, and a wide variety of decorative cuts. In plunge routing, the router is turned on with the bit free of the work surface. The bit is then fed into the work surface to the depth set. In most instances, some sort of template and guide bushing are required. And again, a wide variety of templates are available. One practical use of a plunge router is in cutting hinge mortises. You can cut precise interior and exterior door hinge mortises with a plunge router and the Milescraft Hinge Mortise Guide set.

The magic comes in the wide variety of other techniques and jigs that can be used with a plunge router. One fun technique is creating inlays. This is done using the Milescraft TurnLock Inlay kit. A 1⁄18" spiral router bit is fitted in the router collet and the workpiece clamped to a bench. A Kreg **dog** clamp fitted in a workbench slot makes this easy. The template chosen is then secured to the workpiece with double-faced tape. The depth is set and the router used to make a pass around the inside edge of the template. The excess material is then routed within the template to create the pocket. The inlay material must be the same or slightly thicker than the pocket depth. Set the depth of cut so the bit will go completely through the inlay material. Secure the inlay to a backing board and the template to the inlay material. Carefully make one pass around the template guide. Dry-fit the inlay into the pocket and sand the inlay or pocket to create a good fit, then glue in place.

122

The TurnLock SpiroCrafter is an absolutely fun kit. Although it works best with a Milescraft Plunger Model 1000 or Dremel Model 330, it can be used with almost any router to create thousands of unique designs in wood and plastic. The TurnLock base plate is installed on your router and the guide bushing installed. First, make a design on paper, and then select a template and pattern. The template has a rotating center that fits in cogs. Determine the rotation interval from the Design Guide. Place your paper pattern on the workpiece and secure it in place. Center the template base and secure it to the work surface with clamps. Align the template so the selected pattern window is in the desired starting position and secure the template in place by pushing the template cogs into the appropriate template base grooves. Place the pencil guide on the pencil with the desired end directed toward the pencil lead. Mark the pattern by allowing the pencil guide to follow the edge of the selected pattern. Rotate the template to the next desired position and repeat the steps. Once the design is complete to your satisfaction, choose the appropriate bit and guide bushing. Set the router bit to the appropriate depth, bring the router bit and guide bushing into the selected pattern window, turn on the router, and rout the pattern in a clockwise direction. Rotate the template to the next position.

You can create your own routed wood or plastic signs with the Router SignCrafter from Milescraft. Once the tool is assembled, choose the letters you need to spell the words you intend to engrave, and place them in the letter slot. Use the TurnLock router base plate and guide bushing. Fasten the template to the workpiece and secure the workpiece to your bench with clamps. Choose the appropriate router bit, turn on the router, lower the bit into the template, allowing the guide bushing to follow the letter template, and rout out the letter. Repeat for the rest of the letters.

TurnLock from Milescraft offers a wide variety of router accessories for some quite unusual projects. Creating inlays is a fun technique using the Milescraft TurnLock Inlay Kit. The recess is cut following the template provided, then the inlay cut with the same template. The inlay is then glued in place.

The TurnLock SpiroCrafter is also a lot of fun. The kit includes a rotating template with designs cut in it. After determining the design, rout out the design, turn the template to the next position, and continue routing until you complete the pattern.

Another fun tool is the CMT 3D Router Carver System. This can be used with a plunge router to create hand-carved accents on drawers, doors, or panels. The system comes with templates and holding frames, a 3D Router Carver Bit, 3D Carver video, and full instructions.

Pattern routing is a great way of duplicating items, for instance creating curved upper rails and panels for raised panel doors. The Frame and Panel Templates from Woodcraft make it easy to precisely cut a number of parts. The Templates include cathedral and arched. Each set is machined for precise fit. After rough-sawing the work, the templates are fastened to the work with double-faced tape and a flush trim bit used to rout the shape precisely. You can also make up your own templates of W plastic, HDPE, or plywood for other shapes.

Router Tables

For many operations, the router is used in the portable fashion, moving the router across the workpiece. An easier, safer, and more productive method for some operations is to fix the router in a stand or table top with the bit protruding up through the table. In this method, the stock is moved against the rotating bit. Any number of operations may be made with this method. A router table can be handmade or manufactured. One of the tables I've tested is the Craftsman Large Stationary Routing Center. The unit features a heavy-duty floor stand that holds a large, benchtop table. The table has a cast-aluminum top with clear, antifriction coating. Parallel adjusting, expandable, extruded aluminum fence with jointing feature and dust port are other features, as well as a miter gauge and router bit storage panel. You can also build your own router table, tops, fences, and other parts are available from a number of suppliers, including Woodcraft, Woodline USA, Kreg, and Rockier. Some routers come with depth adjustment from the base plate, making them more suitable for use in router tables.

Featherboards are often used on router tables to aid in holding the workpiece in position when routing. Push-sticks should always be used when cutting narrow stock. Basic table operations include: full-edge cutting or jointing, edge-cutting with nonpilot bits, edge-cutting with pilot bits, and grooving, fluting, or veining. A miter gauge can be used with many tables to ensure accurate cuts on the ends of workpieces.

Creating your own routed wood signs with the Milescraft Router SignCrafter. The jig holds letters in place as a template for the router to follow.

Another handy jig is a circle or arc cutter, such as the milescraft shown. It guides the router in an arc or circle.

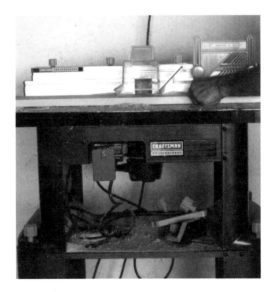

Many routing chores require the use of a router table.

Making Frame-and-Panel Doors

Frame-and-panel doors are traditional with many classic furniture styles, as well as cabinets. Frame-and-panel doors offer several advantages, including their beauty, but more importantly, they are less prone to warp and twist than solid doors. With the inset panel loose in the frame, they more readily adjust to changing humidity and hot and cold conditions.

Although frame-and-panel doors appear complicated, they aren't difficult to build if you take your time and measure carefully. Frame-and-panel doors consist of the rails, the top and bottom pieces, the stiles, the side pieces, and the panel. The panel may be flat or raised. Flat panels are the easiest to construct and install. Raised panels take more work, and arched raised panels require the most work. Arched panels may be simple arches or a cathedral design.

One of the best methods of making raised panel doors is with a router, router table, rail-and-stile, and panel-raising bits. The rail-and-stile bits not only create the rail-and-stile joints that are then glued together, but also a profile on the inside front edge of the frame, as well as the rabbet for the panel. These come in sets of two, one for the cope and one for the inside profile and rabbet in the rails and stiles. Different profiles are available with the most common being Roman Ogee, Roundover, and Cove and Bead. Many companies sell the bits in a set with a mating raised-panel profile for cutting the raised panels. The CMT Sommerfeld Cabinetmaking Set includes a matching drawer-front cutter.

Woodline USA carries a full line of rail-and-stile, raised-panel, and bit sets, including their three-piece Raised Panel Door Set and the Sam Maloof Signature Series 6-piece Cabinet Set. Woodline also sells setup blocks to match their bit sets. These HDPE blocks make it easy to mate cuts for rails and stiles. Slide the profile block next to the bit and raise or lower to determine the mating cuts.

Frame-and-panel is a popular door style for cabinets and furniture.

One of the best methods for creating frame-and-panel doors is using a rail-and-stile bit set in a router table.

Individual bits may be purchased, such as these from Bosch, for creating frame and panel.

CMT offers a single bit with two cutters. Simply raising and lowering the bit allows you to make the profile and cove cuts.

Complete sets with the profile, cove, and raised panel bit are also available.

You will need a heavy-duty, variable-speed router with a ½" shank and chuck and a sturdy router table for using these large-diameter bits. First step is to make the cope cuts on the cross grain ends of the rails. Set the fence almost flush with the cutter bearing. Use wooden push blocks to push the ends through the cutter head. Then set up the profile and rabbet cutter head and cut the inside of both rails and stiles. This usually takes two bits, but CMT makes a single bit that can be used to cut both profiles by changing the bit height.

With the rails and stiles cut, the next step is to cut the panel. Flat panels are easy. You can use ¼" plywood or plane solid stock to ¼" thickness for the panels. Raised panels can be cut in several ways. Square or rectangular panels can be raised by tilting a table-saw blade, removing the splitter and guard, and running the edges of the panel across the blade. Vertical panel cutters that are used in a router table are also available for square panels. They can operate with less powerful routers.

Arched and cathedral raised panels are mated with a top-arched rail. Both must be cut on a router table. The large bit must be run slowly and the wood fed slowly into it. You can design the arch, cut the rail and door to match with a band saw, and then rout. These techniques are more difficult, so practice on scrap wood. The CMT Sommerfeld Cabinetmaking Set, combined with their arched rail templates, makes the chore easier and more precise. First step is to cut all pieces to size and shape. Note the rails must be cut long enough for their profiles to fit into the stiles. Cut the arched rails using the selected template sold separately. This should be cut about ¹⁄₁₆" wider for trimming. Set up the cope cutter to make the cuts in each end of the rails. Set the fence even with the cutter bearing and use a wooden push stick to to push the stock through for the cut. Place the template onto the arched rail stock and fasten with nails driven through the template holes and about ⅜" into the stock. Cut the arch using a band saw and cutting to within about ⅛" of the template. Place the flush trimming bit in the router table and position it so the template meets the bit bearing. Trim the rail, remove the template, turn it around, and use it on the raised panel stock to cut and trim it. If making several doors, do all doors through each step. Set up the pattern cutter for the inside profiles, and use the template against the bearing to cut the inside of the top arched rail. Reinstall the fence and cut the inside profiles on the straight bottom rail and the two stiles.

To cut the raised panel, set the fence so it is even with the bearing on the panel cutter, and set the cutter to the correct height. Run the router at about 10,000 rpm and use wooden push blocks. Rout the straight cross-grain bottom edge first, and then cut with the grain on the left side. Using a half-fence setup, recut the left side and continue around the curved top of the panel freehand. Carefully and slowly feed the arched panel against the cutter using push blocks. Reinstall the full fence and complete the panel by cutting the right side.

The Woodline USA Raised Panel Door System utilizes templates and a holding jig that makes it much easier and safer to make the arched rail and panel cuts. In this case, the template is used to mark the shape of the arch, which is cut on a band saw to about ⅛" to ¹⁄₁₆" of the final shape. The template is fastened to the holding jig and the stock clamped in place. The flush-trimming bit is set so the bearing rides on the template edge and the stock flush trimmed. The holding jig slides on the router table and has a pair of handles that make it easy to guide the stock into the cutter. The flush trimming bit is removed and the cope bit installed. The fence is reinstalled and the cope cuts made on both the upper and bottom rails.

Arched rails and matching panels are precut using a template on the stock with a bandsaw.

The edges are then flush-trimmed using a template riding on the bearing of a flush-trim bit.

The cove or crossgrain cuts on the rails are first cut using a fence and push sticks.

The profile bit is installed. The Woodline set-up block makes it easy to set bit height for mating the two and the proper cut made.

The profile cuts on the stiles and bottom rail are then cut with the profile bit. The fence is removed and the inside profile cut on the rail freehand, again using the handles to feed the stock into the cutter.

The template is reversed on the holding jig and the panel door arch cut to match the template. The flush-trimming bit is then used to flush trim the panel arch. The panel raising bit is installed and the jig used to guide the arched panel portion through the cutter. The fence is reinstalled and the bottom crossgrain cut made, followed by the two side cuts.

The Legacy Revo Router Milling Machine

The Legacy Revo Milling Machine is a machine that can be used for many standard router chores, as well as techniques normally requiring lathe work. A plunge router mounted in a precision-controlled bed is used to create almost any type of contour on both flat and round stock. You can create tapered legs, round legs with flutes, coves, reeds, spiral-round stock, rope, hollow spirals, diamond, and even pineapple patterns. The machine will also do surface planing, create dentil moldings, raised panels, contours, and rosettes. An interchangeable gear system regulates the rotation speed of the workpiece, as well as the linear travel and the length of spiral pitches. With a template follower you can create Queen Ann or other style legs. And, using a template, you can easily and exactly duplicate as many legs as you desire. With the Vertical Vise kit you can rout tenons and finger joints. All operations are performed above the table and secured between the center of the uniquely designed four-pronged index center and hub system. A number of optional accessories are available that expand the capabilities to create tabletops, round plaques, shallow dishes and bowls, and joinery, such as dovetails. Other accessories allow you to create pens, as well as do pin-routing. A plunge router is required.

ROUTERS

Joints you can make with a router

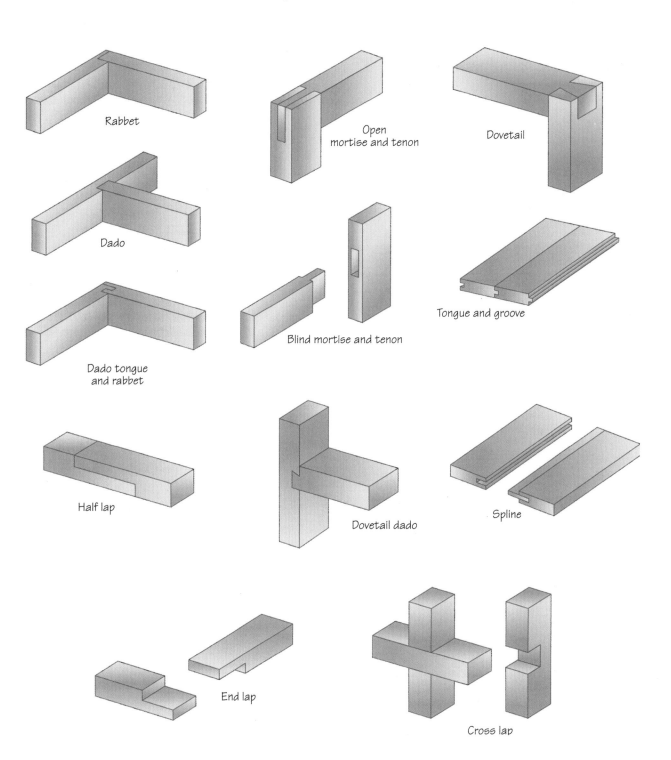

Rabbet

Open mortise and tenon

Dovetail

Dado

Blind mortise and tenon

Tongue and groove

Dado tongue and rabbet

Half lap

Dovetail dado

Spline

End lap

Cross lap

Woodline has created a unique Raised Panel Door System that takes a lot of the guesswork and hassle out of the chore. It comes with a set of templates and a jig to hold the template and work stock.

The jig holds the selected template to match the stock profile and the inside profile cut on the arched rail. Simply guide the jig and stock against the cutter with the handles.

The holding jig then is used with the reverse side of the template for the raised panel.

I utilized the Revo Milling Machine to do two projects shown here, cut flutes in a candlestick project, and to simulate a turned pedestal table with a rope-cut column. In the old days, the column was turned into the round on a lathe, then the rope design was cut with wood rasps and sanded smooth, a very time-consuming chore. The Revo makes the chore quick and easy, taking about an hour to complete the column.

You will need a good quality plunge router, as well as four specific router bits to create the design shown. The bits designed specifically for the Legacy Revo Mill are available from Magnate.

You will need a #3952 Classical Spiral, a #2704 Bottom-Cleaning bit, a #7581 Rope Molding bit, and a #7801 Bowl and Tray Plunge bit.

The table column is made from a 3½"x3½" x17" turning block. The table shown was made from walnut, but any hard, closed grained wood will do. Similar to spindle turning on a lathe, the first step is to make sure the ends are cut square. Mark diagonally across the ends of the block to locate the center of each end. The headstock of the Revo utilizes a metal holding clamp with fingers that is screwed to one end of the turning blank. The fingers are then inserted into a mating clamp on the headstock end of the machine. The opposite end of the turning blank is held in place with a tailstock center point, much like a lathe. With the diagonals marked and the centers found, cut the corners off the blank with a table saw set to 45°.

With the router fastened in place on the milling table, install the bottom-cleaning bit. Lower the router bit, lock it in place, and raise or lower the milling support guide so the bit rests on a flat area of the stock. Lock the milling support guide in place. Raise the router plunge depth guide about ⅛". Release the plunge lever and allow the router to raise completely. Move the milling table to one end of the stock and lower the router bit to establish the starting point. Lock one of the milling table guide stop-locks in place at this location. Move the milling table to the opposite end of the stock and lock that stop-lock in place, as well. Move the milling table back to the beginning and note the starting point of the table on the ruler of the support guide. Lock the milling table to the threaded rod. Turn on the router, lower it in place, and turn the milling machine hand crank. As you crank, the stock revolves at the same time the milling table moves forward, cutting off a spiral of wood to round the stock. Move the milling table back to the starting point, loosen the lock that holds the milling table to the threaded rod, and move the milling table one inch. Repeat the cranking and routing steps until the stock is in the full round.

Remove the bottom-cutting bit and replace it with the classical spiral. Move the milling table so the center of the bit is located 3" from one end of the stock. Using the stop-locks, lock the milling table so it can't slide lengthwise in either direction. Remove the lock to the threaded rod. Set the router bit depth to cut about ¼" into the stock. Turn on the router, lower it in place, and move the sliding milling table to center the router bit over the stock. As you turn the handle of the machine, the bit cuts the pattern into the stock, resembling a lathe-turned shape. Continue lowering the bit and turning the crank until you achieve the depth desired. Repeat this step on the opposite end of the stock.

Remove the spiral bit and insert the rope bit and the magic begins. Locate a starting point for the bit about 1" from the previously turned profile. Lock the stop-lock in place and move the milling table to the opposite end and repeat the step. Determine the cutting depth to create the rope and lock the router

The Legacy Revo Milling Machine utilizes a plunge router to make a wide variety of milling cuts.

One example is a pedestal table with a rope-cut design, a traditional turning project.

The project usually required hours of hand rasping to create the rope design but is done quickly with the Legacy. The first step is to mill the blank to round. As the hand-crank is turned, the stock is turned at the same time the milling table moves the router bit across the stock's surface.

The rope carved.

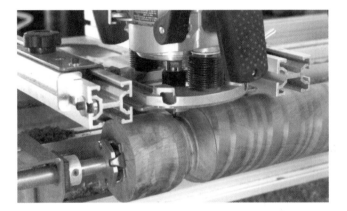

Then a decorative profile is cut in each end.

plunge depth guide in place. Move the milling machine back to the starting point, and reinstall the milling table/threaded rod lock. Turn on the router, plunge to the preset depth and turn the crank to revolve the stock, and at the same time move the milling table. This will create the first of three spirals utilized to create the rope design.

Again, move the milling table back in place, remove the table/rod lock, and move the table 1". Lower the router bit to make sure it is correctly positioned to cut the next rope twist. Turn on the router and repeat the steps to make the next cut. Repeat for the third cut.

The last step on the table column shown was to insert a bowl-and-tray plunge bit and cut a design to clean up the rope cuts. The cuts are extremely precise and require just a little sanding to complete the column.

The table bottom, top support, and top were cut to shape with a band saw, their edges routed and then sanded smooth. Fasten the bottom in place to the bottom of the column and the top-support to the top of the column with screws. Then fasten the top support to the underside of the table with screws. Sand and finish.

The Legacy can also be used to cut flutes in columns.

PORTABLE ELECTRIC SURFACING TOOLS, SANDERS, AND PLANERS

Portable electric sanders and power planers are important tools for the woodworking shop, contractors, do-it-yourselfers, and homeowners. In addition to the portable electric sanders mentioned here, air-sanders are also available. They're covered in the next section about air tools.

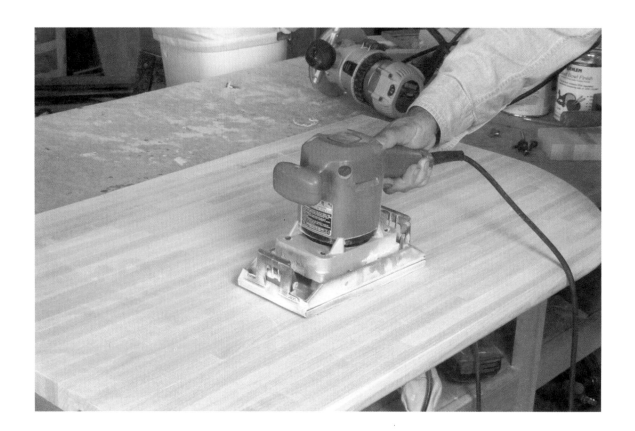

Sanders

Working in my father's custom cabinet and furniture shop as a youngster, I stood and sanded for hours. I hated sanding then, and I hate it now. Sanding is, however, a necessary evil for woodworkers, homeowners, do-it-yourselfers, and auto-finishers. The basic styles of sanders haven't changed much from forty years ago. However, the quality, durability, ease of use, and safety features have greatly improved. Sanders are available in both bench and portable models. We will cover bench sanders in Section 3. Basic portable sanders include: belt, orbital, random orbit, spindle, ¼-sheet (palm) finishing, and ½-sheet finishing. Specialty sanders are also available, including profile and detail sanders.

Belt Sanders

Portable belt sanders are made for fast removal of stock. They will quickly smooth down and level a surface and remove paint or glue lines. Used unwisely, however, or without careful attention, they can turn your project into a mess of gouges, grooves, deep scratches, and a wood surface that is almost impossible finish. Try it once on plywood or veneer, and you'll be sorry.

   You wouldn't think a belt sander to be particularly dangerous, but I still carry a deep scar as a result of misuse of a belt sander. I was building a wooden boat in the summertime, wearing shorts and squatting down sanding the boat side with a belt sander. I started to set the sander down without allowing it to stop thoroughly and it brushed the top of my leg, instantly rolling the skin and flesh of the top of my leg up in the sander. And then I realized, with flesh and skin pinched tightly, I couldn't stand up. After a longtime of yelling, my wife Joan came to my rescue. We had to completely dismantle the sander to release my skin and flesh.

   Belt sanders are available in several sizes, determined by the belt size. Sanders for most home and shop use run from 3x18 up to 4x24.

Belt sanders are primarily used for rough sanding surfaces, such as when several boards have been glued up.

Belt sanders are available in a variety of sizes.

Proper adjustment of the belt tensioning mechanism is important on belt sanders.

Amps can range from 5 up to 11 in home shop models. As with any power tool, more amps translate into more power and faster cutting. The speed of the belt also determines the amount of cutting power, and this can range from 700 up to over 1,400 feet per minute. I keep two belt sanders, a small version for light work and a heavy-duty 4x24 model for rough surfacing of glued up panels and other chores. Variable speed is also a feature, although it can add to the cost. Some models feature a dial for speed control, others utilize a finger control. Most also have a trigger switch allowing you to use the tool in continuous use.

Belt sanders are available in two motor types. A transverse motor belt sander has the motor positioned above the sanding mechanism and drives power via a belt. Once the most common, these types are now more commonly found on the larger sanders, particularly floor sanders. A reduction gear is used to reduce the motor speed to the rpm needed to drive the belt. In-line motor belt sanders have become more popular because they are more compact. The motor is positioned in-line with a gear drive reducing motor speed and, again, a belt to drive the sanding mechanism.

All belt sanders utilize a belt-tensioning mechanism. This is basically a spring-loaded roller that forces the front roller away from the drive roller. The first step in loading the belt or adjusting the sander is to release the belt release lever. This causes a cam on the inner end of the release lever to draw the front roller back toward the rear roller, allowing you to install or remove the sanding belt. Position the sanding belt in place, paying attention to the arrow direction of the belt, if it has one. Then push the cam-locking lever back in place to tighten the front roller against the belt. A tracking knob on the front roller allows you to adjust the belt so it tracks true and straight on the platen.

Belt sanders also create a lot of dust. Most sanders have their own dust collection system, but few really work well when you're really aggressively sanding. Shop-Vac attachments work best.

In addition to their usual fast wood-removal chores, some belt sanders can be turned over on their tops and mounted upside down to be used as stationary bench-top sanders. And you can also use them for rough sharpening of tools, such as chisels.

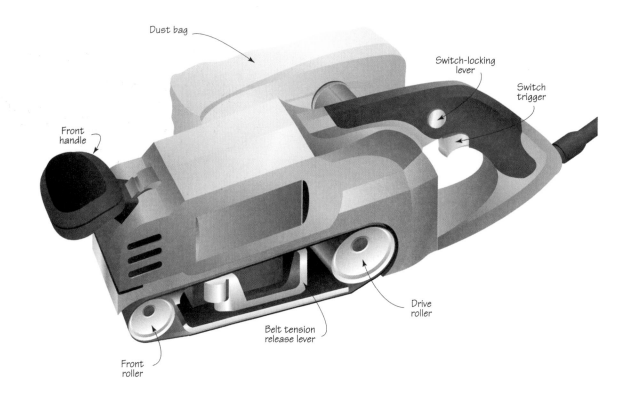

How to Use

Pull the trigger and let 'er rip. That method of sander use can be a serious mistake. The first step is to secure any loose workpieces. A belt sander can cause a piece of wood to fly across your shop like a military projectile. One tactic I use for sanding glued up and other flat pieces is a bench stop. Actually I don't keep a permanent stop, but simply temporarily fasten a section of wood thinner than the workpiece to my workbench, then remove when I'm done. Place the workpiece against the stop and sand against the stop. This allows you access to sanding the full workpiece, rather than clamping one end or side. And I like to grasp the sander cord in one hand and make sure it doesn't get close to the work surface. You can jerk a cord into the sander before you can stop it.

Incidentally, belt sanding is a better way for smoothing glued up surfaces than using a planer because the hard glue lines can dull planer blades in a split second.

Belt sanders can remove a lot of material in a hurry and ruin a wood surface if you're not careful with them.

Orbital and random orbit sanders are the next step in the sanding process to remove marks left by belt sanders.

To prevent gouging the wood surface, grasp both sander handles firmly. Start the sander with the belt off the surface. Never start the sander while resting the belt on the wood surface. With the sander running, lower the heel of the sander to the surface, then with a forward motion, lower the rest of the machine and begin a sanding stroke. Keep the sander moving at all times to prevent digging or gouging the surface. This is simply a back and forth motion with most of the sanding done on the pull stroke. Lift the sander up from the work surface before turning it off. Do not press down on the sander. Always allow the weight of the sander alone to do the work. Pressing down cuts down on the action and is harder on the sander motor. If the surface is glued up with a very uneven surface or you need to do a lot of leveling, I like to first sand diagonally across the grain. But take your time, sand a little, check the surface, then sand again. With a big sander and lots of contact with the surface, I actually allow the sander to move in sweeps holding by the back handle rather than with both hands. This creates a "floating" sanding action that doesn't tend to dig in. On soft woods, however, you'll cut in before you believe it. Regardless, I then sand lightly with the grain to remove cross-marks. Panels are usually bigger lengthwise, and this is where you can really gouge a fine piece of work.

It's important to match the belt coarseness to the job. If heavy-duty sanding is required, start with coarse or very coarse grit open grit (36) belt. Then switch to a medium open coat (60 to 80) belt. For the final smoothing, switch to an open or closed-coat fine grit (100) belt. You may wish to do some final smoothing with an old fine-grit belt.

Orbital and Random Orbit Sanders

Once the surface has been leveled with a belt sander, the next sander to use might be a random orbit model. Random orbit sanders utilize an oscillating action that removes swirl marks.

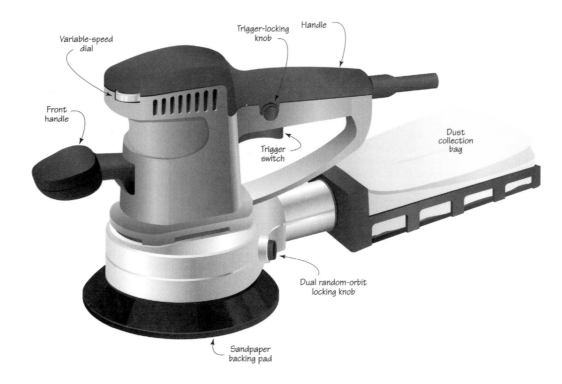

Variable-speed dial

Trigger-locking knob

Handle

Front handle

Trigger switch

Dust collection bag

Dual random-orbit locking knob

Sandpaper backing pad

With the same grit sandpaper in each, straight-line sanders are not quite as aggressive. You may wish to start with a random orbit to remove any belt-sander marks, and then move to the straight-line/or-bital sanders for further smoothing. Random orbit may be a palm or grip design and the sanding pads may be held by adhesive or hook and loop. Hook and loop is the easiest to use. Both orbital and random orbit sanders are available with dust collection systems or adapters for shop vacuums. Other features to look for include: dual random settings for fine sanding or more aggressive material removal. An electronic speed control and soft-start, as well as a pad brake control also make it easier to sand gouge-free. The type of orbit is also important. The faster the orbit and the smaller, the more effective the sanding cut.

Finishing Sanders

Finishing sanders normally utilize a straight-line or vibrating action. They may be large, ½-sheet sanders or small palm sanders, also often called 74-sheet sanders. The ½-sheet sanders are more commonly used in high-production work, such as cabinet and furniture shops. Halfsheet sander motors run from

2 to 3 amps. The ¼-sheet sanders usually run from 1 up to 2 amps. Features to look for on both styles include an on-board vacuum system with through pad dust collection and easy-to-use sanding paper release tabs. Both random orbit and finishing sanders should have dust-free switches. These finishing sanders have the ability to accept virtually any type of sandpaper. A number of finishing sanders are also available with pointed tips. Called detail sanders, they provide the ability to get into corners.

How to Use

Halfsheet production sanders usually have a front and back handle to provide more control. Again, it's important to start with the coarser grits and move progressively to the finer grits. In order to save steps, start with the finest grit that will do the job. For softwood, a good sequence is 60-80-120-180 grits. For hardwoods, a good sequence is 80-120-180-220. Both orbital, random orbit, and finishing pad sanders can easily round-over edges. Be careful not to cut into sharp edges, such as tabletops, leg edges, door and drawer edges, and routed patterns. In use, the orbital sander is usually turned on and then placed in contact

The final step is with finishing sanders, and these are available in large ½-sheet sanders for production work.

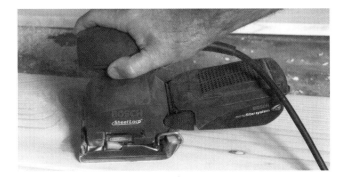

As well as ¼-sheet sanders for smaller chores.

with the wood surface. Random orbit sanders are best first placed in contact with the wood surface and then turned on, preventing the spinning edge from gouging the surface.

Specialty Sanders

A number of specialty sanders have evolved in the past few years. One style is the profile sander. These come with a number of rubber profiles fitted with sandpaper and then into the sander. This allows sanding down in grooves, sanding angles, and other areas. One of the more unusual portable sanders is the portable oscillating spindle sander. This style utilizes an oscillating spindle or drum and is great for sanding larger objects, such as countertops, sink openings, architectural woodwork, and for scribing custom cabinets in place. The Porter-Cable model has variable speed control allowing rotation from 2,400 to 3,600 rpm and comes with an edge guide that allows accurate, preset removal of material for edge smoothing operations. It also mounts in a Porter-Cable router table to create a fixed drum-style sander.

The Intelligent Mouse from Black & Decker gives feedback while sanding. A three-position Zone light indicator communicates the most efficient sanding modes.

The Craftsman 3D Sander is unique in that it consists of three separate sanding discs that can conform to either convex or concave surfaces. The variable speed discs operate independently from 800 to 2,600 rpm.

Power Planers

Another tool my carpenter dad would really have appreciated is a power planer. One of the most common chores in days past was hanging doors, both interior and exterior. That was before today's prehung door units became so popular. And one important chore in hanging a door was to plane the edges to allow the door to properly fit the jamb. This, of course, was done with a hand plane. A portable electric plane can quickly and easily do this, as well as other chores, such as creating chamfers and edge-planing stock. The latter can substitute for a jointer in a small home shop.

What to Look For

Portable electric planes are available in both corded and cordless models. Corded models range from 5 up to 7 amps; cordless models are available in 18- and 24-volt models. The speed of the rotating blades ranges from around 12,000 to 16,000 rpm. Basically, the faster the rotation, the better the cut. Most have a 3¼" planing width. Depth of cut can range from ⅛" to ³⁄₃₂". Most quality planers will come with an edge guide, a rabbet guide, and dust adapter. Soft-start is another good feature. A tip-down support can prevent planer blades from becoming dulled when not in use.

How to Use

The first step is to make sure the workpiece is held securely in place. The work should be positioned so the planing operation is on your right. If edge planing, use a vise to hold the stock. Using the depth adjustment, and set the blades to the proper depth. Do not attempt to remove too much stock in one pass. It's best to make several light cuts. Always use two hands when using

Detail sanders are great for getting into corners.

Profile sanders come with a variety of profiles.

A number of specialty sanders are also available, including the Porter-Cable Oscillating sander used for sanding edges of large surfaces, such as countertops.

The unique Craftsman 3D sander can sand concave or convex surfaces.

a power plane, holding the front handle with your left hand and the rear handle with your right hand. Position the front of the planer base on the workpiece, making sure the blade does not touch the work piece. With pressure applied to the front handle to hold the front shoe completely flat on the workpiece, start the motor and allow the plane to reach full speed. Holding the plane firmly, push it forward on the workpiece, using a slow but steady motion. As you reach the end of the cut, apply slight downward pressure on the rear handle. This helps keep the planer base flat on the surface and prevents gouging. Do not lift the planer from the work surface until you have completed the cut or you will have an uneven surface. Make sure you do not plane through nails or other foreign objects. And make sure you plane slowly. Planing too fast not only results in a wavy surface, but also increases chip buildup in the chip exhaust. Keep blades sharp and the chip exhaust free. Do not attempt to clean out the chip exhaust until you have shut off the motor and unplugged the plane or removed the batteries.

Some planes have a chamfering groove in the front shoe. This allows you to use the groove to guide the plane to chamfer edges. If planing edges, an adjustable edge guide provides for more precise planing. And you can also use it for making rabbet cuts in edges.

A portable power planer can also be a valuable tool for such chores as jointing edges, planing doors, and others.

An edge guide makes it easier to plane 90° edges.

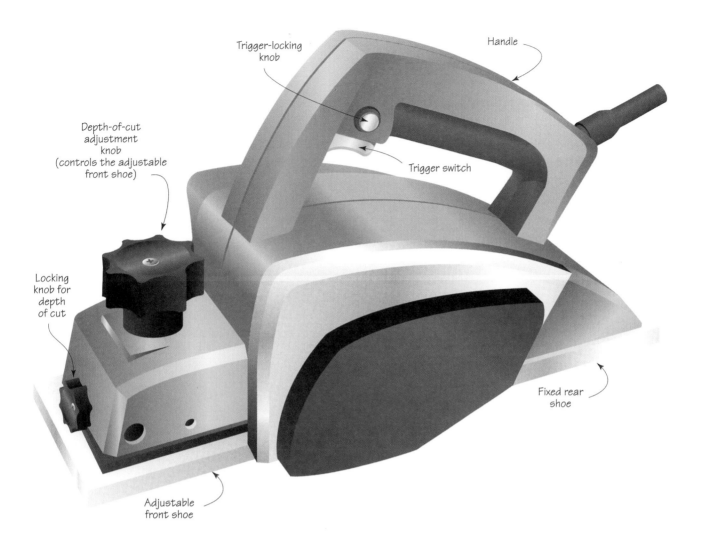

Trigger-locking knob

Handle

Depth-of-cut adjustment knob (controls the adjustable front shoe)

Trigger switch

Locking knob for depth of cut

Fixed rear shoe

Adjustable front shoe

Make sure the stock is secured, and hold the planer with both hands.

OTHER PORTABLE ELECTRIC TOOLS

In addition to specific portable electric tools, other tools are handy around the shop and house. In some instances, certain tools are necessary for certain chores.

Mini Hand Grinders

One of the handiest tools in the shop is a Dremel hand grinder. I use one for everything from cleaning paint and varnish for refinishing furniture to creating carvings in furniture. The Dremel can also be used to sharpen gouges and chisels. I also use the tool with an attachment for sharpening my chainsaws. With the right accessories, the Dremel can be used for a wide range of other chores, including using it as a mini router. This tool can also be used to cut holes in ceramic tile.

Biscuit Joiner

If you're a serious woodworker, one of the handiest tools you can own is a biscuit joiner. Two traditional means of joining wood are with dowels or splines. Dowels are quite common and create extremely strong joints, but it's often difficult to align the dowels and workpieces. Spline joinery is one of the strongest methods used in woodworking. Applying glue to the spline and to the joint area of the wood pieces being connected creates a large surface area to provide more adhesive properties to the glue, forming a strong joint. In the past, spline joinery required cutting slots or grooves with a router, table saw, or radial arm saw. Splines, thin strips of wood, are cut to fit the slots or grooves. A plate or biscuit joiner makes spline joinery easier, quicker, simpler, and more accurate. A biscuit joiner is a plunge-cutting tool used to cut slots in the wood surface into which thin wooden wafers, called biscuits, are placed along with glue. When water-based glue, such as white, yellow, carpenter's, hide, or aliphatic resin is used, the glue causes the biscuits to swell in the joints, creating a strong joint. This bonding technique has traditionally been limited to making edge-to-edge joints. The latest generation of biscuit joiners, however, can easily be used to create butt, miter, and T-joints. Biscuit joining can be as strong as mortise and tenon, tongue-and-

One of the handiest tools you can have in your shop or home is a mini hand grinder, such as the Dremel.

One of the most popular portable eletric tools for serious wood-workers is a biscuit joiner.

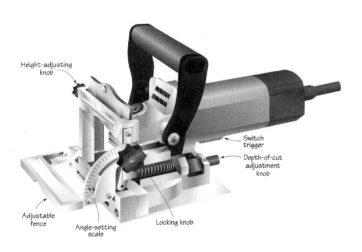

Height-adjusting knob

Switch trigger

Depth-of-cut adjustment knob

Adjustable fence

Angle-setting scale

Locking knob

Biscuit Joints

Miter Joints

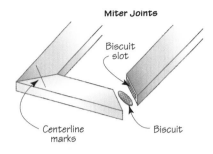

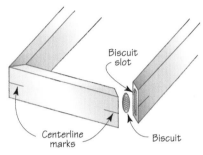

Biscuit slot

Centerline marks

Biscuit

Biscuit slot

Centerline marks

Biscuit

Edge-to-edge Joints

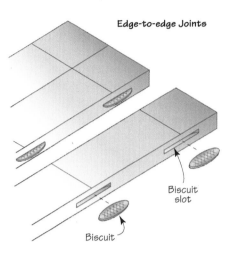

Biscuit slot

Biscuit

T-joint

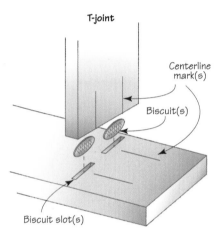

Centerline mark(s)

Biscuit(s)

Biscuit slot(s)

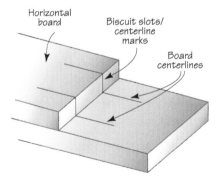

Horizontal board

Biscuit slots/ centerline marks

Board centerlines

Butt Joints

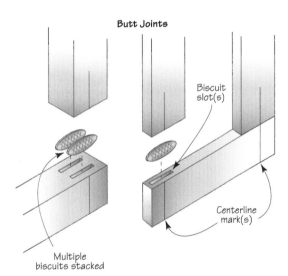

Biscuit slot(s)

Centerline mark(s)

Multiple biscuits stacked

Offset Butt Joints

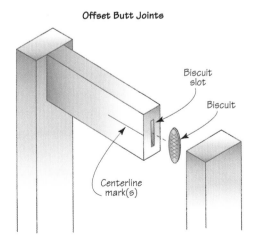

Biscuit slot

Biscuit

Centerline mark(s)

End slots in horizontal board

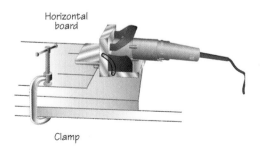

Horizontal board

Clamp

groove, standard spline, and doweled joints. You can even substitute biscuits for dado joints. The great advantage of biscuits, however, is even if you aren't exactly accurate cutting the slots, the biscuits can slide around a little, making it easier to align the pieces precisely.

What to Look For

Although a fairly new tool category, a number of biscuit joiners are available. One of the differences is handle types. Joiners are available with a straight handle and a D-style handle. I personally find the D-style handles to be more comfortable, but it's primarily a matter of purchasing a tool that fits you. The Ryobi model has a dual-grip handle that allows you to choose from different hand positions. A fence that can also be adjusted to 45° and 135° adds more versatility to the tool, allowing you to use it for miter and other angle joints. A fence with the capability to set at any angle is even better. The fence should move up and down easily, and better models use a rack-and-pinion system. Also, make sure the adjusting and lock knobs work easily and lock securely.

Biscuits are available in several sizes and even types and materials. Standard biscuits are thin, wooden, oval-shaped wafers available in sizes #0, #10, and #20. The sizes refer to the length and width, not the thickness. Biscuits are also available in plastic, metal, as round, and even as hinges. The number and size of biscuits needed for each joint depends on the thickness of the wood and the length of the joint. In general, the small #0 biscuits should be used for miter cuts in ¾" materials. The larger

biscuits should be used for edge-to-edge joinery. When making edge-to-edge joints for tabletops, cutting boards, and cabinet and furniture sides and doors, the more biscuits you use, the stronger the joint. When joining 1½"-thick materials, stack two biscuits, one above the other.

How to Use

Using a biscuit joiner is easy. Lay the workpieces to be joined together in the desired position. Mark across both pieces and mark each joining piece with a letter, for instance A-A. Before making any adjustments, unplug the joiner. If the joiner has an adjustment for depth, set it for the appropriate size biscuits. Set the joiner fence height so the cutter is at the halfway mark of the materials to be joined or at the desired depth. For instance, I've used biscuits to join legs to furniture sides, such as desks and nightstands. If an angle is to be cut, set the fence angle desired. Make sure the workpiece is secured or against a bench stop and resting on a flat, smooth surface. Place the joiner on top of the workpiece, move the fence up against the workpiece, and align the alignment mark with the pencil mark. Move the fence up against the workpiece, turn on the joiner, and, holding it with both hands, slowly push the blade into the workpiece. Allow the spring-loaded cutter to return to the rear position and turn off the switch. Move to the next location and repeat. About the biggest problem you can run into is pushing the blade against the workpiece before you turn it on. When you turn it on, it can grab and shove the tool away and down the workpiece edge, creating a damaged area, as well as unsafe use.

The most common use of the biscuit joiner is gluing narrow stock to create wider boards for table tops, furniture sides, and so forth.

This popular portable electric tool set includes a circular saw, reciprocating saw, drill/driver, work light, charger and two batteries.

Many portable electric tools come in sets of a combination of tools plus batteries and a charger.

3

STATIONARY TOOLS

ALTHOUGH HAND TOOLS, and more so portable electric tools, can be used for any number of homeowner, home shop, and contractor chores, sooner or later most do-it-yourselfers and woodworkers are going to want stationary power tools. These often do the job quicker and easier than portable tools. They take up more space, however, and are more costly than portable power tools. Acquiring a shop-full of stationary power tools requires not only a fair amount of space, but also a nearly full pocketbook. If you're just beginning, it's a good idea to start with just one, such as a table saw, then add to your tools. You can sometimes find used stationary power tools for sale at auctions and garage sales. Be aware, however, many older tools don't have proper safety equipment or the safety equipment has been removed.

TABLE SAWS

The most important stationary tool in a woodworking shop, as well as with home-building contractors, is the table saw. A table saw can be used for all types of straight line cutting, including all six basic woodworking cuts—crosscutting, bevel crosscutting, rip, bevel rip, miter, and bevel miter. And it does all these cuts precisely and easily. The right table saw and accessories can be used to cut the largest pieces of wood or large sheets of plywood, or it can be used for tiny intricate cuts with purchased or shop-made jigs. A table saw can also be used to create rabbets and dadoes and, fitted with a molding head, can be used to create many different types of moldings.

What to Look For

Table saws come in several sizes and types. It's important to choose the saw based on your needs. The size of a table saw is rated by the blade size it will accommodate. Saws for do-it-yourselfers and contractors range from 9" up to 12", but are available up to 24" for industrial use. A 10" saw is the most popular for most home shops and contractors. Table saws are also available in three basic styles. Small bench top models come without a stand and are often placed on a workbench. These saws are lighter in weight, so they can be moved around quite easily. Benchtop saws are suitable for craft and hobbyist work. Next up in size are the contractor models. These are rugged and big enough to handle larger sheets of plywood and other materials, yet are lightweight and portable enough to be transported easily in the back of a truck. Job-site saws have become increasingly popular and are designed to fold up and easily be transported and set up on site. A collapsible steel stand with hard rubber wheels and a retractable handle allows the portable saw to be transported like a rolling suitcase.

Heavy-duty floor model table saws with rugged, often enclosed stands and cast iron tables are the choice for the serious woodworking shop. These saws feature more precise fence control, usually larger table surfaces, and are available with either 115- or 230-volt motors. Some may be labeled contractor saws, but most are actually too heavy for easy transportation.

An excellent example of a quality do-it-all saw I've tested is a Delta Industrial 10" Contractor's model. The saw utilizes a 1½ horsepower induction motor, 30" x 27" cast iron table with cast iron extension wing and 30" Biesemeyer Commercial Fence System with a 24" x 27" laminated table board. The latter system allows for precise cutting of larger panels, crosscutting longer pieces, and more versatility for other operations. The table has T-slots for the miter gauge and the extremely

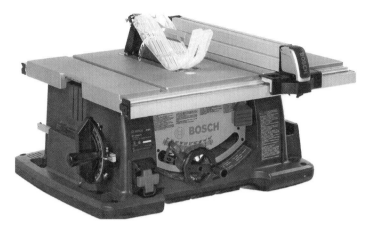

Table saws are available in several sizes and types. Benchtop saws, made to sit on a bench or table, are small, lightweight, and economical.

Job-site saws are designed to be used by contractors or home builders on site. The stand folds up, allowing the saw to be rolled on wheels.

Heavy-duty models, including the Delta Industrial 10" model shown, are the choice of serious woodworkers, cabinetmakers, and finish carpenters. The Delta model shown features a 30" Biesemeyer Commercial Fence System with a 24x27-inch table. This allows easy cutting of large panels and provides a versatile saw.

TABLE SAWS

heavy-duty fence also extends well past the rear end of the table. This prevents any turn-out problems when stock is almost through the blade. All controls are easily worked and precise. The Auto-Set Miter Gauge has adjustable stops at 45° and 90°. The see-through blade guard locks in the up position and automatic insert release makes for easy and quick blade changing. The model also features a cast iron carriage for minimal vibration and up-front on/off paddle switch. The model has a maximum 3½" cut capacity at 90° and 2½" at 45°.

Table Saw Safety

Follow all safety rules provided by the saw manufacturer. Kickback is one of the most dangerous conditions. Always use the guard, splitter, and anti-kickback fingers whenever possible. Always wear safety glasses. Keep blades sharp and clean. Keep the saw blade and fence parallel. Push the workpiece past the blade prior to release. Do not rip a workpiece that is twisted, warped, or does not have a straight edge to guide along the fence. Use featherboards when the antikickback device

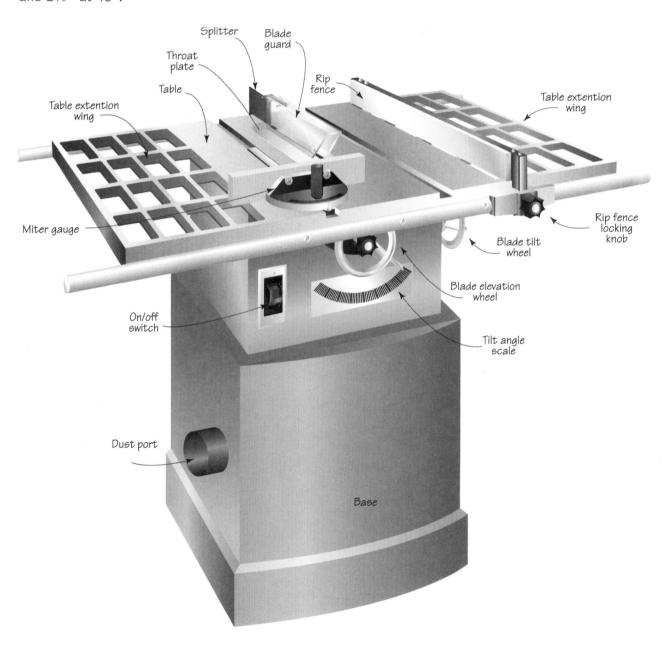

can't be used. Do not saw a large workpiece that can't be controlled. Never use the fence as a guide when crosscutting. Never saw a workpiece with loose knots or other flaws. Use push sticks to finish all cuts. Properly support long workpieces. Avoid awkward operations and hand positions. Keep arms, fingers, and hands away from the blade.

Creating a Super Saw

With upgrades or add-ons and a variety of accessories, you can create a super table saw that is more versatile, more productive, more precise, and easier to use. The saw shown is a Delta Contractor's saw, and many of the add-ons are Delta accessories, although table saw accessories are available from a number of other sources.

These Contractor saws are available with a choice of three extremely accurate fence systems. The three fence systems have front locking mechanisms and are functionally the same, but offer different benefits. The Delta Unifence is surface adjustable, which allows for fine-tuning without removing the fence from the saw. It can be used in a high or low position and is capable of being positioned forward and backward to add support in front of the blade or to be used as a cut-off fence. The T-square design of the Biesemeyer commercial fence is made of welded steel, and the fence faces are made of laminated plywood, hand-sanded to .006". The fence itself is accurate within 1/64" using the scale system. Similarly, the Delta T2 fence system includes a one-piece front rail and T-square fence design. The steel construction is lighter than the Biesemeyer, and the aluminum fence faces are removable. The saw shown is with the Delta T2 fence system.

Tricked out with optional accessories, the Delta Contractor's saw will handle a lot more chores easier and with more precision. The first addition we made was a Biesemeyer over-arm basket-style guard and splitter. This blade guard system is extremely versatile and easy to use. The

You can create a super table saw starting with a quality saw, such as the Delta 10" Industrial Contractor's model. Saw add-ons include a Delta rear table extension and a Biesemeyer over-arm removable basket guard and a quick-removable splitter.

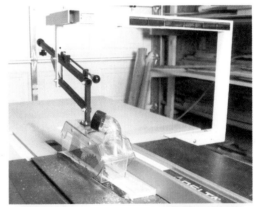

The large, clear basket guard makes it easy to see the workpiece. The overhead arm allows the guard to be positioned sideways for various cuts, including narrow cuts.

The system also features a tool-less splitter for quick and easy removal of the splitter.

basket blade guard is large and easy to see through. The basket guard can also easily be lifted up out of the way on the support arm, which bolts to the table saw rear rail. Or the basket guard can be removed. You can also move the overhead guard back away from the cutting line of the blade with a crank. One of the great features of the Biesemeyer system is the splitter can be removed without tools. You can change from the blade guard and splitter system in seconds to a no-guard, no-splitter system for cutting dadoes, rabbets, creating mortise and tenons, or cutting raised panels. A blade guard and splitter, however, should be used for all through-cutting chores.

The next addition to the saw was a Delta rear table extension. The large table surface provides plenty of support for longer boards and plywood sheets. The extension bolts to the rear rail and has adjustable feet. This does, however, practically eliminate the mobility of the saw.

We also upgraded from the standard miter gauge to a Delta miter gauge. This extremely precise gauge is also very adjustable, has a longer slot arm, and features a long 24" fence. A hold-down holds work down against the saw table surface, and a stop-block allows for cutting multiple same-length pieces.

We also added a Delta Tenoning Jig. Mortise and tenon joints are classic and some of the strongest

joints. The Delta Tenoning Jig, made of heavy-duty cast iron and riding in the saw table top slot, is extremely adjustable and accurate. A clamp holds the stock tightly against the jig fence. The jig is used to create the cheek cuts of the tenons and makes the chore extremely accurate and fast. It's great for cutting a number of tenons. The table saw with miter gauge is then used to make the shoulder cuts of the tenons.

The third Delta accessory we added was a Zero-Clearance Table Saw Insert. The lack of gap between the blade and the insert allows for splinter-free cuts in plywood and chip-free cuts in laminates for a fraction the cost of a dedicated blade. An adjustment screw eliminates side-to-side and front-to-back movement, which allows the insert to be used in a wide range of Delta table saws. Zero-clearance inserts are also available for dado and molding cutters.

How to Use

In a table saw, the blade stays stationary and the workpiece is guided into the blade. The workpiece is most commonly guided with either a rip fence or miter gauge. A sturdy, easily used, and precise rip fence is an important feature of higher quality saws.

For precise and easy use, the table saw must be set up properly. The fence must be precisely aligned with the saw blade. Today's table saws also come with a splitter and a blade guard. The splitter must also be

The cantilevered basket guard can be lifted away from the saw tabletop and held in place to the arm with a spring-loaded pin. The basket guard can also be completely removed from the overdhead arm and the support arm cranked back out of the way for making vertical cuts in panels, or the arm cam be removed entirely for large panel cuts.

An upgraded Delta miter gauge holds stock firmly against the gauge, and a stop block allows for cutting duplicate lengths.

The most common use of table saws is ripping. A push stick should be used to continue pushing narrow stock past the blade.

The table saw blade can also be set to rip at an angle.

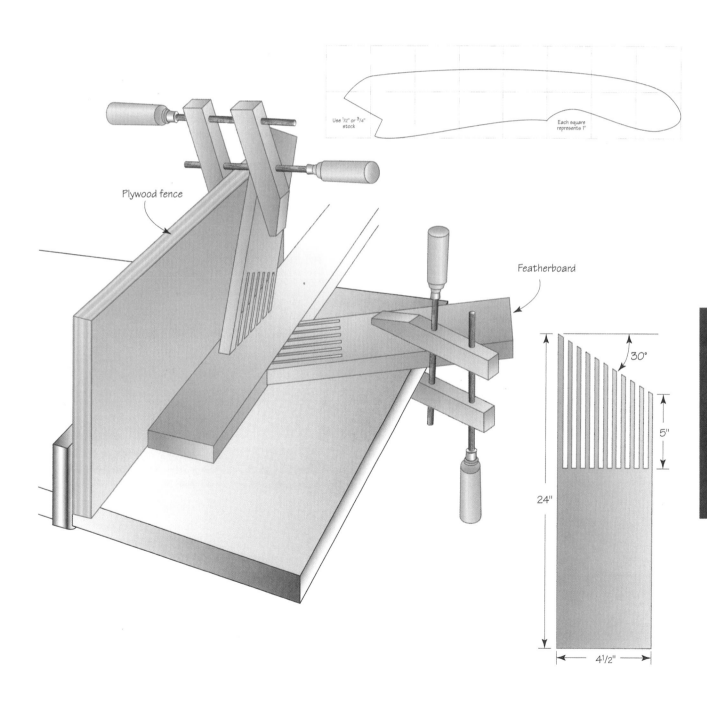

Plywood fence

Use ¹/₂" or ³/₄" stock

Each square represents 1"

Featherboard

30°

5"

24"

4¹/₂"

aligned properly with the blade so the cut made in the workpiece slides freely and the antikickback points must be properly working. Check to make sure the saw guard works up and down easily and is properly aligned with the blade. Table saws are fairly simple to operate. The only adjustments made once the saw is set up are raising and lowering the blade as needed or tilting the blade for angle cuts. One accessory you may desire is a zero-clearance insert. This is especially important when cutting thin strips that may fall between the blade and the insert opening.

Before beginning the cuts, adjust the saw blade height so it protrudes ¼" to ⅜" above the material thickness. The most common cut is the straight rip. The fence is set to the width needed, the stock held against the fence, and pushed into the blade. As the end of the stock nears the blade, a push stick is used to push the stock past the blade. A push stick can be purchased, or made as shown on page 153. When the

cut is completed, turn off the saw, wait for the blade to stop spinning, and then remove the cut pieces.

Bevel ripping is just as easy. Set the blade to the angle desired and then feed the stock through the saw. Long stock must be supported as it comes off the table. My dad used a 4x8 table positioned behind the saw in his cabinet shop, and I used the same principle for a number of years. The problem is the table is usually full when you want to use it. Any number of height-adjustable roller supports are available that make this chore easy and don't take up the space.

One unusual ripping technique is creating tapers, such as for table or chair legs. A purchased taper jig can be used, or you can create your own. The flat face of the jig rides against the fence to create the angled cut in the workpiece.

Another technique involves cutting a straight edge on an irregularly-edged stock. This is common on wood purchased in the rough, which does not have the outer

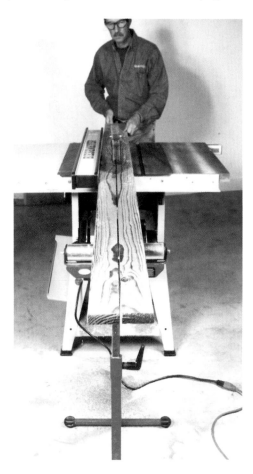

Tapered legs can be cut on a table saw using a hand-built jig.

Guide strips can be fastened to boards that have uneven edges to make a straight cut.

Adjustable-height roller supports can provide support when ripping long stock.

edges sawn. In this instance, a straight edge is fastened to the underside of the stock to be ripped. Fasten with either a pair of clamps or even screws. This guide strip rides against the outer edge of the table saw to guide the workpiece. Once one edge has been cut straight, the stock can then be ripped to cut the opposite edge straight and to the width needed.

Crosscutting is most commonly done using the miter gauge (for narrow stock) or of a size to fit between the miter gauge and saw blade. Table saws with T-slots keep the miter gauge in place better than flat-sided slots. Remove the fence, make sure the miter gauge is set at 90° or the angle desired, place the stock against the miter gauge, and then push the stock through the blade. Keep both hands well away from the blade as the stock passes through the blade. Making crosscuts in long stock is not easy, however table extensions can help. I use the table saw primarily for ripping or cutting large panels and the radial arm or miter saw for crosscutting. Miter crosscutting on the table saw

is achieved by setting the miter gauge to the angle desired, then feeding the stock against the blade. If you have a number of 45° angle cuts, for instance in picture-frame material, a sliding miter table can be used. Compound miter cuts are made by setting both the blade and the miter gauge at the angles desired. The blade can also be set at an angle to create decorative V-grooves, or even raised panels.

One of the most common uses of table saws is cutting large panels, such as plywood. As you can guess, heavy-based saws with table extensions are the best for this chore. A helper can also be a great help on large, heavy sheets. Fence extensions may be needed in order to cut to 24", or the center of 48" sheets on some saws.

Other Uses

Table saws can be used for any number of other cutting chores. This includes making rabbets, dadoes, tenons, and even for creating molding. For most of these chores, the splitter and saw guard

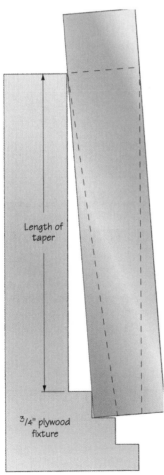

Length of taper

¾" plywood fixture

Tapering fixture

Crosscutting is done using the miter gauge to guide the stock.

Angles can be cut using the miter gauge set at the angle desired. Compound miters can also be cut using the miter gauge with the saw blade tilted.

must be removed. Be extremely careful of the saw blade or accessory blades when doing any of these operations.

Rabbets, dadoes, and tenons can be cut using the blade alone. Make a cut, move the fence the width of the saw blade, and make another cut. Smooth up any unevenness with a sharp chisel. A dado set makes this chore must faster and more precise. Dado sets are available as multiple pieces that are added together to make the width needed or adjustable. Regardless of which set is used, you'll need a table insert with a wider throat to accommodate the width of the dado head. A guide-fence protector board should be made and used when cutting dadoes in the ripping mode. A dado set is extremely handy for creating a number of specialty joints, including mortise and tenon finger, and box joints. A tenoning jig can also be extremely handy for these techniques.

Another unusual technique is cove cutting, or cutting a rounded concave cove. This sounds complicated, but a variety of cove shapes can be cut fairly easily. A guide strip is clamped to the tabletop to guide the stock at an angle across the blade. The blade is lowered so it is no more than ⅛" above the table surface. A cut is made, the saw raised another ⅛" and a second cut is made. The procedure is repeated until the desired cove shape and depth is achieved.

A table saw can also be used for kerf-cutting to create curved stock. A simple jig attached to the miter gauge allows for precise cuts in the stock.

A variety of moldings can also be created with the saw blade. Dentil moldings are easy to create using the same basic procedure as for kerfing. The guide pin in the auxiliary miter gauge fence provides precise cuts. Make the cuts on one side of the stock, turn the stock over, and make cuts on the opposite side in the same manner, spacing the cuts between each other. Then rip thin strips off to create the molding.

Another common use of table saws is cutting large panels. Saws with table extensions, such as the Delta model shown, make the chore easier.

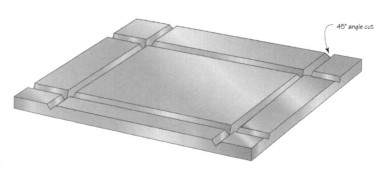

Decorative cuts in panels and molding can also be made with a table saw.

Raised panels can be cut with the saw set at an angle.

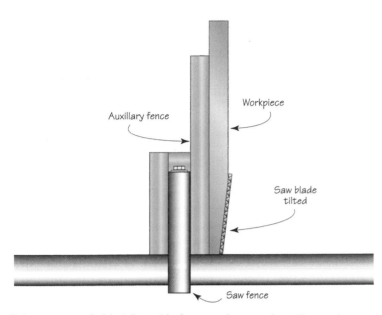

Using an extended-height guide fence makes panel cutting easier.

A dado head in a table saw can be used to quickly and easily cut dadoes and rabbets. Dado heads are available as multipiece or adjustable.

An auxiliary fence allows the use of the dado head to create rabbets.

Molding can also be created using the saw blade in a variety of straight and bevel cuts in the ripping mode. Or use a combination of ripping and crosscutting to create moldings or even to decorate panels. The use of a molding cutterhead greatly expands the possibilities of creating almost any type of molding or even decorating panels. Molding cutterheads consist of a cutterhead in which various shapes of steel knives are fastened. These commonly come in sets with a variety of knife patterns that allow for an almost infinite number of combinations. Because of the width of the cutterhead, a special table insert must be used, and the splitter and blade guard must be removed.

An auxiliary wooden fence should also be installed. A two-sided fence that slips over the saw fence is easily made. Thin stock should have hold-downs or a special fence to hold it precisely against the knives. It's safer to mold on the edge of wide stock and then rip off the molding. The knives come in sets of three and each is held in place in the cutterhead with a set screw. Make sure the knives are solidly locked in place. Unplug the saw while installing the cutterhead and then turn the blade by hand to make sure everything clears the saw and insert before plugging in the saw and turning it on. Cutters can remove a lot of wood, so it's best to make several shallow passes to remove a little wood at a time. This is especially important when making deep cuts in hardwoods. Cuts can be made across or with the grain. With-the-grain cuts, however, are the easiest and produce the smoothest result. If molding several sides of a stock, make the crossgrain cuts first. With-the-grain cuts can then remove any splintering that occurs on the ends.

Choosing Saw Blades

A variety of saw blade styles are available. Regardless of the tooth shape or design, all are designed with the teeth slightly wider than

The cast iron Delta Tenoning Jig makes quick and easy work of cutting tenons and is accurate.

Coves can be cut in stock by clamping a guide board at an angle to the saw blade and pushing the stock against the guide board.

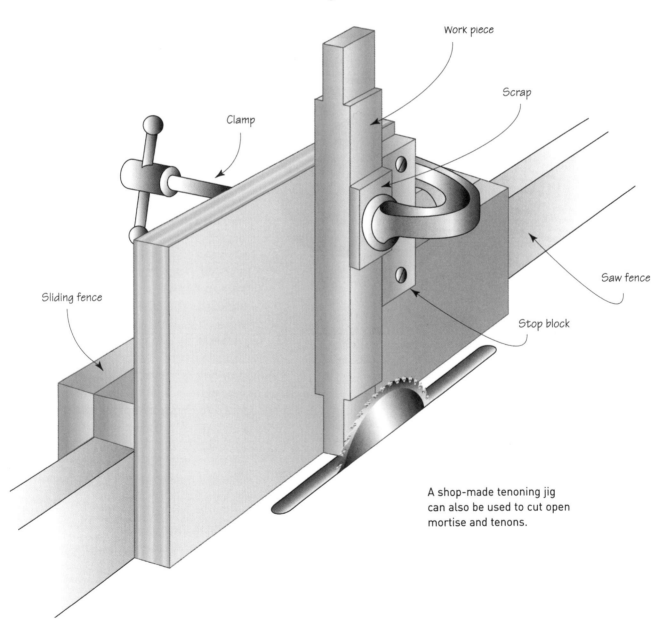

Work piece

Scrap

Clamp

Saw fence

Sliding fence

Stop block

A shop-made tenoning jig can also be used to cut open mortise and tenons.

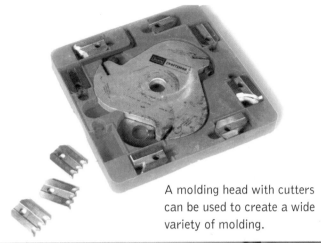

A molding head with cutters can be used to create a wide variety of molding.

You can also create dentil molding using the saw blade alone. A jig with a pin is used to position the stock for each cut.

the blade thickness to create a kerf and prevent the blade from binding or becoming overheated. This clearance is accomplished by either setting the teeth to one side, called a flat-ground blade, grinding the blade so the edge is thicker, hollow grinding or tapering the blade, or by adding carbide-tipped teeth slightly wider than the blade thickness. In addition to the type of blade, the shapes and sizes of the teeth vary depending on the intended use of the blade. It's important to choose the correct tooth and style for the work being done.

The most commonly used blade is the combination blade. It may be used for general construction crosscutting or ripping, although some other blades produce smoother cuts. The blade may be standard or carbide-tipped. Blades are available specifically for crosscutting, fast or finish ripping, and for cutting laminates and melamine. Blades are also available with a larger number of teeth for cabinet and finish cabinetry work. These blades can have up to eighty teeth and might be called miter, cabinet, fine-cut, smooth-trim, or planer blades.

Common cutters

A variety of cutters is available to create different shapes.

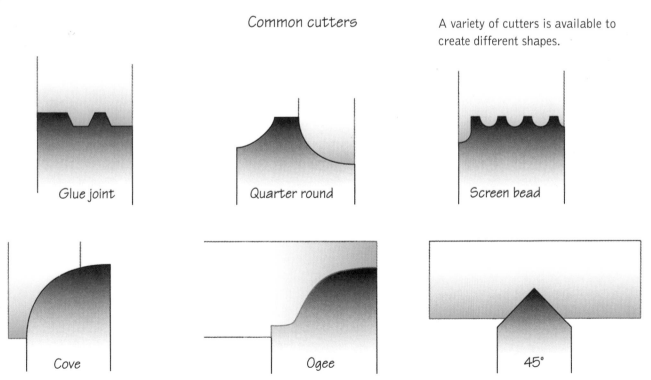

Glue joint · Quarter round · Screen bead · Cove · Ogee · 45°

RADIAL ARM AND MITER SAWS

I own two radial arm saws and three miter saws. One radial arm saw is permanently set up with a dado blade. The miter saws consist of a big 12" compound miter for shop work, a 10" model on a stand for construction work, and a cordless Bosch for trim work.

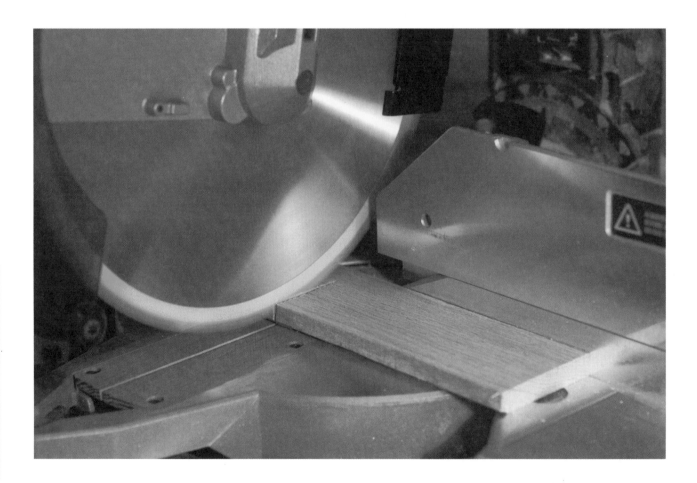

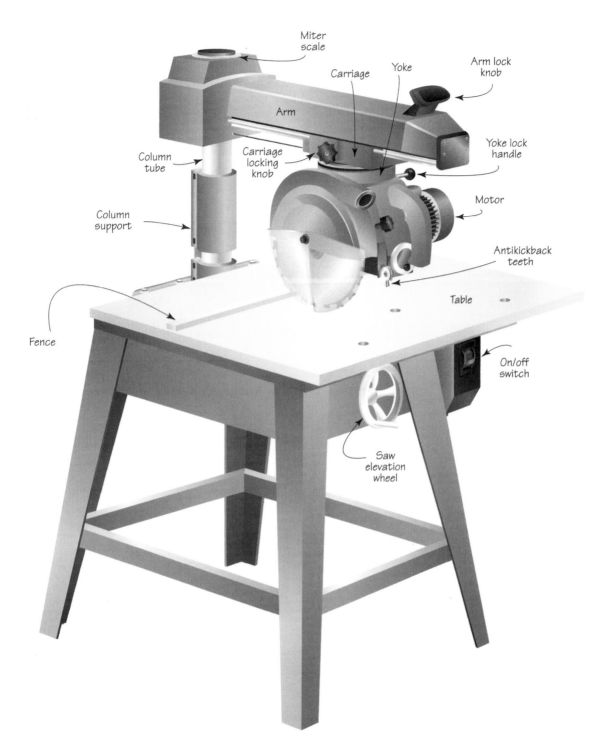

Miter scale

Carriage

Yoke

Arm lock knob

Arm

Column tube

Carriage locking knob

Yoke lock handle

Column support

Motor

Antikickback teeth

Table

Fence

On/off switch

Saw elevation wheel

Radial Arm Saws

If, for some unknown reason, you had to pick only one stationary power tool for your workshop, a radial arm saw would be a wise choice, although they are not as popular as they once were due to the creation of miter saws.

No other stationary power tool, however, can perform as many chores as easily as a radial-arm saw. Woodworking consists of six basic cuts: crosscutting, bevel crosscutting, ripping, bevel ripping, mitering, and bevel mitering. The radial arm saw will make all of these cuts efficiently and precisely. With attachments and accessories, the radial arm saw can also be used as a boring machine, router, sander (either drum or disk) and buffer/polisher. It can also do jointing and shaping chores, as well as make dadoes.

What to Look For

Radial arm saws are available in several different sizes; the size is indicated by the size of blade the saw will accept. Common sizes include 8", 10" or 12", with 10" the most popular for the home workshop. Larger 14", 16" and 18" sizes are also available for heavy-duty commercial work. The size of the blade determines the depth of cut possible with the saw. A 10" saw blade will cut to a 3" depth. Most quality saws today have automatic blade brakes to slow and then quickly stop the saw once the motor has been turned off.

The reason for the versatility of radial arm saws is their ability to configure for the different cuts. A radial arm saw consists of a motor on a rotating arm positioned over a tabletop with a fence located near the back of the tabletop. The arm can be lowered or raised as desired. The radial or travel arm supports a sliding saw/motor. The arm rotates around the support column. Indexes precisely position the motor at 90° to the saw fence or 45° in either direction. The column can also be locked in place at any degree between. Regardless of whether set at 90° or some other degree marking, the primary use is for crosscutting. Radial arm saws also allow for precise cutting because the upper surface of the wood is facing you and your marks are easily seen. A number of saws feature lasers, which provide a laser line giving a clear indication of blade travel for ripping or crosscutting operations. A centrifugal switch, built inside the module, triggers the laser's operation once the blade reaches 1,500 rpm.

The saw/motor unit is held by a carriage with a yoke. The yoke allows the saw/motor to be swiveled 360° on the carriage, while still allowing the carriage to travel the length of the support arm. With the saw blade turned 90° to the arm, or parallel to the saw fence, ripping operations can be done. By setting the blade slightly off 90°, coving cuts can be made with the blade, creating rounded cuts.

A radial arm saw can be configured to do any number of chores.

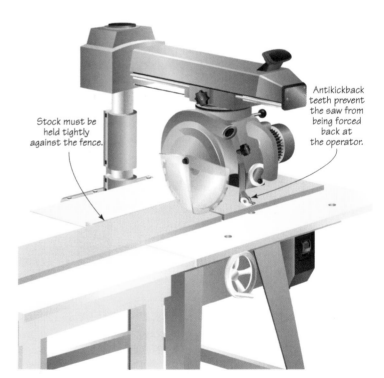

Stock must be held tightly against the fence.

Antikickback teeth prevent the saw from being forced back at the operator.

The primary use is crosscutting. The stock is positioned in place, and the saw is drawn across the stock., providing precise cutting.

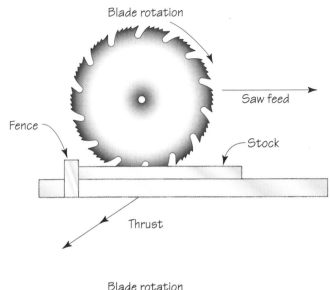

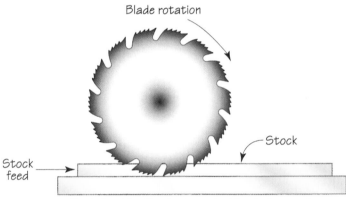

Feed direction for ripping cuts. View is from column.

The motor and blade can also be turned in a second yoke, allowing the spindle to face towards the tabletop or at any angle and be locked in place. This provides a position for any number of accessories.

In addition to the bells and whistles, several features are important in radial arm saws. First are the controls. The controls should be easy to access and grouped according to logical progression. The on-off switch should be easily within reach and large so you don't fumble turning the machine off. The switch should also be lockable or have a removable key. The miter and bevel cut stops should be adjustable to make precise 45° and 90° bevel and miter cuts. The scales should be large and easy-to-read. The saw table should be of a comfortable working height, usually 36" and should be large enough to securely support stock. The fence should be easily adjustable and the table top smooth. The motor should be large enough to handle heavy-duty chores. A 1½ horsepower motor is a good choice with a 10" saw. The motor should have a double spindle. After removing the saw blade, accessories can be attached to the opposite spindle end and used for a number of chores.

Radial arm saws come with safety guards, and the guard should be clear so you can see through it. The guard should move easily out of the way as it touches the workpiece, but should drop down immediately once past the workpiece. Antikickback fingers are also positioned on the saw, and they should be adjustable and work easily. Last, check the accessories available from the manufacturer, as well as those available from other manufacturers before purchasing a specific saw.

Radial arm saws come with a saw blade, normally a carbide-tipped 40-tooth combination blade, which is a good all-around blade. For ripping, use a blade that has fewer but larger teeth, normally 24, for ripping hardwoods. Cabinet work requires a hollow-ground planer or fine-cut blade with 80 teeth.

How to Use

When doing crosscuts, mitering, beveling, and dadoes, the workpiece is positioned on the saw table and the saw pulled through the cut. One advantage radial arm saws provide is the force of the blade pushes the workpiece against the fence in crosscut operations. In ripping and grooving operations, the blade is turned parallel, the motor locked in place, and the stock fed into the blade in much the same manner as for a table saw. In ripping operations, it's important to feed the stock into the blade against the blade rotation, so the bottom teeth are turning toward you.

To begin a basic crosscutting job, first make sure the saw is behind the fence. The blade should be adjusted about ¹⁄₁₆" below the surface of the table and in a precut kerf. Position the workpiece on the table, making sure the ends of long boards are supported level with the table. Before turning on the motor, make sure the blade isn't binding on the tabletop and all clamps and locking devices are tight. Position the pawls and riving knife to clear the workpiece or the fence, whichever

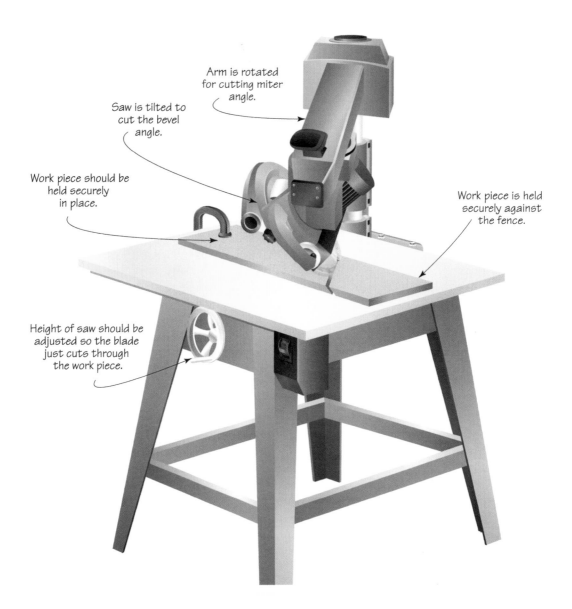

Arm is rotated for cutting miter angle.

Saw is tilted to cut the bevel angle.

Work piece should be held securely in place.

Work piece is held securely against the fence.

Height of saw should be adjusted so the blade just cuts through the work piece.

is higher, by at least ¼". Make sure the guard is down and working properly. Use a crosscut or combination blade. Hold the stock firmly against the table fence with your hand at least 6" away from the path of the saw blade. Clamp the stock in place if necessary if the piece is 6" or fewer. Turn on the saw, grasp the saw handle, and pull the saw firmly and slowly through the cut. The blade may tend to feed itself in some cases, especially with hardwoods. Make sure you keep complete control of the rate of feed with a sturdy grip on the handle. After completing the cut, move the workpiece to the side, return the saw to behind the fence, and turn it off. Keep your hand on the handle until the blade stops rotating.

A miter cut is made with the blade vertical and the arm angled. Move the fence to the front position, or

next to the front of the table, and tighten the clamps. Set the saw to the desired angle. If a kerf doesn't exist in the table, as well as a slot in the fence for the miter angle desired, make one, approximately ¹⁄₁₆" deep in the table top. To make the kerf, raise the blade so it doesn't touch the table, turn on the saw, grasp the handle, lower the blade into the table, and then pull the saw to make the cut. Return the saw to behind the fence.

A bevel cut is made with the blade and motor angled and the arm straight or 90° to the fence. Again, move the fence to the front position, set the blade to the correct angle, and make a kerf if there isn't one. Then make the cut in the same manner as for crosscutting. Make sure the saw guard is in proper position and the riving knife and pawls clear the workpiece and fence. After the cut has been made,

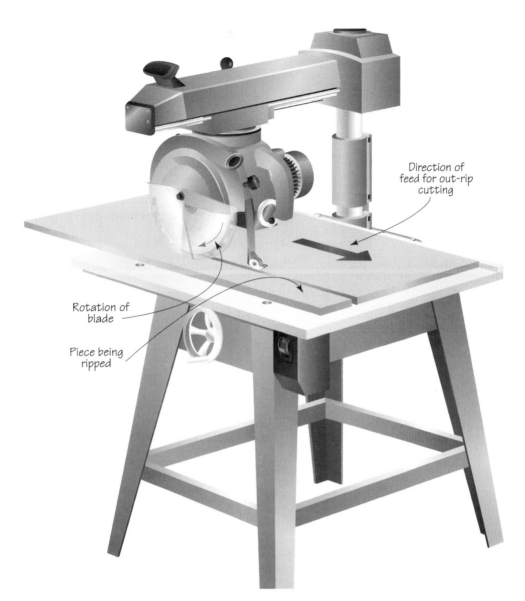

Direction of feed for out-rip cutting

Rotation of blade

Piece being ripped

move the workpiece to the side, turn off the saw, and move it back behind the fence. It's a good idea to practice this on a piece of scrap. A compound crosscut is made with both the blade and the arm angled. It's a good idea to practice both bevel and miter cuts before making a compound cut, then again, practice on scrap wood. Again, the fence should be in the front position, and you must first make a kerf cut in the fence and table. In this cut, the saw guard can tend to hang-up. Make sure it is free and clear to operate properly.

Ripping is a bit more difficult, so I do all my ripping on a table saw. Two hazards specifically associated with rip cutting: wrong-way feed and the out-feed zone. Wrong-way feed happens when the workpiece contacts the blade from the outfeed side. This is very hazardous and can jerk the workpiece

and throw it violently. You can be injured or cut if holding the workpiece. In the outfeed zone, or behind the blade, the blade teeth point down. The slightest contact while the blade is still spinning can snag clothing, jewelry, the workpiece or even your body, causing serious injury. Stay completely away from the outfeed zone.

Establish the rip cut line and lock the carriage in place. Set the blade to just about 1/16" into the table. Point the antikickback pawls away from the blade teeth to snag the workpiece if the blade grabs. They should be positioned to rest lightly on the workpiece. The flat side of the pawls should be level and horizontal. Set the riving knife to just clear the table. Set the hold down in front of the blade to just clear the workpiece. Start and finish the cut from the infeed

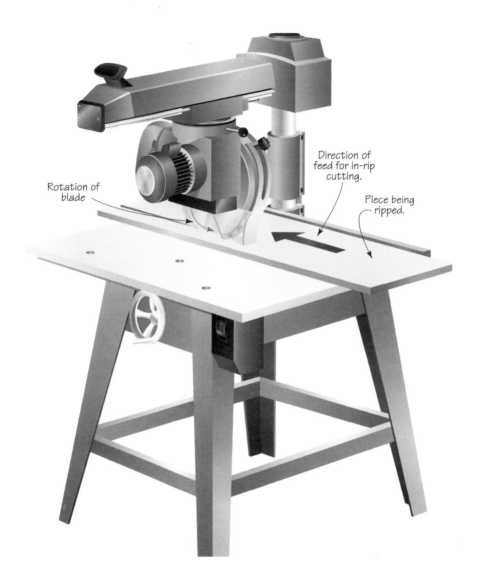

Rotation of blade

Direction of feed for in-rip cutting.

Piece being ripped.

side. Push the workpiece past the cawls with push blocks and push sticks to finish the cut. Never allow your hands closer than 6" from the blade. If the blade jams, turn off the saw, remove the yellow key, and wait for the blade to fully stop before freeing it. Make sure the blade is parallel to the fence and the workpiece is not warped or twisted. Make sure there is no pressure applied to the workpiece on the outfeed side. Make sure the blade guard is lowered and is working properly. Always set up the workpiece so the wider part of the wood is between the blade and the fence to stabilize the workpiece. A precise and safe rip-cut requires a careful setup.

Bevel ripping has the blade set at an angle. When bevel ripping, make sure the plastic lower guard is raised to keep it from jamming. Once the bevel has

been set, test the guard to make sure it will clear. A rip cut can be set up as in-rip or out-rip, depending on the width needed for the cut, but again, the feed must always be from the infeed side. In all cases of rip cutting, never stand directly in line of the cut. Stand to the side to reduce the chance of injury should the workpiece be kicked back at you.

Non-through cuts, such as dadoes or rabbets, can be made with a dado head in either cross cutting or ripping modes. Dadoes, tenons, grooves, lap joints, and other wide cuts are made using a dado blade or dado set. The cuts can be made with the saw in either the crosscut or rip position. Dado sets consist of a set of two outside blades with chipper blades between. Removing or adding the chippers creates the different dado widths. Adjustable dado heads create the different width cuts by

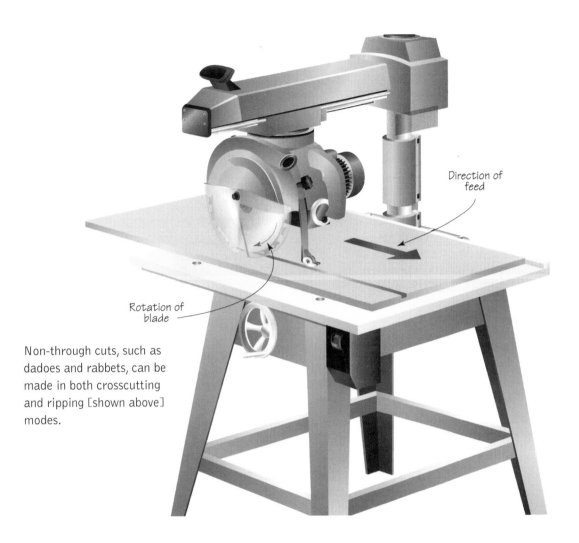

Direction of
feed

Rotation of
blade

Non-through cuts, such as
dadoes and rabbets, can be
made in both crosscutting
and ripping [shown above]
modes.

turning a dial. Because of the volume of
wood and the force exerted when making
these wide cuts, it's extremely important
that the stock be held solidly in place
and the antikickback fingers are working
properly. Special guards are required for
use with dado cutterheads.

To use a dado head, unplug the saw
and/or remove the safety key. Turn on
the switch to make sure the saw is not
receiving power. Remove the blade guard
and blade. Adjust the dado head to the
width needed, then mount on the saw arbor.
For a cross cut, pull the saw out away
from the fence, position a scrap block
against the fence and against the dado
head teeth, and raise or lower the saw to
reach the desired depth of the dado or
rabbet. Return the saw back behind

Radial arm saws may be fitted with a wide variety of accessories, such as
dado sets, adding to their versatility.

the fence. Holding the scrap stock solidly, turn on the saw and slowly and firmly pull the dado head across the scrap stock. Dado heads can grab violently, so you must have a firm hold. And you may wish to clamp the stock in place. My technique for cutting deep and wide dadoes is to cut a scrap stock, cutting the dadoes only about ⅛" deep at a time. Then cut the final workpieces, again a little at a time. Use the scrap stock to gauge when you have reached final depth of the workpiece. If running several dadoes, do them all at the same depth each time until you reach final depth. For rip dadoes and rabbets, the same basic set-up is used, but push sticks and blocks are necessary to push the stock against the rotating dado head, and the saw hold-down must be positioned correctly.

A drill chuck, fitted to the outfeed spindle end of some saws, can turn the radial arm saw into a drill press. Or a drum sander can be fitted into the chuck for precise contour sanding. A router bit or drill press planer can also be inserted in the chuck for a number of other chores.

A radial arm saw mounted on lockable casters can be moved to any position needed. The one accessory that can provide better and easier use is an outfeed stock support. Trying to crosscut long stock is hard

and dangerous, but a support makes the chore easier. By the same token, when ripping long stock, the outfeed end tends to drop down, creating irregular cuts and a possibly dangerous situation. One of the best tactics with radial arm saws is to build a 6' outfeed table on each side of the existing table. Although this takes space, they will provide support during both operations.

If the radial arm saw provides versatility in its many configurations, the drawback to that feature is more can go wrong with the alignment. It's important to assure the machine is properly set and aligned correctly in order to make precise cuts and wood joints. The machine should also be regularly checked to make sure it doesn't get out of alignment.

Miter Saws

One of the reasons for the lack of interest in the radial arm saw is the increasing popularity of miter saws. Although they can be used for ripping chores, the primary job of radial arm saws is crosscutting. Miter saws do this same job with less complicated adjustments. Many are smaller, portable, and less costly. Contractors and home remodelers were the first to discover their uses, and do-it-yourselfers quickly joined the crowd.

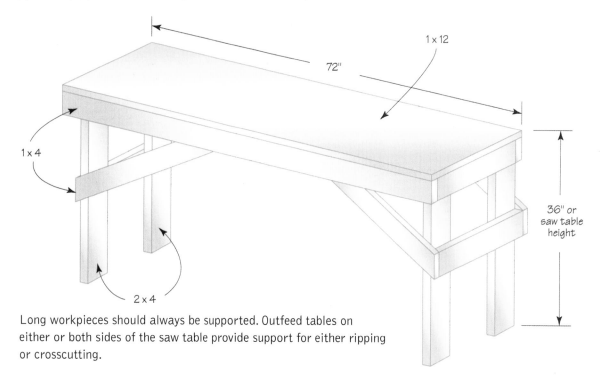

Long workpieces should always be supported. Outfeed tables on either or both sides of the saw table provide support for either ripping or crosscutting.

What to Look For

The first miter saws consisted of a small table with a rotating head. The head could be set to 45° in both directions, or any degree between. These compact, portable saws made cutting framing materials much quicker. Then came compound miter saws allowing you to cut compound angles for cove and other moldings, and they became the trim carpenters, tool of choice. These tools, however, were limited in the width of work they could cut. Then came sliding compound miter saws, enabling the saw to cut wider stock and still maintain the ability to cut compound angles.

Prices, as well as weights, vary with simple miter saws the smallest, lightest, and most economical, many running less than $100. Sliding compound miter saws are the most expensive, and they are also the heaviest but are more versatile in the chores they can do. The first step in choosing is to determine your needs. Miter saws are also available in different sizes, based on the size of the blade, and may range from 7¼" up to 12" saws. A 10" compound miter saw will typically cut 2x6 stock at 90°. Motor power also varies from around 9 up to 15 amps. For the small additional cost over a standard miter saw, a compound miter saw is probably the best bet for most users. A 10-inch, 15-amp compound miter saw is probably the best all-around choice for the money. Many saws today can also cut wider angles both left and right. And, if you have ever tried to fit molding and trim to a room that is not exactly square, you'll appreciate the few extra degrees. The better saws also have detents at specific angles. Some, such as the Ridgid models, have specific crown molding detent stops. In the past, tables and fences were normally cast iron, but these days most are cast aluminum. Saws can weigh from 34 up to almost 80 pounds. Better saws have blade brakes, a sliding left fence to provide support for wider materials, and a left-side table extension. Most also come with a dust

Miter saws have become more popular than radial arm saws because they're more portable and will do all the crosscutting chores for homeowners, remodelers, and builders.

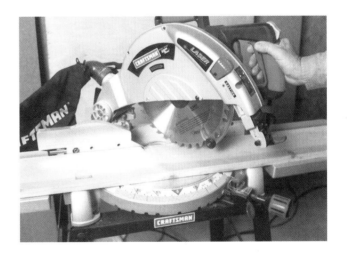

Miter saws are available in several sizes and compound miter saws are the best choice, as they can be used to cut coving and do other compound-angle chores.

bag or dust portthat allows you to connect to a shop vacuum. The dust bags aren't usually very efficient. A laser guide is also a great feature on these types of saws. Miter saws come with two types of handles, a D-handle and a pistol grip. In both instances, a trigger is fitted inside the handle with a built-in safety switch. Both have to be squeezed to start the saw operation, and some people find one or the other type of handle easier to use. You probably should check this out on the showroom floor before purchasing. Another thing to look for is hold-downs. Miter saws can fling objects, especially small cut-off ends. Some

clamps are top mounted, some front. All of today's miter saws have a swinging blade guard that moves up and out of the way during the cut but drops down instantly when you raise the saw from the cut. I have a friend with an older model without this feature, and I cringe when I see him use it.

Cordless miter saws are also available. As I've discovered, nothing can be handier for builders, home shops, trim carpenters, and especially those framing buildings away from electrical power than the Bosch 24-volt, compound miter saw kit. The 24-volt motor runs at 3,600 rpm and the kit

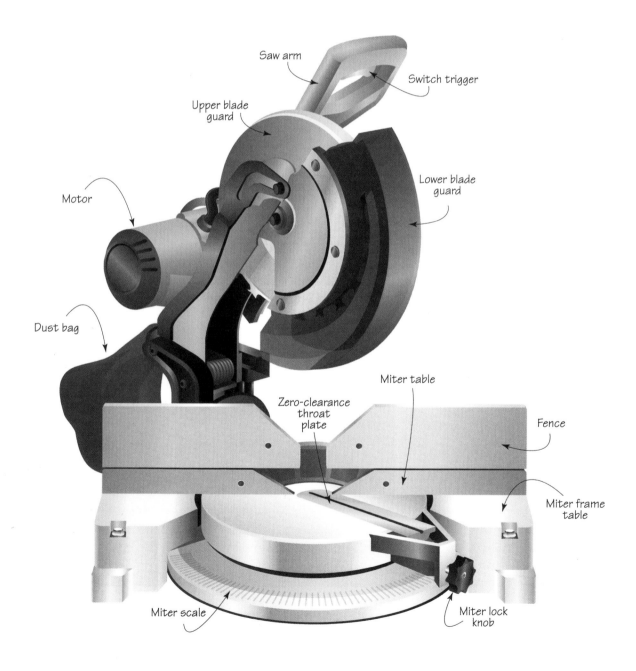

Saw arm

Switch trigger

Upper blade guard

Lower blade guard

Motor

Dust bag

Miter table

Zero-clearance throat plate

Fence

Miter frame table

Miter scale

Miter lock knob

includes battery, 1-hour charger, 10-inch 40-tooth blade, quick clamp, wrench, and dust bag. The large 20¾-inch aluminum base has a 3¼-inch sliding extension for 24 inches total length support. The saw has crown miter detents, 31.6 miter and 33.9 bevel detents for quick accurate crown cuts. The Speed Track sliding fence system allows base and fence to slide independently. The tall, 3½-inch sliding fence allows for easy bevel set ups and increased crown molding cutting capacities. The exclusive wedge-and-slot detent system provides for consistent and precise miter angles. A miter detent override is also available. An electric brake stops the saw in seconds. With one battery in the saw and one on the charger, I've used the Bosch cordless miter saw day-long for numerous chores.

Sliding compound miter saws are normally larger, with 12-inch blades and bigger motors. These saws can usually crosscut 2x12's. The saws are much heavier and bulkier, but a great help in cutting joists and other framing chores. They will also easily cut 4x4 materials, even the tougher pressure-treated lumber.

Miter saws should be anchored to a solid surface for use. Contractors often bolt them to tables, to wooden strips that can be clamped to sawhorses, and other supports. The best bet, however, is a miter saw stand. These lightweight stands fold down for transport, yet provide a good means of holding both the saw and the workpiece. One of the best I've tested is the Ridgid Miter Saw Utility Vehicle. It is quick to set up and provides 8 feet of support.

How to Use

Miter saws, like radial arm saws, need to be adjusted to precise cutting, following the owner's manual. Few come from the factory cutting exactly, although adjustment is easy. Make sure you follow all safety rules. It's important to use proper body and hand positions when using miter saws. Never place your hands near the cutting area. Keep your hands out of the No Hands Zone. which may be marked on some saws. If not marked, keep your hands at least 3" from the blade. Tools with pistol-grip handles can be activated with either hand, but it's important to never cross hands. Hold the workpiece firmly, make sure it is well-supported and is firmly against the fence. Make sure you are standing well-balanced with your feet firmly on the floor. Follow the miter arm when mitering left or right. Stand slightly to the side of the saw blade and sight through the lower guard if following a pencil line. With the power off, lower the blade to test for the proper cut before making the cut. Turn on the saw, and lower it into the workpiece until the cut is completed. If using a sliding compound saw, pull it away from behind the fence to start the cut at the front of the workpiece and lower it in place, then push it back behind the fence. Turn off the saw and allow the blade to stop turning, then raise it from the workpiece. Do not take your hands off the saw or workpiece until the blade stops. If you lift the blade while it is spinning, it can catch and fling small pieces.

Straight cuts are made with the saw set at the 90° detent. Miter cuts are made by moving the saw control

Sliding compound miter saws are able to cut wider stock.

One of the handiest saws for trim work is the Bosch cordless miter saw.

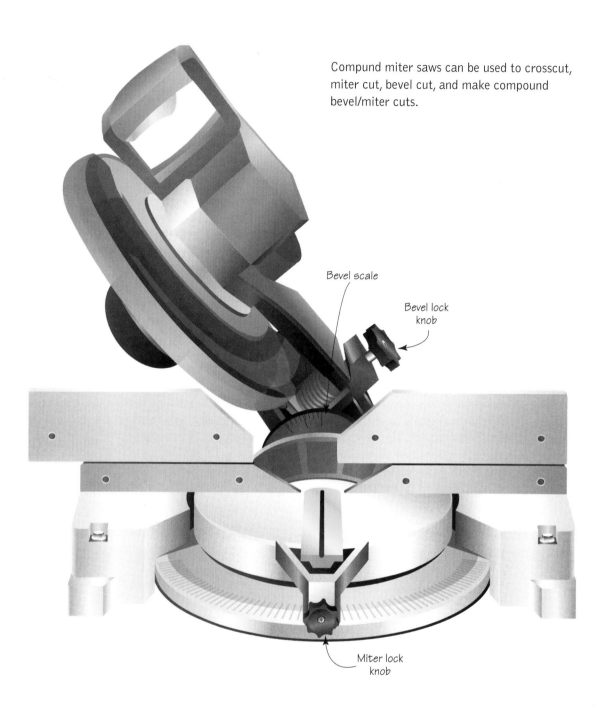

Compund miter saws can be used to crosscut, miter cut, bevel cut, and make compound bevel/miter cuts.

Bevel scale

Bevel lock knob

Miter lock knob

arm left or right to the desired angle between 0° and 45° or a greater angle if the saw provides for it. After moving the control arm, always make sure to tighten the miter angle lock handle before making a cut. A bevel cut is made across the grain of the wood by tilting the saw control arm to the desired degree between 0° and 45°. After setting the control arm to the desired angle, make sure to tighten the bevel lock knob before making a cut. A compound miter cut is made using a miter angle and a bevel angle. This

type of cut is used to cut moldings, especially crown molding, make boxes with sloping sides, make picture frames, and, for some, roof framing cuts. To make a compound miter cut, you must set the bevel angle, as well as the miter angle. Make sure all controls are locked solid and practice on scrap stock. Because of the interaction between the two angles, it may take some scrap cutting and resetting of the angles to achieve the final desired cut.

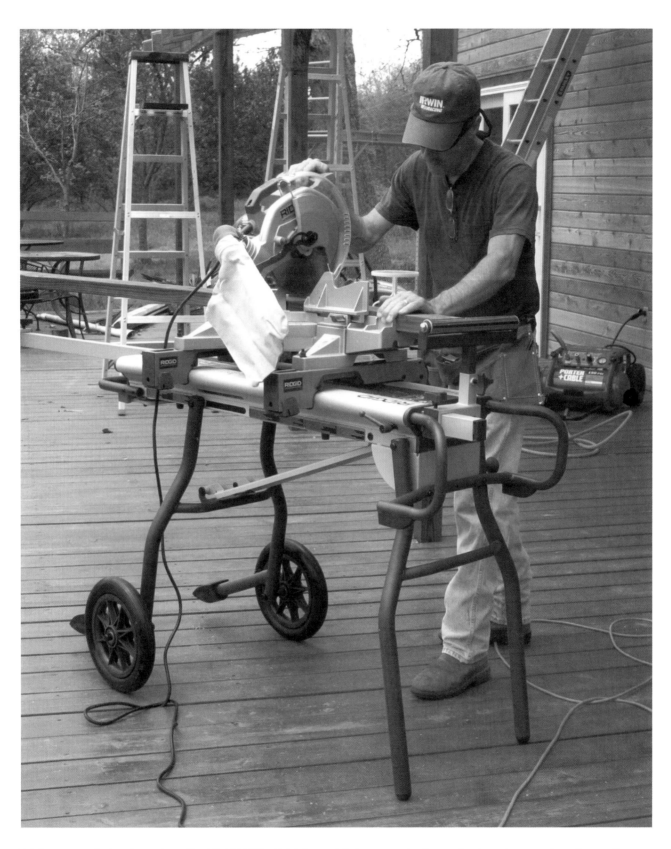

Folding support stands, such as the Rigid Utility Vehicle model shown, make it easy to store, transport, and use miter saws.

RADIAL ARM AND MITER SAWS

BAND SAWS AND SCROLL SAWS

Although a band saw is rarely the first stationary power tool purchased for a shop, it is one of the most versatile. A scroll saw cannot only be used for fun craft work, but also for cutting decorative moldings and other furniture and cabinetry pieces.

BAND SAW

A band saw can be used to cut curves, even in thick lumber, such as in creating cabriole legs, to rip lumber, and to crosscut short pieces. The most common use for the band saw, however, is in cutting irregular shapes. The second most common use is in resawing or ripping lumber into thinner slabs. A band saw also makes the smoothest cuts and, with the appropriate blade, can be used to cut materials other than wood, including metal.

What to Look For

Band saws are basically a pair of wheels, or occasionally three wheels, holding a thin rotating blade, a table to support the work, and a motor to run it. I built my first band saw many years ago using a kit from the Gilliom Mfg. Company. The company supplied the wheels and other parts, you supplied the motor and constructed a wooden cabinet. Band saws are available in a variety of sizes, ranging from small benchtop to huge floor models. Benchtop saws are portable and can be placed on a workbench or bolted to a stand for support. These usually don't have the capacity or the resawing capabilities of floor models but are much more economical. Benchtop models are also handy if you are limited on shop space. Band saw size determines the stock size it will handle and the size is based on two dimensions. First is the distance between the inner edge of the blade and the throat of the saw. A 14" band saw has a 14" measurement between the two. This measurement may range from 10" up to 24". Some manufacturers may go by the wheel size, which will make the measurement smaller. The second dimension is the depth of cut—the distance between the table and the underside of the blade guide/guard. On a saw with a 6" depth of cut, you can actually cut about 5⅞" due to the clearance needed for the guide to assure easy movement of the work.

The type and size of table on the saw is also important. The larger the table, the easier it is to hold and guide stock through the saw. The table should also have the capability to be set at an angle up to 45°. One use in this mode is removing the corners of a large turning block to speed up stock removal when turning on a lathe. Most band saws also come with a fence, used for resawing, and a miter

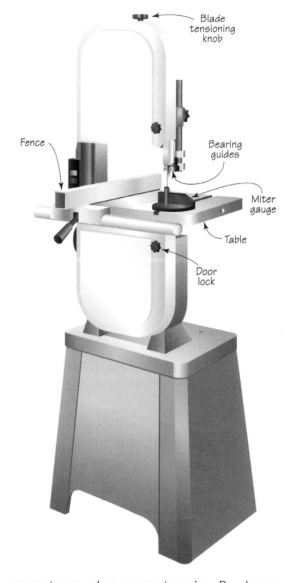

gauge to use when crosscut sawing. Band saws do tend to vibrate, and regardless of bench or floor model, it should be well-built with a sturdy cabinet. Bench models should be bolted, screwed, or clamped to a solid surface. For the most part, band saws can be used as they come from the factory. You can purchase riser kits for some saws to increase the depth of cut. And more accurate blade guides are also available as aftermarket additions. If you are purchasing a good quality saw, however, you probably won't need these items initially. Band saws are also available with different size motors, typically ranging from ⅓ up to 1½ horsepower. If you intend to cut only thin stock, the smaller size motors will suffice. If you intend to do any resawing, a larger motor is required.

It is important that all the guides be adjusted properly. Better quality band saws feature roller-bearing guides.

Band saw blades ride on rubber-covered wheels. It is important to have proper blade tension to match the blade width.

Band saws have a tension guide in order to match tension with the blade width.

How to Use

Having your band saw in proper adjustment is important. The blade must be tensioned properly and the guides adjusted. Follow your manufacturer's directions for proper adjustment. The tension is loosened to install or change blades. The blade is positioned in the center of the wheels and the tension set according to the width of the blade, per instructions that came with the tool. The wider the blade, the more tension required. Blade tension keeps the blade tracking properly. If the tension is set too high, however, the blade will break. With the guard open and the machine turned off and unplugged, slowly revolve one wheel a couple of turns to determine if the blade is aligned properly. If the blade is tracking properly, close the guard and turn on the machine to make sure the blade stays tracking properly.

The next step is to make sure the blade guides are adjusted. The back of the blade should barely touch the rear guide, with the teeth running clear of the guides.

Most band saws today have bearing guides. The guides should be set so the blade just touches the guides when pressure is applied with the wood. Some models have brass or metal side bearings that must be adjusted in or out and replaced or filed or turned around as they become worn.

Using a band saw is fun. As with any tool, proficiency comes with practice. Follow all safety rules with your saw. Keep your hands clear of the cut line. A band saw is a relatively safe tool, but the blade is sharp and fast and can inflict serious injury in a fraction of a second. Hold your hands on both sides of the cut line and clear of the blade. If a small piece of waste is being cut off, keep both hands on the main piece. If your hands are on the small waste piece,

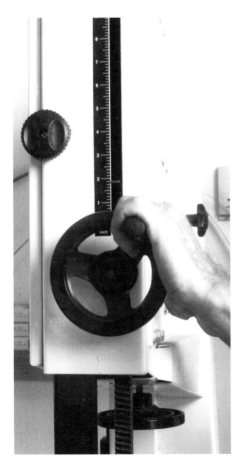

The blade guides are adjustable up and down to match the thickness of the stock being cut. Quality saws, such as the Jet shown, utilize a wheel for adjustment.

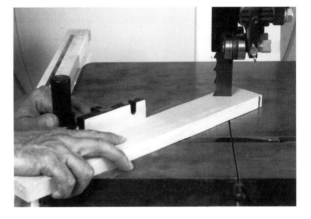

Most band saws come with a miter fence for crosscutting.

Better quality band saws have locking fences for ripping materials.

they may slip into the blade as the piece is released by the cut. Always wear safety glasses. If you haven't used a band saw before, make practice cuts on scrap softwood stock and then try hardwood scraps. Mark the cut line and move the stock slowly, steadily, and firmly against the blade. If you push the stock out of line to one side, the blade will bend and the cut will not be vertical. Do not cut a smaller radius than the blade size can handle. The blade will bind and can jump off the wheel. Instead, cut sharp curves by making a series of relief cuts up to the cut line. Then make a series of short whittling cuts to remove the waste between the relief cuts. When making irregular cuts, if possible, keep the waste portion on the outside. And make any short connecting cuts first. It is difficult to back out of a long curved cut, especially if the workpiece hits the frame of the machine.

Cutting compound curves is a fun practice that can be used to create cabriole legs and other designs. Mark the cuts onto adjoining edges of stock. Cut the waste pieces from one side, tape them back in place, turn the stock 90°, and make the two cuts on the adjoining side.

You can also cut perfect circles on a band saw with a shop-made jig. First, scribe the circle on the wood and locate the center of the circle. Drill a hole through the center. At the point where the cut is to start, make a cut a couple of inches long tangent to the circle. Fasten an auxiliary table to your band saw table. Position the stock on the auxiliary table with the started cut against the saw blade. Drive a nail or screw through the hole in the stock to be cut and down into the auxiliary table at right angles to the saw blade. Turn the stock into the band saw blade allowing the stock to pivot on the screw or nail. You can cut a large circle in this manner, relative to the capacity of your band saw.

If you have a number of identical pieces to cut, the best method is to use a template

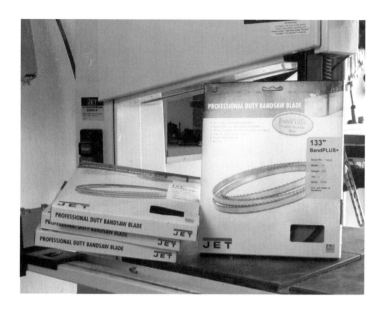

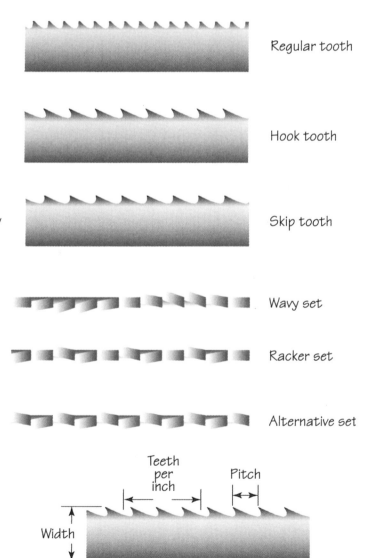

Regular tooth

Hook tooth

Skip tooth

Wavy set

Racker set

Alternative set

Teeth per inch

Pitch

Width

Band saw blades are available in different widths and types for different chores.

The most common use of a band saw is making curved or irregular cuts.

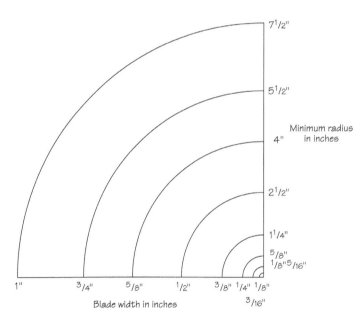

Minimum radius in inches

7¹/₂"
5¹/₂"
4"
2¹/₂"
1¹/₄"
⁵/₈"
¹/₈" ⁵/₁₆"

1"   ³/₄"   ⁵/₈"   ¹/₂"   ³/₈" ¹/₄" ¹/₈"
³/₁₆"

Blade width in inches

When making irregular cuts, it's important to match the blade size to the radius being cut.

and a follower jig clamped to the saw table. Attach the template to the stock to be cut with double-faced tape. Then run the template against the follower.

One of the biggest band saw chores is resawing, or sawing thick stock into thinner stock. This is often used when highly figured wood is chosen for a door panel or other furniture project. Set up correctly, you can even saw your own veneer. Wide blades must be used. The saw guides must be set properly to keep the blade from wandering or running out. A fence, of course, must also be used. Even with all that, some lead will happen as the blade tends to saw to one side or the other. The Jet saw shown has a resaw guide that attaches to the saw fence and alleviates the lead problem. A high fence can also be made from wood stock and clamped to the saw table. Saw a scrap stock to determine the lead, and adjust the ends of the fence to account for the lead.

Band saw blades are also available in a variety of sizes and tooth styles, and it's important to match the blade to the chore. Sizes range from ⅛" in width up to more than 1". It's important to choose the proper blade for the chore. To cut sharp curves in thin stock, choose narrower blades. Move up to wider blades for thicker stock. Resawing requires the bigger blades. The pitch or number of teeth per inch (tpi) of the blade is determined by the hardness of the wood being cut and varies from 4 up to 15 tpi. Basically, the coarser the teeth, the faster the blade will cut. More teeth per inch, however, produce a smoother cut. Hardwoods require a finer pitch, or a blade with more teeth. Regardless, there should be three teeth in contact with the stock, no matter how thin.

Choosing Blades

Blades are also available with different tooth patterns for the various chores. These are commonly called hook tooth, skip tooth, raker-set, and wavy-set. Hook tooth blades have wide

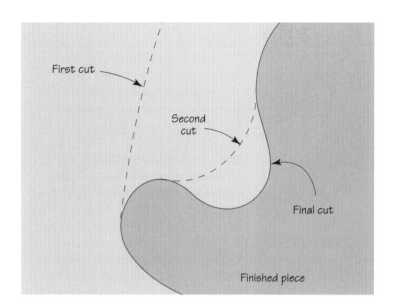

When making cuts with sharp curves, use several cuts to release various portions of waste stock.

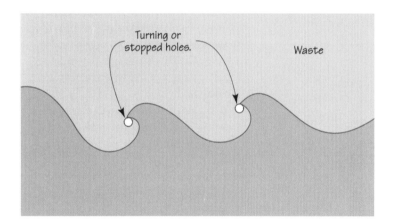

Turning or stopping holes can also be used for sharp corners.

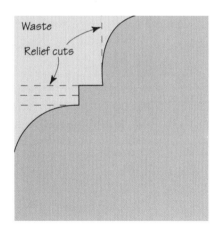

When cutting square corners, use relief cuts, as well.

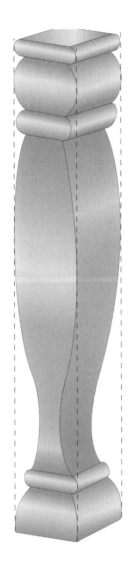

Cabriole legs and other multiple-cut pieces can be created with a band saw.

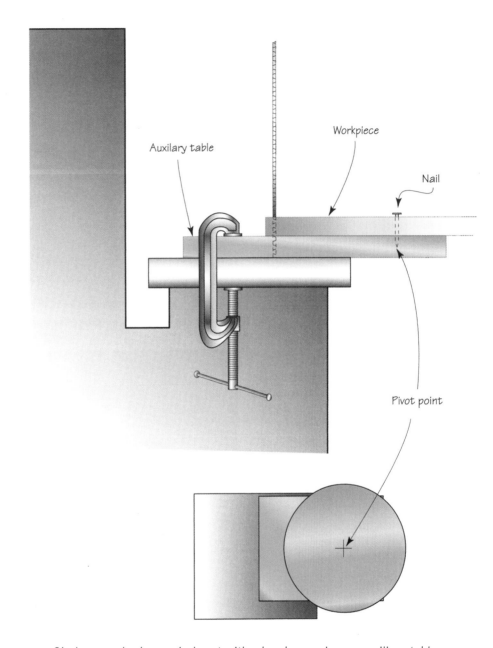

Auxilary table

Workpiece

Nail

Pivot point

Circles can also be precisely cut with a band saw using an auxiliary table.

teeth and are more closely spaced. They are best for hardwoods, harder nonferrous metals, as well as plastics. Skip tooth blades have widely spaced teeth to provide better chip clearance when cutting the softer metals and for soft nonferrous metals, such as aluminum. Wavy- and raker-set tooth blades are primarily used for cutting ferrous metal. A wavy-set blade is used with horizontal band saws used primarily for cutting ferrous metal. Some manufacturers also sell blades categorized to a purpose, such as general woodcutting, scrolling, and nonferrous or ferrous metal-cutting blades.

Blades are also available in various widths, ranging from ⅛ up to 1". When making straight cuts, such as crosscutting or ripping, including resawing, the blade should be as wide as your saw will handle. The wider the blade, the straighter the cut will be. When making irregular cuts, the blade should be matched to the radius being cut. It's important to have a variety of blades on hand for the different chores. Changing blades is fairly quick and easy on most band saws. Blades come coiled, and it's important to release them from the coil carefully so they don't snap out and cut you. Wearing protective gloves is also suggested. If you want to recoil a blade, hold it with the back of the blade facing you. Rotate the left wrist down and the right wrist thumb up simultaneously. At the same time, move your hands inward. Keep twisting your wrists to force the blade to coil into a triple loop. Tie the coils together in three places, and then lightly spray with a rust-preventive spray.

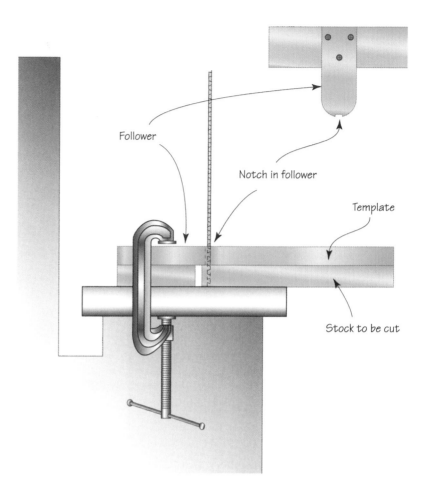

Identical pieces can be cut using a follower and a template.

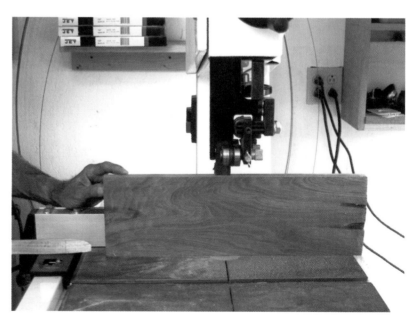

Band saws can also be used for resawing thick stock into thinner stock. The Jet model shown features a bolt-on resaw accessory.

Scroll Saw

If a band saw is fun, a scroll saw is even more so. In addition to fretwork for craft items, a scroll saw can also be used for creating inlays, molding, and intarsia. And they're great tools for introducing youngsters to the fun of woodworking. Scroll saws are available as economical and simple tools or expensive professional models, as well as a number of in-betweens. As you can imagine, a variety of features are available. The first is size, as determined by the throat width. This is determined by the distance between the front of the arm and the blade and can range from 12" and up to 30". The most common sizes are 16" and 18". Wider throats will cut larger stock, but it's a good idea to determine your needs. The next step is the arm design. Three arm designs are available, parallel arm, C-arm, and link arm. Parallel arms are the most common and move the blade up and down in a straight action. This produces a clean cut. A C-arm also adds a forward and backward cut, which is the most aggressive cutting, but it produces a rougher cut. The link arm is found on the more expensive models and creates a smooth cut with the least vibration of the machine. This type of arm also can be used with tighter radius cuts. Some saws come with variable speed. Different types of wood, as well as different cuts, are best done with different speeds, and this can definitely be a good feature. A foot-control for the variable speed adds even more ease-of-use. This not only provides good cutting control, but allows you to keep your hands on the work for better workpiece control, as well as safety. Most saws have a tilting table. Some will tilt only one direction, others will tilt both directions. In most instances, scroll saws are used for making inside cuts, threading the blade through a starting hole in the stock. This means you'll do a lot of removing and reinstalling of the blade. In the past, and still today, some saws require the use of a screwdriver or hex-head wrench to remove and reinstall the blade. Changing a blade in this manner is very time consuming, making a tool-free blade changing feature very important. Two other features to look for include a blower to keep dust out of the cut line and a work light. Some models also offer a foot-operated hold down for holding the workpiece more securely.

A scroll saw is a fun tool that can be used for craft projects, as well as cutting embellishments for furniture.

How to Use

Again, a scroll saw is relatively safe, but any saw can create a serious injury. Make sure you follow all safety rules. If the saw is to be used in a permanent location, mount it to a stand or workbench. Or you can mount the saw to a board that can be clamped to a solid work surface when in use.

A scroll saw can be used to make outside cuts, but is used primarily for inside cuts. Remove the saw blade and drill a ¼" hole in the stock on the inside or waste area of the work-piece. Place the stock on the saw table with the hole in the stock over the access hole in the table. Install the blade through the hole in the board, and attach the blade to the saw mechanism. Adjust the hold-down foot, grasp the stock, turn on the saw, and make the cut or cuts. After making the cut, remove the blade and slide the stock from the saw table. It's a good idea to make

practice cuts on scrap stock. You can also use the saw to make stack cuts or cut more than one piece at a time to create duplicates. Simply stack thin wood pieces together with double-faced tape between them and cut as one piece.

Choosing Blades

Scroll saw blades are also available in different tooth per inch and blade styles. It's important to choose the proper blade for the job. Teeth per inch can vary from 9 to 25 tpi with, again, the finer teeth best for harder materials. The finer tooth blades also cut smaller radiuses, but are slower cutting. Blades are available as pin-type or plain-end with skip-tooth or reverse-tooth. The skip-tooth blades cut the fastest. Reverse tooth blades provide splinter-free cuts on both top and bottom surfaces.

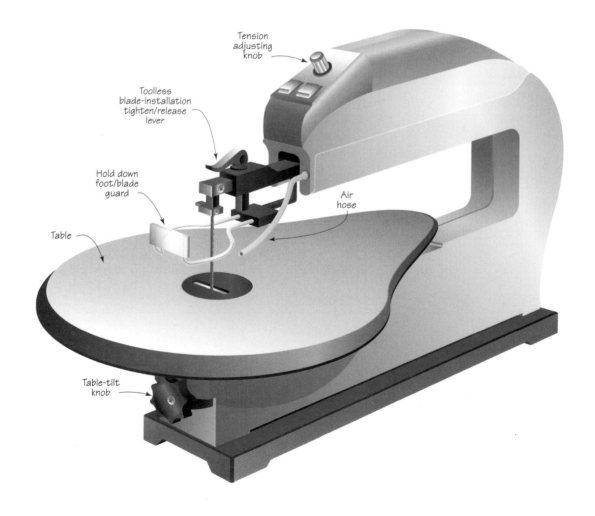

Tension adjusting knob

Toolless blade-installation tighten/release lever

Hold down foot/blade guard

Table

Air hose

Table-tilt knob

A starting hole is bored in the work-piece and the scroll saw blade threaded through it and locked in the machine.

The saw is then used to cut out the interior.

BORING TOOLS

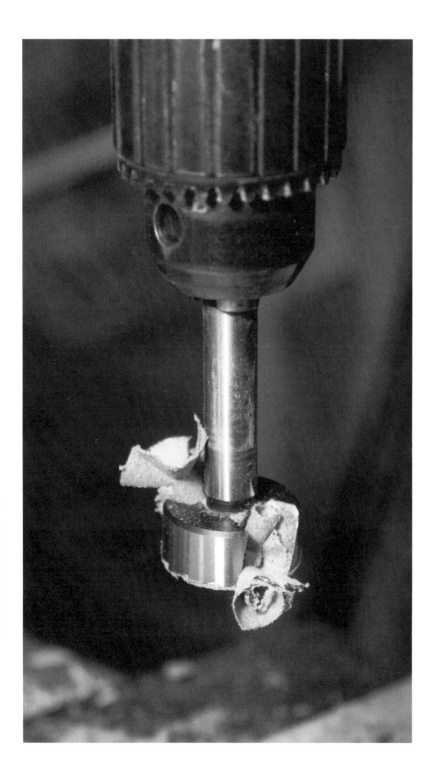

Stationary boring tools include a drill press and a hollow chisel mortising machine. A drill press is almost a necessity in a shop. The mortising machine less so, but it is still important for serious furniture builders. A drill press is invaluable for drilling in metal, wood, and other materials, as well as for a wide variety of other metal and woodworking chores. Floor models allow for boring in long pieces of wood.

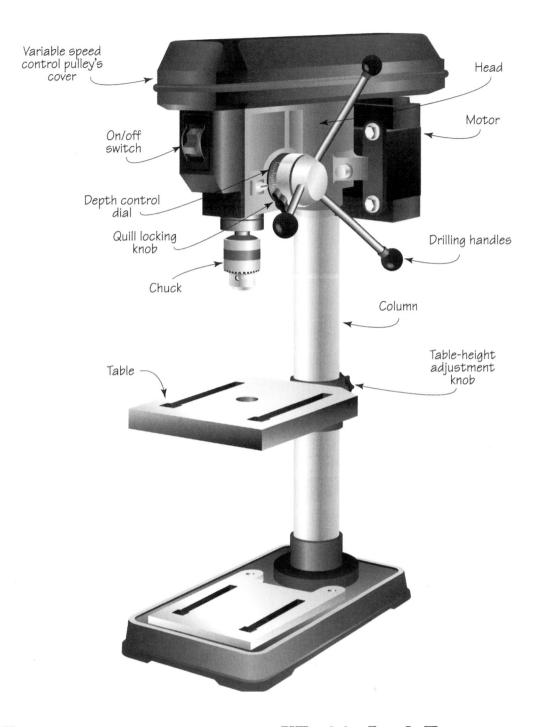

Variable speed control pulley's cover

Head

On/off switch

Motor

Depth control dial

Quill locking knob

Drilling handles

Chuck

Column

Table

Table-height adjustment knob

Drill Press

A drill press is a versatile shop tool for working with both metal and wood. Some chores simply can't be done without a drill press; other chores in both wood and metal can be done by substituting a drill press for other specialty machines.

What to Look For

A drill press consists of a base, column, table, and head. The latter contains the motor, spindle, and the quill. The spindle revolves in the head and the quill is moved up and down with a rack-and-pinion system. Turning a feed lever moves the quill up and down. When the feed lever is released, the quill and spindle are carried back up to the starting position by a spring.

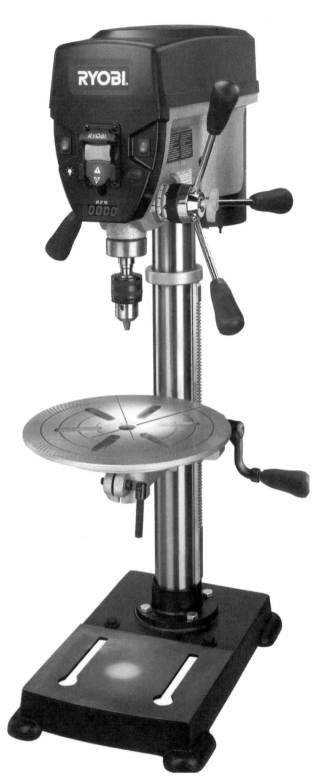

Bench models are more economical and just as efficient for drilling in flat objects and doing other chores.

The quill can also be locked in place or a depth adjustment can be set to stop the quill's travel at a preset measurement. The length of quill travel in most home workshop drill presses is 3" to 4". The spindle has a keyed chuck used to hold the various drills and accessories. Most home shop models feature a ½" to ⅝" chuck.

Drill presses are available in several sizes. The size, or capacity, is denoted by the distance from the center of the chuck to the front of the column, expressed as diameter. This means a 12" drill press will drill a hole through the center of a 12" round. The actual distance will be 6". Most home workshop drill presses range from 10" to 16½", but models are available up to 20". The motors will also vary in size. Most home models range from V4 up to 2 horsepower. The larger horsepower models provide for easier boring in harder materials.

Both bench and floor model drill presses are available. Bench models normally have only about 8 to 14" between the chuck and the table. Only shallow or fairly small items may be bored, although the press can be used for any number of other purposes. Most floor models will allow for boring in a 36" or larger workpiece. With these models, you can bore holes in table legs and other long pieces. And you don't need a bench or stand because they're free-standing. These models, however, are heavy and awkward. They can weigh several hundred pounds.

A lever moves the bit into the work surface.

Drill presses are available with both fixed and radial heads. Fixed heads are fixed in one place. Radial heads are more versatile, as the head swivels 360° around the column and also tilts 90° to the left or right. This provides almost infinite angle drilling capabilities. Radial heads, however, are not as common with home shop models. I had an ancient Delta model I used primarily for drilling angled holes for installing chair legs, but I eventually gave it up for a modern press with variable speed. The only radial drill presses I've found are from Grizzly. Some upper-end drill presses have tilting tables that allow for a variety of drilling angles. Tilting work surfaces that fit over tables are available as accessories.

Because of the need for different speeds for different operations, drill presses must have a means of speed control. The most common method in the past, and the most economical, utilizes dual-stepped belts. By changing the belt from one set to the other, you can obtain different speeds. Models with several speeds are available. Variable speed models have also become increasingly popular. Speed is controlled by a switch on the head and infinitely variable speeds are easily obtained. This makes changing speeds much faster and easier.

The Delta 16½" variable speed drill press shown in my shop is an example of a top-end home workshop model. The variable speed drive system includes a jack shaft for providing full torque at any speed. The ¾ horsepower induction motor provides plenty of power for a variety of drilling and other chores. The 14" table features rack and pinion for easy raising and lowering, and tilts 90° left or right. A microadjustable depth stop provides quick and accurate drilling. The unit comes with a lamp and an accessory tray.

How to Use

The wide range of bits and accessories is what makes the drill press so versatile. The most common use, however, is drilling holes with drill bits, and the most common bits are twist drill. Twist drills, although designed primarily for use in drilling in metal, can be used in wood, plastic, ceramic, and

The quill can also be locked in place at any location for use with any number of accessories.

The quill can also be stopped at any spot with a depth adjustment for creating blind or stopped holes.

A variable speed model makes changing speed instant and easy.

other materials. You really get what you pay for with twist drill bits. Good quality bits will work better, stay sharper, and sharpen easier. Bits are available in several high-tech materials that afford easier drilling in materials, such as steel alloys, stainless steel, armor plate, and titanium alloys. New designs also make it easier to drill in many materials. For example, the Craftsman Zirconium drill bits feature an exclusive split-point and groove design that breaks up chips for faster penetration and more precise drilling. Quality bits such as these also offer a point design that eliminates walking or skidding of the point when starting the bit.

It is important to use the proper bit or cutter for the chore and the recommended speed for the drill press bit and the workpiece material. The best speed is determined by the type of material being worked, the size of the hole, the type of drill or other cutter, and the quality of cut that is desired.

Like other shop tools, follow all safety rules when using these machines, and always wear a face shield or safety glasses.

Boring in Wood

Although intended for metal drilling, twist drills can also be used for boring holes in wood with a drill press. The best choice for wood, however, is machine spur bits. These bits cut a flat bottom hole and are designed for fast removal of wood chips. Hand bits with a screw tip should not be used. At drill press speeds, they can turn into the wood rapidly, catch, and cause the workpiece to lift from the table and spin. For through boring, position the table so the bit will enter the center hole of the table as it exits the workpiece to prevent damage to the bit. One trick is to scribe a vertical line on the front of the column and a matching mark on the table bracket and drill press head. This makes it easy to align and clamp the table for center position at any height. You can also use a scrap piece of wood for a backer or

Twist drills are the most commonly used bits. It's important to select quality bits, whether for metalworking or woodworking.

Forstner bits are used for cutting clean and accurate holes in wood.

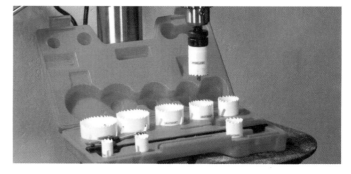

Hole saws can be used for cutting holes in metal, wood, plastic, and other materials.

A mortising bit allows for drilling a series of square holes to create mortises for mortise and tenon joints.

Plug cutters are used to cut plugs to match specific woods and cover screw heads.

support block on the table. In this case, make sure to set the depth control so the bit doesn't go entirely through the backer block. A backer block also prevents splintering on the back of the workpiece. Feed slowly, especially as the bit is about to exit the back of the workpiece to prevent splintering.

For precise boring of holes, particularly larger holes in wood, the Forstner-style bits can't be beat. Forstner bits are also used for drilling blind holes, or holes that do not run all the way through. Forstner bits leave the bottom of the hole flat. The Woodcraft 16-piece boxed set will handle just about anything you can think of. Sizes run from ¼" up to 2⅛", all in ⅛" increments. Bits larger than one inch have saw-toothed edges to keep the cutting edge cool while boring. Forstner bits should be run slowly, at 450 rpm or less, to prevent burning the wood. One trick to creating a splinter-free hole is to set the depth stop to allow the point to barely protrude. Then remove the workpiece turn it over, and drill from the back, starting the point in the small point hole to realign the bit. When using the smaller diameter bits, especially on deep holes, chips may clog the bit and can eventually make it difficult to pull the bit out of the hole. It's a good idea to frequently back out the bit to remove the chip buildup. One technique to creating mortises is with Forstner bits in a drill press. Bore overlapping holes to create the mortise, and then clean up the edges and corners with a wood chisel.

You can drill a square hole in wood with a drill press. Mortising attachments allow you to bore a series of square holes to create a mortise for inserting a tenon. This is a quick and easy method of creating these joints. The mortising chisel kit clamps to the quill of the drill

Drum sanders make quick work of sanding contours.

press, and the work is clamped against a fence to align a hollow chisel in which a bit turns.

A similar operation to drilling is using plug cutters to cut wooden plugs to cover countersunk wood screws. This allows you to conceal screws in fine furniture, matching the plugs to the wood being used. For instance, you may have a beautiful piece of walnut furniture. It's easy to conceal the screws with walnut plugs cut with a drill press and plug cutters. Another handy drill-press tool is a countersink bit that makes quick work of drilling precise countersunk holes for screw heads.

Sanding is another useful woodworking chore that can be done with a drill press. Drum sanders are available to fit into the drill press chuck. These range in size from ¼" up to 3". The Craftsman set features rubber-cushioned, self-expanding drums, along with a buffing wheel. These drums can sand curves and rounds on stock. One example is in creating cabriole legs. If you use a drill press for a lot of rotary sanding, you might consider purchasing a Shop Fox Oscillating drill press. Its up and down action duplicates spindle sanders. Rotary rasps and files of different sizes can also be chucked in a drill press for quick removal of material. Metal can also be polished using abrasive discs. One unusual metal working technique is lapping, or creating overlapping polished spots. This can be done with a lapping tool and abrasives, available from Brownell's, or a shop-made tool consisting of a cork held in a tube and used with abrasives.

One of the most interesting woodworking uses of a drill press is surface planing or shaping. Back in the 1970s, when I was Associate Editor of Workbench magazine, one of the tools I really enjoyed working with was the Wagner Safe-T-Planer. The tool, available from Woodcraft Supply, fits into the drill-press chuck and can be used to freehand thickness plane stock. Boards too wide

The Safe-T-Planer and a drill press can be used to surface-plane stocks.

It can be used to cut tenons.

Or to cut coves for raised panels.

A rosette cutter amd drill press can be used to make decorative blocks for door and window lintels.

A drill-press vise is a must for boring many materials. The vise holds the work solidly in place not only for more accurate boring, but also to prevent the workpiece from spinning and causing a danger if the bit catches.

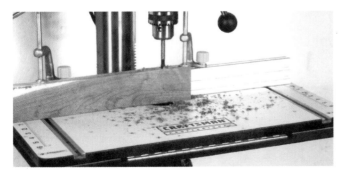

A drill-press table, such as the Craftsman model shown, creates a larger work surface and provides a fence for some operations.

for a planer can easily be surfaced with the tool. And, it's guaranteed not to grab or kickback. In addition, the tool will also do rabbets, cut tenons, make cove cuts, and create raised panels. With a fence, the unit can also be used to joint wood edges for joining together wood pieces to create wide stock. A shop-made planing table makes jointing and planing easier. A radial-drill press is the best choice if you intend to do much with the Safe-T-Planer.

Another form of surface shaping utilizes rosette cutters. These tools allow you to quickly make door and window plinth blocks or cut wheels for wooden toys. Four different patterns in two different sizes, $2\frac{1}{8}$" and $2\frac{3}{4}$" are available. The Grizzly Rosette cutterhead and knives feature a unique cutterhead with a variety of knives that can be fitted into the cutterhead. These include rosette patterns, planer patterns, and raised-panel patterns.

A drill press table helps in making more precise cuts and holes with a drill press. A drill press table can also be used to help clamp the workpiece solidly in place. These tables offer a larger work surface for easier positioning of larger pieces. The Fasttrack model from Woodcraft Supply is one such unit. Rockier also carries an excellent drill press table and fence. Another model is the Craftsman Universal Drill Press Work Center with Dust Port. It tilts from 0° to 45° for angle and compound angle drilling. An aluminum fence has adjustable stop and hold-down clamps.

Drilling Metal

Drilling holes in metal is a common drill press chore. Extra care must be taken when drilling metal, especially steel and other hard metals. It's important to match the bit and the speed to the chore. Generally, drilling in metal requires slower speeds and a lubricant should be used.

Most workpieces must be clamped or held securely in position for precise drilling with a drill press. This is especially so when drilling metal, using larger wood bits, and other such chores.

A drill bit that catches in a piece of metal or other workpiece can cause the workpiece to spin dangerously. Any number of clamps, wood, or C-clamps can be used to hold the piece to the table. Drill press vises, used to hold the workpiece, are handy for many items, especially round stock or small pieces. Drill press vises can also be another safety factor in keeping your fingers and hands away from spinning cutters and blades. Drill press manufacturers, such as Delta, offer accessory drill press vises that mount directly to their machines with bolts through the slotted table. These vises have jaws that can be moved in precise measurements and angles and secure a variety of workpieces. Grizzly also offers a number of reasonably priced vises.

For cutting larger holes in mild steel, bronze, copper, brass, aluminum, wood, plywood, plastics, and laminates, the Craftsman Bi-Metal hole saw set is a good choice. The set includes bits from ¾" to 2½".

Hollow Chisel Mortiser

Although a hollow chisel mortising attachment can be used in the drill press, a dedicated mortising machine can be a great helpmate to the serious furniture or cabi-net builder. These units can cut precise and snug-fitting mortises for mortise and tenon joints, freeing up your drill press for other boring jobs. And it does take some time to change out the drill press from drilling operations to a mortising machine. A number of these machines are available from different manufacturers and are available in benchtop models, as well as floor models. The latter are primarily used in production shops.

What to Look For

A number of these machines are available from different manufacturers, including Shop Fox, Craftsman, and Grizzly. For the most part, the more affordable benchtop models are adequate for most home shop chores. It is important the unit be sturdy with rigid cast iron construction. Most come with ¼", ⁵⁄₁₆", ⅜", and ½" chisels. These allow you to not only create mortises of this width, but double that by moving the fence.

How to Use

Select the appropriate size chisel and install it in the machine. Set the depth if the mortise is to be stopped. If making through-mortises, use a backer board to prevent

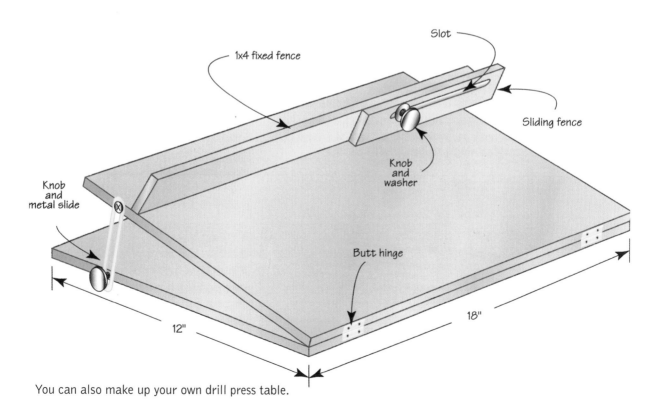

You can also make up your own drill press table.

chip out and table damage. Adjust the hold-down to secure the workpiece. To move the work to the left to continue a mortise length, set the chisel opening to the left. To move to the right, set the chisel opening to the right. This helps keep the chips from obscuring the work area. Using a steady, firm hand on the lever, feed the bit and chisel into the workpiece as fast as the workpiece accepts the feed without the mortiser motor stalling. Too slow a speed may burn the tip of the bit. Light smoke is a normal part of the operation with some woods, as resins burn off, and chip friction creates heat. A blued chisel is not a sign of dullness, but of chip friction heat and resin build-up. The chisel is too dull when a lot of force is needed to continue working easily.

A hollow chisel mortiser can be valuable to cabinet and furniture builders.

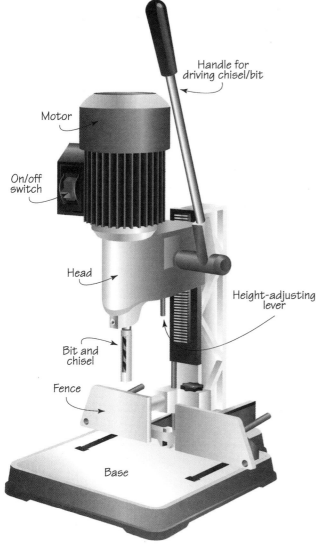

Handle for driving chisel/bit

Motor

On/off switch

Head

Height-adjusting lever

Bit and chisel

Fence

Base

Stock is clamped in the mortiser table and handle-pulled down to make the square cut, then the stock is moved to make succeeding cuts.

SURFACING MACHINES

Sooner or later, serious woodworkers will require surfacing machines. This is especially so if doing furniture or cabinetry work. Hardwood stock is the most economical purchased in the rough. Wood surfacing machines include a jointer and a planer. Jointers can be used for creating smooth, flat surfaces on workpieces as well as precise 90° or desired-angled edges. Planers are commonly used to plane rough-sawn surfaces to smooth them, or to plane wood to the thicknesses desired. Some planers can also function as production molding machines, and some can even create rounded or arched moldings.

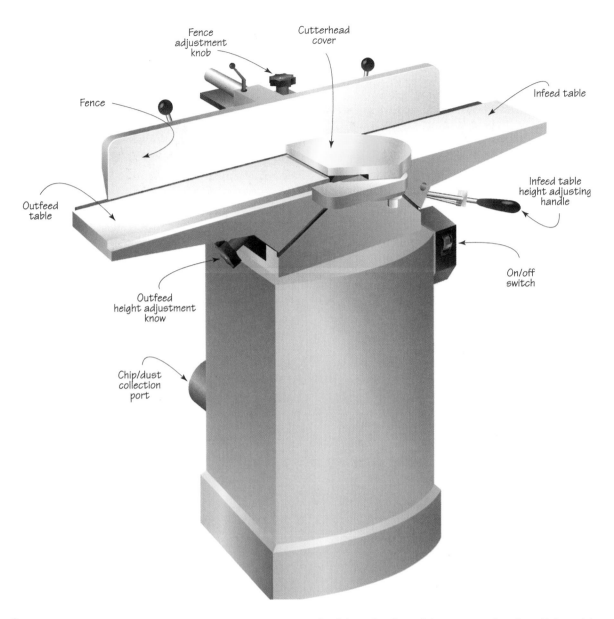

Fence adjustment knob

Cutterhead cover

Infeed table

Fence

Outfeed table

Infeed table height adjusting handle

Outfeed height adjustment know

On/off switch

Chip/dust collection port

Jointer

A jointer can be an invaluable tool for the wood workshop. Jointers are most commonly used for surfacing edges, but can also be used for creating flat surfaces and removing cups or twists in workpieces. They can also be used for a number of other chores, including creating rabbets, tenons, raised panels, and tapers.

What to Look For

Jointers are available in a wide range of sizes, including portable or benchtop models up to behemoth stationary jointers. Sizes range from 6" up to 16". The size denotes the width of the cutterhead or the width of stock that can be run. The most common size is

6", although 8" models are popular. Small, benchtop models are more economical, with a Grizzly model available for a couple hundred bucks. Tabletop models are great for small shops with limited space. You can store them out of the way when not needed, and then clamp them to a bench when needed. These machines typically don't have rabbeting capability. The big production models run into the thousands of dollars. The larger machines can also take up a lot of space because their tables are extended.

A good choice for most home and even serious furniture builders is a 6" or 8" stationary model. If you're limited on space, a mobile base can be helpful. My jointer is set up right next to my table saw as the two operations are often done together—joint an edge, run the stock to width through the table saw, then joint the cut edge. You will also need space in front and behind the jointer to run lengthy stock. My shop has garage doors on one end. Both my jointer and table saw are set up near a door. I can run stock up to 8' in length with the door closed and longer stock with the door opened.

Economical jointers feature two knives; better quality models have three knives. If you do a lot of work with hardwoods, especially figured woods, you may wish to look into spiral cutterheads. These convert normal rotary cutting into side-shearing cuts for smooth cuts. Some jointers or jointer blades come double-edged so you can double your use before sharpening them. Jointer cutterheads with jack screws make it easier to set the knives properly. Without these you'll need a knife-setting jig. The Jointer Pal Knife Setting Jig, from Woodstock International, makes the chore easy. The cuts-per-minute is determined by the rpm of the cutterhead, as well as the number and shape of the knives. This ranges from around 1,400 to over 20,000 cpm. Smoothness of the cut is dependent somewhat on the number of cuts per minute, with the higher numbers typically producing smoother finishes. Depth of cut usually ranges up to $\frac{1}{2}$", but typically a jointer should never be used to cut more than $\frac{1}{8}$" unless rabbeting, with $\frac{1}{16}$" the most common cut depth. The bed, or workpiece support surface, consists of two pieces, an infeed and outfeed table. The outfeed table stays stationary, the infeed table is adjustable. Lever table adjustors have been traditional, but wheel-type adjustors have become more popular, are easier to use, and more precise. A round cutterhead with blades fits between the two. Regardless of size, beds are cast iron for weight. Bed length varies from a little over 2' to over 8' on the commercial models. Most 6" and 8" jointers have a bed length of around 4'. I use a roller support on the outfeed side for longer stock. Motor size also varies from 1 up to 5 horsepower on production models. The most common motor size on 6" and 8" models is from 1 to 2 horsepower. Fences may be center-mounted or offset. Center-mounted fences are more rigid. The fence can be adjusted from the front to the rear of the bed. And most offer tilting fences. These may be tilted at any angle. Jointers, such as the Rigid, also offer stops at 45°, 90°, and 135°. I have actually never used my jointers in any other than 90° degrees, because other tools do angled cuts much simpler. Stationary models come with two base styles, an open frame and an enclosed stand. The latter offers more rigidity and also makes it easier to collect dust and chips. (Jointers do create a lot of dust and chips.) You will need a serious dust collector. Most enclosed bases feature a 4" dust port for connection to a dust collector.

Jointers are available as benchtop models.

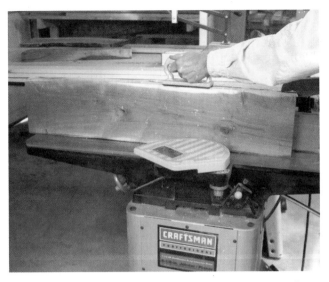

Or as floor models. The 6" jointer shown here is a good choice for home shops.

Some models have the capability of cutting rabbets.

The main purpose of a jointer is to edge materials. Note the author's jointer is set up next to the table saw, as jointing edges and ripping stock are chores often used in conjunction with each other. It's important to always use push sticks and push blocks when using a jointer.

Stock can be surfaced on the jointer up to the width of the jointer cutterhead.

SURFACING MACHINES

How to Use

Up front, I'm going to state unequivocally, a jointer is probably one of the most dangerous tools in the shop. A good majority of my woodworking acquaintances, including my father, have left parts of fingers in a jointer. A swinging blade guard is supposed to cover all portions of the revolving blades except those covered by the workpiece. But it's really easy to get your fingers into the cutterhead. In addition to general safety rules, such as unplugging the machine before making any adjustments, jointers have some specific safety rules that must be followed.

1.   Never perform any operations with the cutterhead guard removed, and make sure it works smoothly and freely. Make sure the cutterhead behind the fence is guarded.

2.   Always used push sticks and hold-downs, especially when finishing the cut at the end of the stock.

3.   Never joint stock shorter than 10", narrower than ¾" or less than ⅝ " These can create kickback, not only throwing the stock at you, but also exposing your hands to the cutterhead.

4.   Never start the cutterhead with the stock on the bed. Start the cutterhead, and then feed the stock slowly and evenly across the cutterhead.

5.   Always hold the workpiece firmly and solidly against the fence and tables. Never perform any type of free-hand operation or without supporting the work with the fence.

6.   Never make jointing or planing cuts deeper than ⅛". On cuts more than 1½" wide, adjust the depth of cut to $\frac{1}{16}$" or less to avoid overloading the machine and to minimize kickback. Only rabbet cuts should be made with deeper cuts, as per the machine operator's manual.

7.   Properly support the work at all times, especially on the outfeed side.

8.   Do not back the workpiece over the cutterhead toward the infeed table.

9.   Make sure all table and other adjustments are secure.

Edge Jointing

The most common chore is edge jointing. First, make sure the outfeed table is properly adjusted so the table

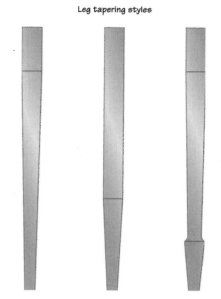

Leg tapering styles

A jointer can be used to create a variety of tapered legs.

is the same height as the knives. Use a straight edge to check. Use a small square to check the fence is correctly set at 90°. Set the jointer for the depth of cut. Examine the stock to determine the grain direction. Whenever possible, you should cut with the grain and not against it. Standing slightly to the outside of the jointer, turn it on and advance the workpiece into the cutter, holding it firmly against the fence and table with push blocks and push sticks. Continue pushing the workpiece onto the rear table while applying pressure with your left hand. Never hook your thumb over the end of the stock to complete the cut. As the rear end of the stock reaches the cutterhead, push it through with the push stick with your right hand. Again, support long stock on the outfeed side. End grain jointing is a bit trickier. If you're jointing entirely around a workpiece, do the end grain edges first, following with the grain.

Planing, or face-jointing, a surface is somewhat similar but also different. This technique is often used to initially smooth a rough-sawn surface or to remove a cup, twist, or warp. Never cut more than $\frac{1}{16}$" with this technique. Always use paddle pushers and push sticks for the chore. Be very careful as you near the end of the cut. A great deal of the cutterhead is exposed as the stock clears the cutterhead and before the guard can snap back. Feather boards must be used when cutting thin stock.

Tapering

One excellent chore for a jointer is tapering, and you can create a variety of tapered legs and other projects. This can be a straight taper the full length, a portion of the workpiece or a stopped taper. These require jigs that are simple to set up.

Planers

A planer is an invaluable tool for serious woodworkers and custom home-building contractors or those wishing to save money building or renovating a home. Purchasing rough or unplaned lumber, then planing it yourself can save money. On many fancier woods, this can be quite a savings. Lumber can also be planed to the exact thickness desired, rather than buying the standard thicknesses available. In many instances, you can also obtain specialty woods from salvaged projects, custom-sawn logs, and other sources. These woods can then be planed into beautiful lumber for creating fine furniture. Builders of custom homes can utilize the planer to plane custom woods for trim and cabinetry. Add a molding head, and the planer becomes even more invaluable. All types of house trim and all shapes for custom furniture are easily and precisely cut with a planer with a molding head.

This allows the builder to satisfy a homeowner's desire for custom-built trim and furniture, utilizing woods not readily available, such as ash, pecan, and walnut. Add in a portable band saw mill, and the possibilities are almost unlimited.

What to Look For

Planers are available in a variety of sizes, denoted by width. Widths range from 8" up to large 30" industrial models. The smaller planers are often called **portable** and can be set up on a benchtop. The more economical models feature a two-knife cutterhead, the heavier duty models have three knives and provide a smoother finish. The smaller models are not designed to be used with molding knives.

The bed of the planer is important. Some smaller models feature rollers to assist in the movement of the stock. Larger models typically have extended outfeed ends for more support. Snipe, or cutting or cupping of the end of the board, has been a common problem in the past and is to some degree on smaller planers. This is basically caused by the cutterhead wobbling as the stock moves against it. Most planers feature four-post design to reduce this problem. Feed rollers pull the stock through the machine, and these may be hard rubber or serrated steel. Rubber rollers are found on most portable units, both steel and hard rubber rollers are found on the larger models. Some models also have return rollers on the top. This allows you to feed the stock back over the top of the machine for repeat passes. Feed rate, or the speed at which the stock is pulled through the planer, varies. This can be a single speed, dual-speed, or in the case of upscale models, variable speed. When thickness planning hardwood stock, you may wish to go at a faster rate for the initial cuts, then slow down for the final finish

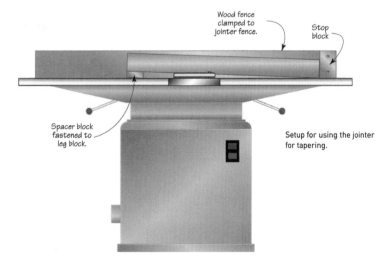

Wood fence clamped to jointer fence.

Stop block

Spacer block fastened to leg block.

Setup for using the jointer for tapering.

cuts. In addition to the feed rate, cutterhead rpm is also important and this can range from around 2,000 to over 5,000. Again, the cuts per minute can vary according to the number of blades, as well as cutterhead rpm. Basically, the faster the rpm, the smoother the cut. The maximum cutting depth is typically $\frac{1}{8}$". The portable planers are fairly lightweight, more economical, but must be bolted or clamped to a solid surface. The larger stationary planers can weigh several hundred pounds and are more rigid. Cutterheads may have two, three, or even four blades on the production units. Blades may come as single edge, double-edged, or even disposable.

The Woodmaster Tools planer in my shop is a stationary, 18" model with three knives. It has two motors; one to power the cutterhead and one to power the feed rollers. The power feed rate is infinitely variable, from 0 to 16 feet per minute, providing power to both infeed and outfeed rollers. This allows using a high speed rate for fast stock removal, and then slowing down for difficult woods or for fine-finishing passes. This is especially important when planing materials such as curly maple, burls, and other figured woods. The unit also features a milled cast iron bed that is a full $18\frac{1}{8}$" x $18\frac{1}{2}$". The 18" size accommodates planing wide cabinet stock, as well as glued up stock. The bed will lower to accept $6\frac{3}{4}$"-thick stock. The tool also comes with steel infeed and outfeed extension tables as standard equipment providing a full $42\frac{9}{16}$" bed length for handling long stock. The Woodmaster's patented Morse-taper cutterhead lets you move from planing to molding, sanding, or sawing using their attachments in fewer than five minutes without the need to change cutterhead bearings or planer knives. A variety of 1" cutter bits can be fitted into the cutter bit holder. A special wide knife holder is also available for wider patterns and custom knives. These holders can be easily moved from one location to another, allowing you to make quick work of combination cuts for fancy trim.

The Woodmaster ripsaw attachment turns the unit into a power-feed, single- or multiple-blade ripsaw. This is perfect for sizing blank molding stock, facing frames, rail and stile work, and more. A Woodmaster quick

A surface planer can be an important piece of machinery for the serious woodworker, custom-home builder, or anyone remodeling an older home.

Planers come in several different sizes and power ranges, including this benchtop model.

The Woodmaster 18" 4-in-1 planer shown is a quality, heavy-duty floor model that can also be used for cutting molding.

change drum-sanding attachment allows mounting a drum sander in fewer than five minutes. Because the stock is power fed at a uniform rate, you can create a smooth surface with no low spots or cross-grain marks.

How to Use

Most in-the-rough lumber is sawn to 1" or thicker, allowing for planing to ¾". Other thicknesses are also available. For instance, red cedar used for lining materials may be ⅝" to ¾", to be planed down to be ⅝" to ⅜" inches. Turning blocks and other thicker materials are also available. In-the-rough lumber may come with two sawn sides or four sawn surfaces. Most lumber will have a **crown,** or cup to it, which must be removed in the dimensioning steps. Planing, however, won't correct a warped piece of stock. The

purpose of planing is to smooth the stock and cut it to a uniform thickness. Examine the end of the stock to determine the direction of the grain. The lines of the grain should usually point upward in making the first pass to remove the crown.

The first step is to index the planer. With the motors off and unplugged, place the stock in the planer bed and adjust the depth adjustment crank until the feed rollers just touch the stock. Remove the stock, turn the depth adjustment to take a very shallow cut, turn on the planer, and then feed the stock with the convex side up. Repeat, making very shallow cuts until you have a smooth, flat surface on approximately 70 percent of the width. Turn the board over and continue making very shallow cuts on the concave side until about 70 percent of it is finished. Continue turning and cutting until the board faces

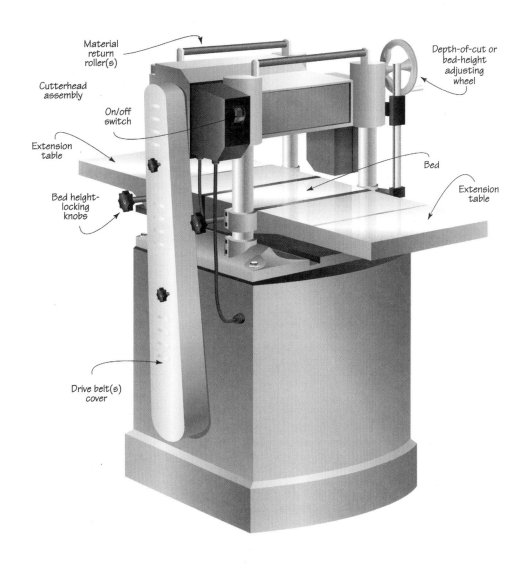

Material return roller(s)

Cutterhead assembly

On/off switch

Extension table

Bed height-locking knobs

Drive belt(s) cover

Depth-of-cut or bed-height adjusting wheel

Bed

Extension table

Surfacing rough stock to size, especially hardwoods used for fine house trim and furniture, and creating a smooth surface is a great cost saver over purchasing lumber already surfaced.

The beautiful grain of this walnut shows the possibilities in custom-planing and surfacing materials.

are smooth and parallel. If the stock isn't crowned, it may take fewer cuts to smooth and surface the faces. If you have several pieces to plane, make the same cuts on each piece.

If planing long pieces, it helps to have someone hold the outfeed end. Or you can use a roller support. The biggest problem with planers is snipe, a slightly deeper cut made on the end of the board as it comes out of the planer. Snipe is most common on long, thick, or heavy stock and is a result of the board being held by only one feed roller as it comes out, allowing the board to be lifted by the cutterhead and the weight of the remaining stock to pivot the stock further into the cutterhead. Proper adjustment of the feed roller pressure will eliminate most

Surface planing also allows for creating precise thicknesses of materials.

snipe problems. Setting the outer ends of the extension tables slightly higher and supporting the stock as it comes out also helps. Butting together workpieces as you feed them will help. When planing stock to a thin depth, use a wooden protection board over the planer bed. Taking too deep a cut can cause kickback, a serious problem if you don't index and set the blades properly. Follow your planer manufacturer's warnings as to settings, and don't stand directly behind the stock; stand off to one side.

In many cases, narrow stock is glued up to create wide stock, and these pieces can be surfaced. Before planing, use a scraper blade, chisel, hand plane, or belt sander to remove squeezed-out glue. The dried glue is hard and can nick or damage the planer blades. Even with the best of clamping techniques, there will be some variation in both sides of the glued up boards. Turn the boards repeatedly to achieve smooth, parallel surfaces. Incidentally, this is a great place to use the Woodmaster drum sander attachment instead of the planer blades.

Molding

The real fun, and actually one of the best uses of the Woodmaster machine shown here, as well as some other planers, is creating custom molding. In about five minutes you can remove the cutterhead and install an accessory shaft holding the molding knife. Over 500 molding profiles are available from the company. You can also have custom knives ground to your design, which allows the renovators of older homes to match unusual trim designs. All pattern knives are made from industry-standard $5/16$" high-speed, M-2 steel. All standard house trim patterns in different sizes, picture frame patterns, dowel patterns, banister rails, bar rails, designer patterns, and many more are available. Other knife patterns include tongue-and-groove, as well as wood plank paneling and siding. One of the more unusual and most popular models, according to Ed Dobbins

After the planer is indexed, or set to the proper feed rate, the bed is then positioned to take a slight beginning cut.

Many rough-sawn pieces have cupped. Begin by removing the cup from the convex side. Remove only a little, then turn the stock and remove from the concave side, repeating until the board has parallel surfaces of the thickness desired.

The Woodmaster has infinitely variable speed control, allowing you to match the feed rate to the wood or type of surfacing being done.

with Woodmaster, is their log cabin siding patterns. A matched set of three knives is used to create the rounded half-log design.

Each molding operation involves 5 steps: stock preparation, knife installation, guide-board installation, test run, and production run. Successful molding operations begin with careful stock preparation. The stock should be planed to within $\frac{1}{32}$" of the thickest portion of the finished molding. Patterns that involve a cut on both sides (crown moldings, bed moldings, picture frame moldings) should be planed to within $\frac{1}{16}$" of the thickest portion of the finished molding (allowing $\frac{1}{32}$" for each pass).

If the molding involves parting legs, the stock should be ripped to within $\frac{1}{8}$" of the finished width (this allows each parting leg $\frac{1}{16}$").

Stock preparation should include 4 or 5 pieces of stock between 18" and 24" long to be used as test pieces prior to the production run. The test pieces should be exactly the same width and thickness as the prepared stock. At least one or two should be the same species of wood, as well. Make sure the cutter knives are installed safely according to the manufacturer's instructions.

Most molding operations involve using cutters with **parting legs.** This refers to the extreme right and left edges of the knives, which surface the edges of the stock. The parting legs are designed to cut below the surface of the stock by approximately $\frac{1}{8}$". A guide board must be used with these operations and is suggested for all molding operations. Otherwise, the knives will strike the planer bed. You can build a guide board for each molding operation or build an adjustable model. An adjustable guide board is available from Woodmaster, which provides the flexibility to use one guide board for various molding patterns. The guide fences ride in slots and are bolted in place where needed.

Long pieces should be supported when they come out the outfeed extension table.

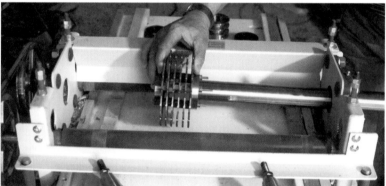

The Woodmaster 4-in-1 planer also can quickly and easily be fitted with accessories, including this gang-rip saw. Thin stakes or strips are quickly ripped to size.

Both a rip saw and molding cutterhead can also be installed, allowing for ripping a stock to precise width for molding with one pass, then moving it over and running it through the molding head.

With the hood off and the power disconnected, place a piece of the prepared stock between the guide board fences and raise the bed until the knife touches the stock. Check the alignment of the knives with the edge of the stock. The parting legs of the knives should be taking an equal amount off each edge of the stock. Make adjustments by either moving the knife or the guide board. Lower the bed, remove the stock, replace the hood, and plug in the planer.

Start the planer and raise the bed until you hear contact between the parting legs of the knives and the guide board. Raise the bed another $\frac{1}{8}$". Make sure the planer is running for this step but also absolutely sure that the parting legs do not cut all the way through the guide board. Lower the bed slightly, turn off the planer, disconnect the power, and remove the hood.

Rotate the head until the knife is at the low point of its arc. Slide a piece of test stock up to the knife. The knife should be touching the highest portion of the molding pattern by $\frac{1}{32}$". If the knife will not cut a full pattern, more relief must be cut into the guide board. But make absolutely sure the parting legs do not cut all the way through the guide board. If the highest portion of the knife is removing more than $\frac{1}{32}$", lower the planer bed to the proper depth.

Install the hood, plug in the planer, and turn it on. Feed one of the test pieces of stock through the planer. When the molding comes out, check to make sure the pattern is cutting to full depth, the parting edges are leaving a clean edge, and that the alignment of the bed and knife is producing a proper profile. Make any adjustments needed, and then run a test piece of the same species as the production stock and set the feed rate for the optimum finish. You're now ready for production runs of that particular molding.

Running molding requires a guide board to guide the stock. This can be a purchased, adjustable guide board, such as the one from Woodmaster, shown above.

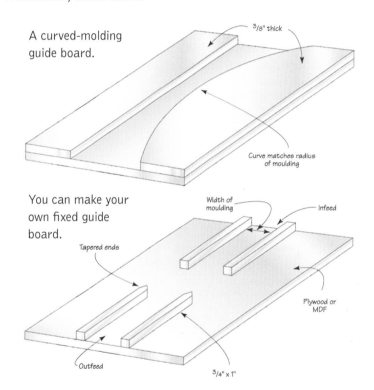

A curved-molding guide board.

You can make your own fixed guide board.

The Woodmaster is easily converted to a molder. The first step is to unplug the machine and remove the hood.

Although straight molding is the most common, radius or shaped molding may also be cut. Radius molding is great for creating unusual custom window trim, as well as for creating moulding for many classic furniture styles. The first step is to cut the molding to size. This can be band saw cuts from a solid piece of stock, joining to make the radius needed. An alternative method is to laminate the shape. Rip thin strips and bend and glue them into a curve using a clamping jig designed for that particular radius. The Woodmaster planer/molder also has a gang-rip saw attachment, allowing for precise ripping of these strips.

The radius molding is formed using a jig attached to the guide board. A straight guide board is attached at one side of the cutterhead and a guide board with a radius attached on the other side, leaving just enough room for the radius stock to feed through. The position of the radius guide and straight guide depend on which direction the radius stock is formed.

Safety

Follow all safety rules and manufacturer's instructions when using a planer/molder. Do not stand directly behind the machine. Wear eye protection, hearing protection, and a dust mask if the planer is not connected to a power dust collection. From many years of working in my father's cabinet and furniture shop, I have only 65 percent hearing in both ears, due to long use of a planer without protection 30 years ago. And my father had very bad lung problems, as well.

Slip off the drive belts and position a 2x4 beneath the cutterhead to support it.

Remove the bearing collars on both ends.

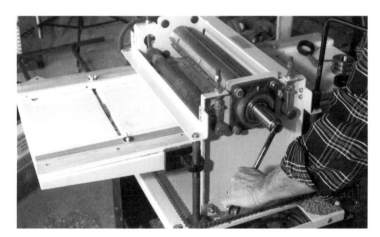

Then remove the Morse-taper head supports.

Wearing heavy gloves, carefully remove the cutterhead.

One of the most interesting aspects of molding with a surface planer is creating radius molding.

Install the selected cutters and tighten securely.

A radius jig is fastened to the guide board.

Install the molding head shaft and the cutterhead. Note the location of the cutterhead in relation to the guide strips.

The molding is first created by bandsawing to shape. Or you can glue up strips into a radius shape. The resulting molding is easily and precisely run through the planer/molder.

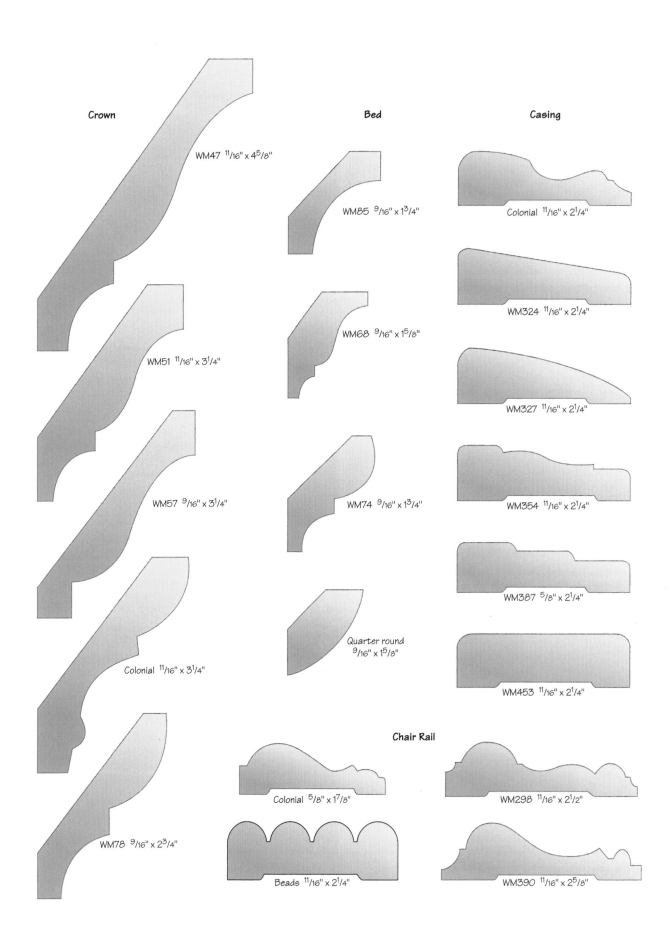

Crown

WM47 $^{11}/_{16}$" x $4^5/_8$"

WM51 $^{11}/_{16}$" x $3^1/_4$"

WM57 $^9/_{16}$" x $3^1/_4$"

Colonial $^{11}/_{16}$" x $3^1/_4$"

WM78 $^9/_{16}$" x $2^3/_4$"

Bed

WM85 $^9/_{16}$" x $1^3/_4$"

WM68 $^9/_{16}$" x $1^5/_8$"

WM74 $^9/_{16}$" x $1^3/_4$"

Quarter round
$^9/_{16}$" x $1^5/_8$"

Casing

Colonial $^{11}/_{16}$" x $2^1/_4$"

WM324 $^{11}/_{16}$" x $2^1/_4$"

WM327 $^{11}/_{16}$" x $2^1/_4$"

WM354 $^{11}/_{16}$" x $2^1/_4$"

WM387 $^5/_8$" x $2^1/_4$"

WM453 $^{11}/_{16}$" x $2^1/_4$"

Chair Rail

Colonial $^5/_8$" x $1^7/_8$"

Beads $^{11}/_{16}$" x $2^1/_4$"

WM298 $^{11}/_{16}$" x $2^1/_2$"

WM390 $^{11}/_{16}$" x $2^5/_8$"

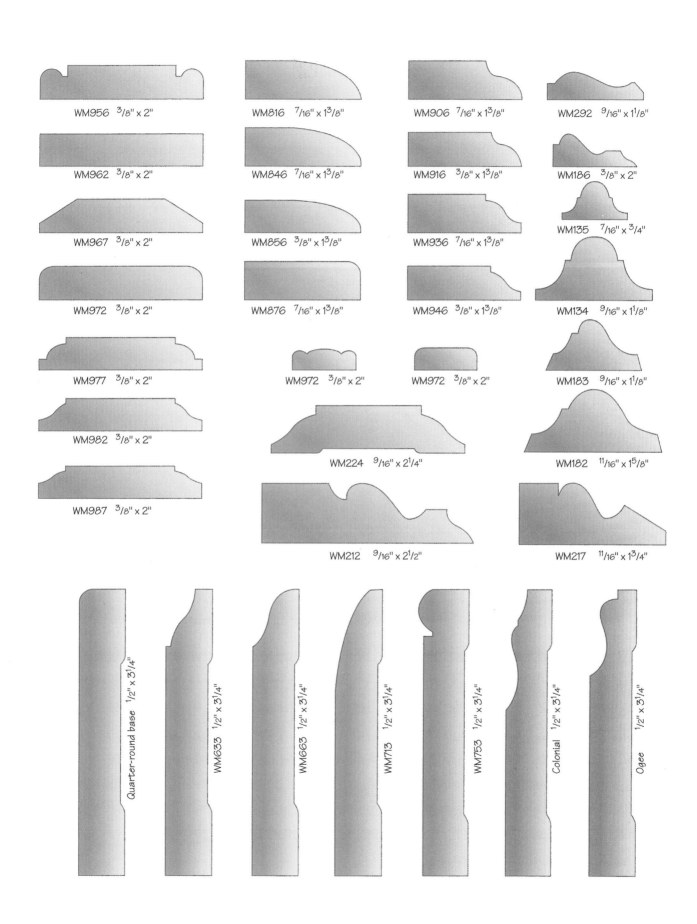

WM956 $^3/_8$" x 2"

WM962 $^3/_8$" x 2"

WM967 $^3/_8$" x 2"

WM972 $^3/_8$" x 2"

WM977 $^3/_8$" x 2"

WM982 $^3/_8$" x 2"

WM987 $^3/_8$" x 2"

WM816 $^7/_{16}$" x 1$^3/_8$"

WM846 $^7/_{16}$" x 1$^3/_8$"

WM856 $^3/_8$" x 1$^3/_8$"

WM876 $^7/_{16}$" x 1$^3/_8$"

WM972 $^3/_8$" x 2"

WM224 $^9/_{16}$" x 2$^1/_4$"

WM212 $^9/_{16}$" x 2$^1/_2$"

WM906 $^7/_{16}$" x 1$^3/_8$"

WM916 $^3/_8$" x 1$^3/_8$"

WM936 $^7/_{16}$" x 1$^3/_8$"

WM946 $^3/_8$" x 1$^3/_8$"

WM972 $^3/_8$" x 2"

WM292 $^9/_{16}$" x 1$^1/_8$"

WM186 $^3/_8$" x 2"

WM135 $^7/_{16}$" x $^3/_4$"

WM134 $^9/_{16}$" x 1$^1/_8$"

WM183 $^9/_{16}$" x 1$^1/_8$"

WM182 $^{11}/_{16}$" x 1$^5/_8$"

WM217 $^{11}/_{16}$" x 1$^3/_4$"

Quarter-round base $^1/_2$" x 3$^1/_4$"

WM633 $^1/_2$" x 3$^1/_4$"

WM663 $^1/_2$" x 3$^1/_4$"

WM713 $^1/_2$" x 3$^1/_4$"

WM753 $^1/_2$" x 3$^1/_4$"

Colonial $^1/_2$" x 3$^1/_4$"

Ogee $^1/_2$" x 3$^1/_4$"

LATHES

A wood lathe is one of the oldest "powered" woodworking tools. A bow-powered lathe was thought to have originated in ancient Egypt. I have a bed made by an ancestor well before the advent of powered tools, and it features beautifully turned posts, evidence of the skills of early craftsmen. I also luckily inherited a full set of antique turning tools many years ago. A lathe can be used to create many different objects, ranging from furniture legs to candlesticks and other decorative turnings. A lathe can also be used to turn large objects, such as posts, tiny fancy writing pens, or it can be used to turn wooden bowls and other items. Lathe turning takes a bit of skill and practice, but it's easily learned and one of the most enjoyable of woodworking techniques.

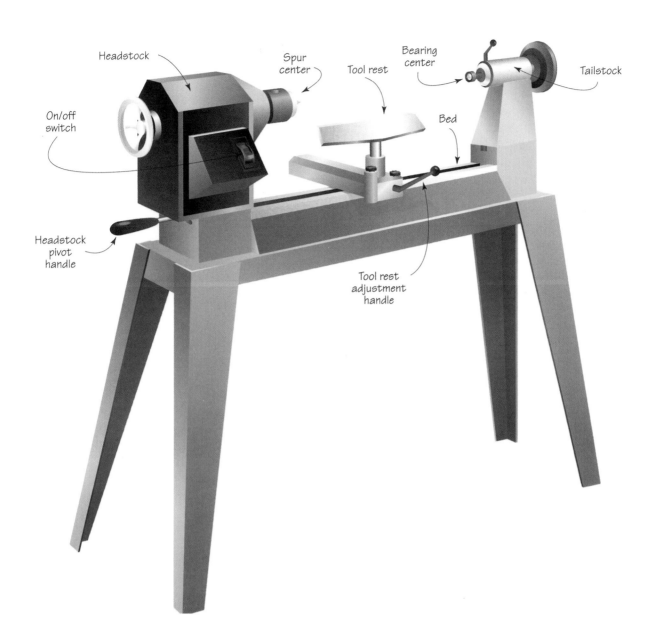

On/off switch

Headstock

Spur center

Tool rest

Bearing center

Tailstock

Bed

Headstock pivot handle

Tool rest adjustment handle

What to Look For

All lathes are of the same basic design, although size, quality, and features vary. A lathe consists of a means of turning a piece of wood stock with a method of holding a tool against the spinning stock or blank to remove wood, creating a symmetrical shape. The size of the lathe is based on two factors, the length of stock that can be turned and the amount of swing, or the diameter of the stock that can be turned over the lathe bed. You will need a lathe with 36" between the centers to turn most table legs. Sizes can range from mini 10" models to models with up to 40" between centers. A 15" lathe will turn a 15" diameter item, with 7½" of

clearance between the bed and the spur center. Lathes are commonly available with a swing ranging from 10 to 17". The size of the swing is most important in bowl and other large-diameter turnings. Some older lathes had outboard spindles allowing for turning on the outer end of the head. Many quality lathes now feature a swiveling headstock. This allows you to turn the headstock outward 90° to turn large-diameter bowls. More economical lathes feature tubes to hold the headstock and tailstock. Lathes can generate a lot of vibration, especially during the roughing out steps. Lathes with a cast iron bed provide more support than tube models. Lathes are available as benchtop models, which can be bolted to a bench or work surface, or floor models with legs and stands—an integral part of the tool or an option. The latter models offer more rigidity. Different speeds are needed for different operations. The more economical models feature step pulleys and belts. To change speeds, you move the belts on the pulleys. Higher quality models are variable speed, allowing you to dial in the speed you desire.

The lathe in my shop is a Craftsman Professional, 15", variable speed model. This heavy-duty lathe has a single-piece cast iron base and cast iron headstock and tailstock housing a 2 horsepower maximum developed induction-run motor. The hand wheel on the headstock yields variable speeds from 400 to 2,000 rpm. The headstock swivels from 0° to 90° for outboard turnings up to 20" in diameter. One of the features I especially like is the indexing head. Twenty-four indexing stops at 15° intervals lock the head for groove cutting with a router. The unit comes with 6" and 12" tool rest, 4" faceplate, spur, and bearing centers.

You will also need lathe chisels. The best bet when you're starting out is to purchase a set of lathe chisels. Woodworking chisels are available in six common configurations—gouge, skew, parting tool, spear point, flat nose, and round nose. The chisels used for cutting include the gouge, skew, and parting tool. The chisels used for scraping include the flat nose, round nose, and spear point. Sharp, quality chisels are a must for productive, easy, and safe wood turning.

These are typically available individually or in sets with five to eight chisels, including the most commonly used chisels. As you get into more turning projects, you'll want to purchase additional chisels, including some specialty chisels for bowl turning and other chores.

Basic Turning Steps

Basic turning consists of two operations, spindle turning and faceplate turning.

Spindle turning is done between the centers for furniture legs, candlesticks, and other items.

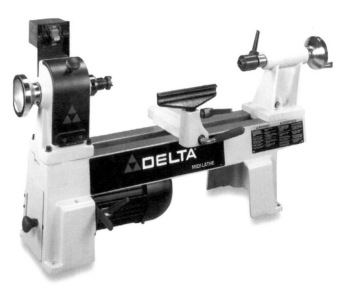

Lathes are available as tiny pen-turning machines and as small benchtop models.

The Craftsman 15" Variable Speed model features a heavy-duty cast iron bed, headstock, and tailstock. The lathe is mounted on the Craftsman lathe stand.

Faceplate turning is done with the stock mounted on a faceplate, which is inserted into the main spindle. Two specific types of techniques are used for both of these operations, cutting and scraping.

Basic Spindle Turning

Make sure you read and understand the operator's manual that comes with your lathe and understand and follow all safety rules. If you're inexperienced, the basics of lathe work should be learned turning a small spindle. Choose a piece of stock 2x2x12 inches. Using a straight edge and pencil, mark diagonal lines from corner to corner on both ends of the stock. Make a saw cut about ⅛" deep on each diagonal line of one end. This is to allow the spur center to hold the stock. Position the point of the bearing center directly over the intersection of the two lines on the opposite end and tap it with a wooden or plastic mallet. A piece of wood can also be held over the end of the center to protect it as you tap it in place. Remove the bearing center and drive the spur center in place on the opposite end, making sure the spurs align with the saw cuts. Then remove the spur center. Place the centers in place, the spur into the headstock and the bearing center into the tailstock. Use a piece of wood to lightly seat them in place. Do not drive them tightly in place. Some lathes have fixed centers instead of bearing centers. In this case, place a bit of wax or oil in the center hole of the stock to lubricate

it. Position the stock between the centers, lock the tailstock in place, and then move the bearing center into the wood by turning the tailstock hand wheel. Make sure both centers are properly seated in the holes previously made. Turn the stock by hand to make sure it is centered properly. Adjust the tool rest so its outer edge is about ⅛" distance from the outer corners of the stock. The rest should also be about ⅛" above the center line of the stock. Turn the stock by hand to make sure it doesn't contact the tool rest. It's important to turn at the proper speed. Roughing requires a slow speed. For example, roughing a 2" square turning of about 18" in length should be done at 1,100 rpm. Finishing can be done at higher speeds of 2,000 rpm for that size. The Craftsman lathe shown has the speeds stamped on the front at the speed dial and a size and speed chart on the top.

The different tools can be held in one of two methods, depending on whether cutting or scraping techniques are used. One hand, depending on whether left- or right-handed, is used to hold the tool down on the tool rest, guiding the end of the tool along the shelf of the rest with the heel of the hand. The opposite end of the chisel is held with the hand palm down. Make sure you hold the chisel firmly in place with both hands. Chisels can be wrenched out of your hands, damaging the workpiece or creating a danger to the operator. Proper position of the tool rest and angle of the chisel are important. The bevel of the end of the chisel should

Different turning speeds are needed for different operations. A variable speed lathe allows instant changing of speeds.

An indexing head on the Craftsman lathe allows for indexing turnings for such chores as fluting columns.

Quality turning tools are also a must. Shown are both the latest modern tools, as well as some tools inherited by the author. Lathe tools haven't really changed much over the years.

always be positioned against the workpiece. If the rest is too low and the angle of the chisel is held more horizontally, it causes the point of the chisel to dig in, creating chattering. If the rest is too low and the chisel is held too high, there is the danger of the chisel being kicked back out of your hands. A face shield is the best choice for eye protection.

Generally, the gouge is used for roughing the stock to round. Position the gouge with the cup upward and facing slightly toward the other end of the rest. Carefully and slowly feed the end of the gouge into the stock until it just begins to touch the stock, and remove a bit of material. Then move the gouge steadily along the rest. At the end of the stroke, turn the gouge slightly back toward the opposite end, but with the cup still up, and draw it back in the opposite direction. Repeat these steps until the stock is round. Move the tool rest

The first step in spindle turning is to mark diagonally across the corners on each end. A saw cut is made on the marks on one end for the spur center.

The spur center and live bearing centers are both tapped in place to create a seat for the centers.

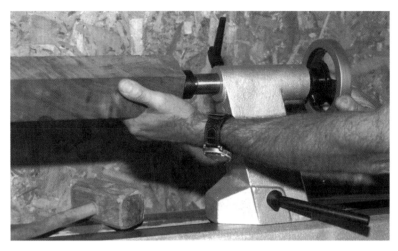

The centers are inserted in the headstock and tailstock, and the spindle blank is then positioned between them. The wheel on the tailstock is turned to tighten the blank between the two centers.

as needed to rough different portions of the stock and to maintain the ¹⁄₈" distance between the tool rest edge and the stock edge.

Once the stock is in the round, it is sized at the various diameters. The tool is held somewhat differently for these scraping techniques, as more control is required. In this case, the tool is held with the palm of the tool-rest hand facing up. The wrist is still held down and the side of the index finger slides along the tool rest as a guide. This allows you to use the fingers of the tool-rest hand to assist in positioning the tool.

Mark the locations of the beads, coves, and turns. Use a parting tool held in cutting position to cut grooves in the stock at the locations desired. Use a pair of outside calipers at each location to make sure the measurements are correct. The speed can be increased for smoother cuts once the stock has been roughed out.

Once you have the stock sized at each diameter, use scraping tools to shape the stock between the cut diameters. A skew chisel can be used to round off the sides of the beads, while a round nose is used to cut coves. To shape concave and convex shapes use the skew and round- nose as needed.

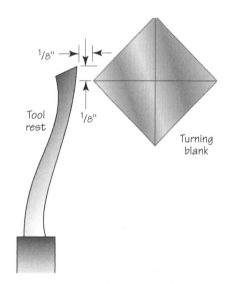

It's important to have the tool rest properly positioned for safe and easy operation.

Small diameter and long pieces should be backed with a steady rest to prevent them from whipping. You can make your own or purchase manufactured rests. Woodcraft Supply has an excellent spindle steady rest.

Once the piece has been shaped, it can be sanded quicker and easier while on the lathe. Be careful as the sandpaper can become quite hot, and sanding on a lathe creates a lot of dust, so make sure you wear a dust mask.

Duplicate Turnings

If you have to turn several pieces in the same shape, make a template of stiff cardboard, thin plywood, or a thin piece of wood. You can then hold it against the turning (with the

LATHES

lathe off) and check for proper shape. A quicker and more precise way is to use a lathe duplicator. The Craftsman Wood Lathe Copy Crafter duplicates spindle or shallow bowl turnings and can duplicate from either a prototype or a template. It can also be used to duplicate taper work up to 38" in length.

Split Turning

One unusual turning technique is split turnings. Stock is glued up to create a square blank with paper glued between the pieces. Once the stock is turned, the pieces are split apart along the paper line using a sharp chisel. Half or quarter turnings are created in this manner. One common use is in period furniture where one quarter

turned and fluted columns are used on pieces, such as Philadelphia highboys. Again, an indexing head on the lathe can make it easy to lay out the flutes.

Face Plate

Face-plate turning is done by first mounting the stock on a face plate, which has a taper to fit into the headstock or, more commonly, threads that screw onto the headstock. Wood plaques, plates, and small bowls or even rounded, ball-style furniture feet can be turned using this technique. While the stock is still in the square, mark diagonally from corner to corner to locate the center of the back of the stock. Then use a compass to mark the outside circumference of the

The first step is to rough the blank into a round, cutting off the corners. Use a gouge tool for this step and position the hands as shown.

Once the blank is in the round, the location of the various beads, coves, tapers, and other design factors are marked on the blank with a sturdy pencil.

piece to be turned. Using a band saw, rough cut the stock to this shape and size (large, square stock is dangerous and hard to rough to the round). Fasten the stock to the face plate with screws from the back of the face plate. Allow extra depth at the back to cut off the screw-hole area. Another method is to glue the stock to waste stock with paper between, turn to shape, then split off the waste stock. Begin the turning by roughing the band sawn outside shape to perfect round. Then you can use a scraping tool to make the various cuts, such as cutting the inside, rounding the lip, creating beads or coves around the outside, or other shapes. It's important to continue moving the tool rest to provide proper support for each tool position. A rounded bowl turning rest is best for turning deep bowls and other shapes, especially for the inside area. These have a rounded tool rest allowing for getting closer to the stock with the tool. The Woodcraft Supply Lathe Tool Rest System has a small and large bowl rest with different size posts to fit different lathe tool rests. Craftsman also has a bowl turning rest for their lathes.

Outboard Turning

Larger items than can be turned over the lathe bed can be turned on a lathe with an outboard feature. The headstock is turned 90° to the bed. The stock is mounted on a face plate, and the techniques are the same as for over-the-bed face-plate turning. Bowl turning rests are required for this technique. They swing out from the tool rest mounted on the lathe bed and over to the front of the stock. Due to the work size often used in this technique, use caution, proceed slowly, and keep speed to a minimum. Experiment with soft woods of a smaller size before attempting larger, hardwood projects. If you are interested in turning bowls, vases, boxes, and other similar projects, check out the special turning tools available from Woodcraft Supply and Packard Woodworks.

The various shaped turning tools are then used to cut the spinning blank into the desired shape. Change the tool rest frequently to maintain the proper position.

Once the shape desired has been created, it is sanded and polished while spinning on the lathe.

Specialty Turning Tricks

One fun tactic is to glue up spindles or flat-work for plates or bowls of contrasting wood colors. When turned, the different segments produce unusual patterns. Small items, such as chess pieces or furniture knobs, can be turned on a screw plate. A number of lathe chucks are also available that allow you to grip smaller items for turning. The stock first has a tenon sized to fit inside the chuck. You can also make up your own wooden chuck for these types of turnings. Again, create a tenon on the workpiece and drive it into the wood chuck, which is screwed to a face plate. Turn the piece, and then drive the tenon out of the chuck.

A lathe can also be fitted with flap sanders, drill chucks, polishing wheels, and other accessories to expand the use of the tool and make it more versatile.

I do, however, have a warning—wood turning is addictive. Once you get the feel for it, you'll be looking for excuses to make more projects.

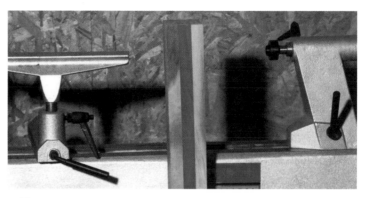

Different colored woods can be glued up to create unusual segmented turnings.

Bowls, boxes, and other shapes are turned with the blank fastened to a faceplate that is fastened in the lathe.

Some lathes can be turned 90° for outboard turnings. A bowl-turning rest makes it easier to follow the rounded shapes of bowls with the tools.

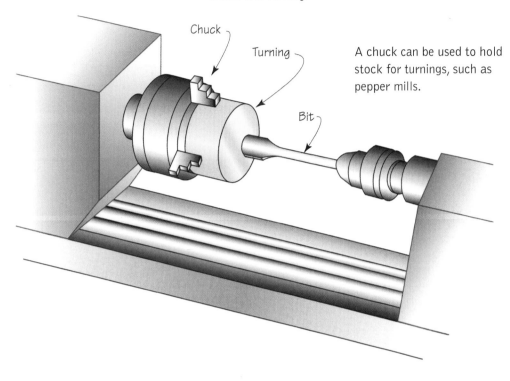

Using a chuck to bore a hole in a turning

Chuck

Turning

Bit

A chuck can be used to hold stock for turnings, such as pepper mills.

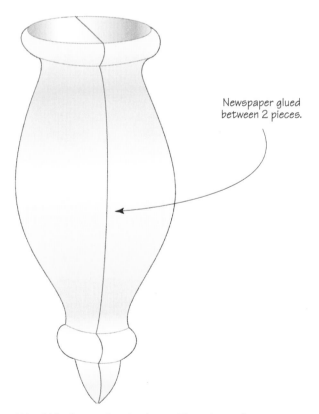

Split turnings

Newspaper glued between 2 pieces.

Wood blanks can be glued up with a piece of paper between them, turned, and then split apart to create decorative split turnings for furniture and cabinet decoration.

SAFETY RULES

1. Do not wear loose clothing.
2. Wear protective hair covering to contain long hair.
3. Wear safety glasses complying with U.S. ANSI Z81.7.
4. Wear a face mask or dust mask.
5. Keep hands away from chuck, centers, and other moving parts.
6. Disconnect tool when changing attachments.
7. Do not force cutting tools.
8. Never leave lathe running unattended.
9. Make sure workpiece is firmly mounted, turn lathe off if workpiece splits or becomes loose.

LATHES

BENCH SANDERS

Although portable electric sanders will handle most chores, eventually the serious woodworker will want to acquire a bench sander. Not only can these sanders smooth surfaces, some can also be used for intricate shaping, as well. Bench sanders consist of three types: disc/belt, spindle, and drum sanders. Depending on the chores commonly done in your shop, you may need one or all three styles.

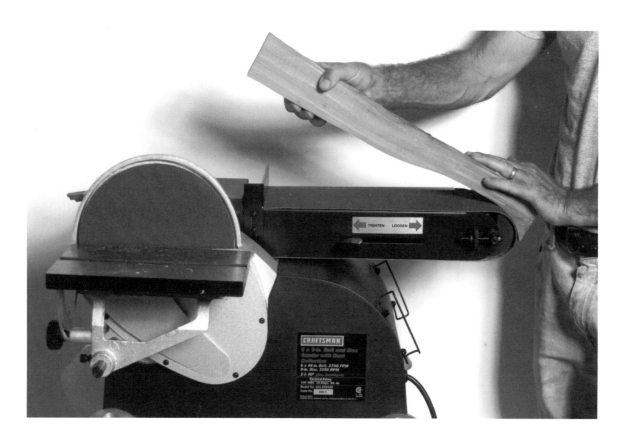

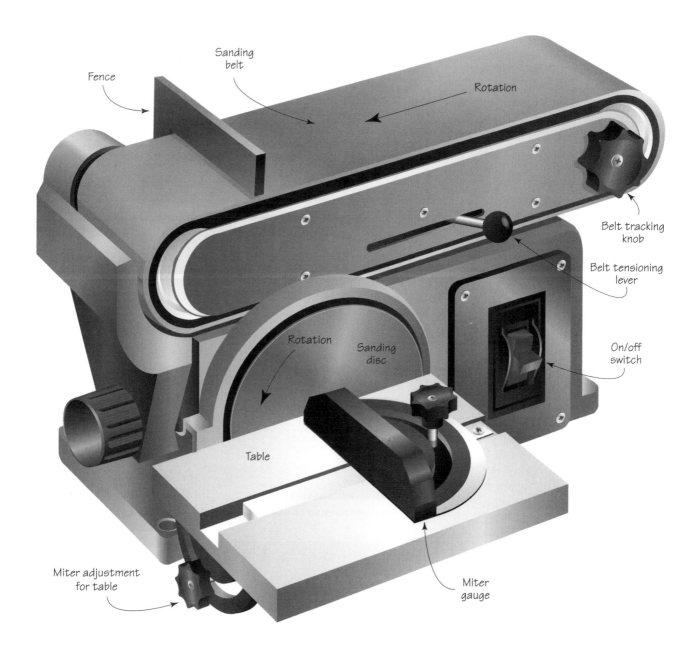

Fence

Sanding belt

Rotation

Belt tracking knob

Belt tensioning lever

On/off switch

Rotation

Sanding disc

Table

Miter gauge

Miter adjustment for table

Disc/Belt Sanders

Disc and belt sanders are often combined into one tool. These are ideal tools for furniture and cabinetry construction. They can be used to shape and smooth convex or concave surfaces, such as cabriole legs, scroll work and other nonstraight items. They can also be used to smooth straight edges and surfaces.

What to Look For

Disc/belt sanders are available both as smaller benchtop models, as well as big floor models. These tools range in size, starting with smaller units with 2"-wide belts and 6"

discs up to machines with 9" discs and 6x48-inch belts. Motors will run from 6 up to 12 amps. Most have cast iron bases to lessen vibration. Some of the larger models also have built-in dust collection systems because these units can create a lot of dust. Disc/belt sanders also feature a universal cast iron table that tilts 45° and can be repositioned to support belt or disc sanding operations. The belt runs around a pair of rollers and over a metal platen. A release lever loosens one roller, allowing you to remove or install belts.

A tracking knob is used to tilt the roller end in or out to make the belt track in the center of the platen. The discs have a tilting table with a miter gauge slot.

Narrow-belt sanders, featuring 1"- wide belts are also available. These are the choice for sanding band or scroll sawn projects. They can also do sharpening chores on knives, planer blades, and plane blades. Some of these belt sanders also come in combination with a disc sander. Belts and discs are available in a variety of grits, ranging from 50 to 120.

How to Use

Depending on the grits used, both the disc and the belt can remove a lot of material in a hurry, a good reason for having them. They can, however, quickly damage a workpiece if you're not careful. Both can also grab and fling a small workpiece violently, so maintain a firm grip when using either the disc or the belt. Keep your fingers away from the belt or discs because they quickly sand off skin and flesh. To finish flat surfaces on the belt, use the belt in the horizontal position. Hold the workpiece firmly down in place and use the workstop to position and secure the work. Keep the end butted against the workstop and move the workpiece evenly across the belt.

Use extra caution when sanding very thin pieces. Use the flat portion of the abrasive belt to sand outside curves. Use the idler drum portion to sand inside curves. Most belts can be adjusted for vertical sanding and some for a variety of angles. It's easiest to finish the end grain of workpieces with the belt in this position. Position the table on the belt side of the sander. Move the work evenly across the belt. For accuracy, use the miter gauge. The table can be tilted for bevel work. The disc is used for finishing small flat surfaces, as well as convex edges. Always move the workpiece across the down-turning side of the disc. Hold with both hands and keep fingers away from the disc. Use the miter gauge for more precise sanding.

Bench sanders can be used to smooth and flatten surfaces. A stop is used to position the workpiece.

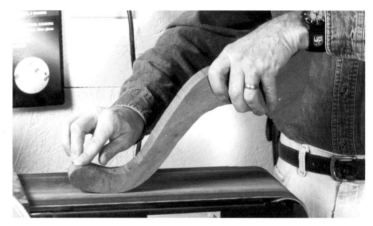

A bench sander can also be used to sand and smooth convex surfaces.

And concave surfaces.

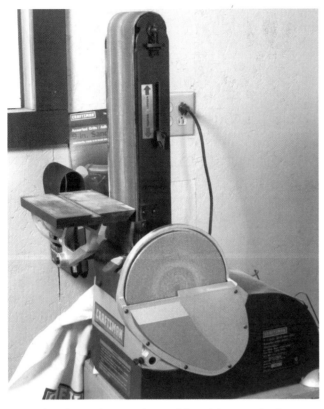

Many bench sanders can be positioned in a vertical position and used with a table.

If sanding small pieces, hold them with pliers or a clamp.

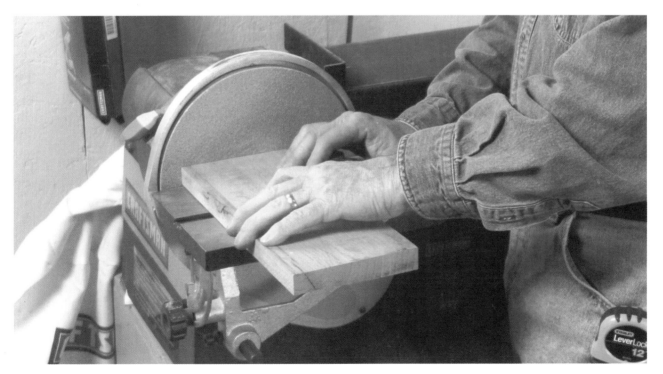

The disk sander is good for sanding end grain and edging.

A miter gauge can be used with the disk sander.

The table can be tilted and the disk sander used to create bevels.

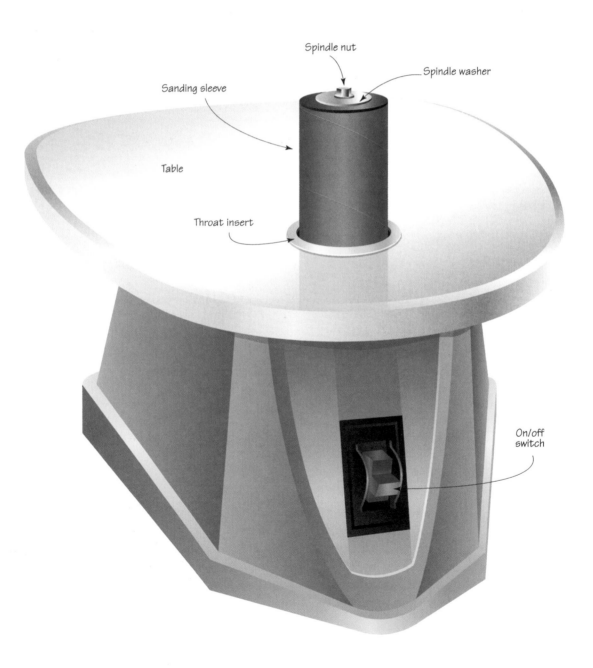

Spindle nut

Spindle washer

Sanding sleeve

Table

Throat insert

On/off switch

Oscillating Spindle Sanders

Oscillating spindle sanders are another style of benchtop or stationary sander, and they have become increasingly popular. They are compact and make fast work of sanding inside curved edges.

What to Look For

Oscillating spindle sanders have a spindle set in the center of a small table. The spindle spins and oscillates up and down at the same time. Most machines come with several sizes of hard rubber spindles and sanding sleeves. The Ridgid model also comes with a detachable edge-belt sander and has a tilting table. Craftsman has a disc/belt sander with an oscillating spindle sander included. Most also come with a dust port for attachment to a shop vac or dust system.

How to Use

Sanding sleeves are available in a variety of grits. Choose the grit needed and the spindle that comes the closest to fitting the contour of the workpiece. Turn on the machine and move the workpiece into the spindle. Keep the workpiece moving evenly to prevent over-sanding one area and creating a depression. I like to sand from one side, then flop the workpiece and sand from the other to obtain the best over-all finish. To use the edge-sanding feature of the Ridgid, install the edge sander and workstop. Keep the end of the stock butted against the workstop and move the workpiece evenly across the sanding belt, holding it firmly. To sand end grain, use a miter gauge.

Drum Sanders

A drum sander is the best choice if you have a lot of surfacing to do, such as sanding glued up stock for bookcases, shelves, tabletops, furniture projects, baseboard, and interior trim.

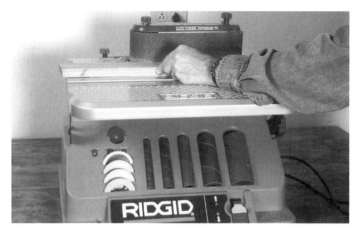

Oscillating spindle sanders, such as the Ridgid model shown here, are great for sanding and smoothing inside curves.

A variety of sleeve sizes can be selected to match the curve.

The Ridgid oscillating sander also has an edge-sanding feature.

BENCH SANDERS

What to Look For

Drum sanders are not as common as the other sander types and are primarily large, stationary models weighing several hundred pounds. Some bench models are available as both closed and open-end models. The open-end models can sand wider stock because you can sand one side of the workpiece, turn it, and sand the other side. These sanders create a lot of dust, and most have stand-alone dust collection systems. Grizzly has an excellent small 12" closed model. As mentioned earlier, the Woodmaster planer/molder also has a sanding drum that can be installed in minutes. The Craftsman 18" open-end drum sander is a good choice for the home shop and the one I have in my shop. It sands workpieces up to 36" wide and 5" thick and has a maximum removal rate of $\frac{1}{64}$" per pass. It also incorporates an integrated dust collection system to safely exhaust dust into a 30-micron **half bag**. The half bag dust collection system feeds sawdust directly into a heavy-duty plastic waste bag or a 30-gallon garbage bag for quick cleanups. Many units also feature top rollers so you can move stock across their tops to make another pass.

How to Use

Drum sanders are a good choice for surface sanding glued up stock rather than using a planer. You'll quickly discover, however, that these machines use a lot of electrical power and they should be installed on their own circuit. The feed belt has a variable speed. Stock can be removed more quickly by using a fast speed, but the machine works harder, and the wood is left with a rougher finish. Slowing the speed lightens the load on the sander and creates a finer finish but takes more sanding time. Hardwoods and wide boards will require a slower feed speed. Lower the table until the stock will run through without sanding. Then increase the height of the table V4 turn for initial material removal. Run the stock through one side, turn over, and run the opposite side. For finishing cuts, raise the table only $\frac{1}{16}$" to create a smooth finish and slow the feed speed.

If you have a lot of stock to be smoothed for bookcases, shelves, and furniture projects, a drum surfacing sander is the answer.

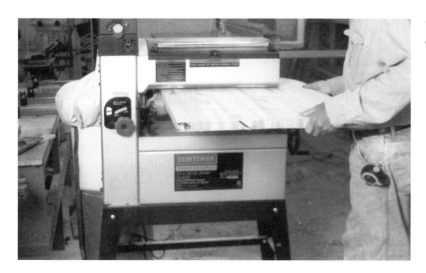

The Craftsman 18" drum sander can sand workpieces up to 36" wide and 5" thick.

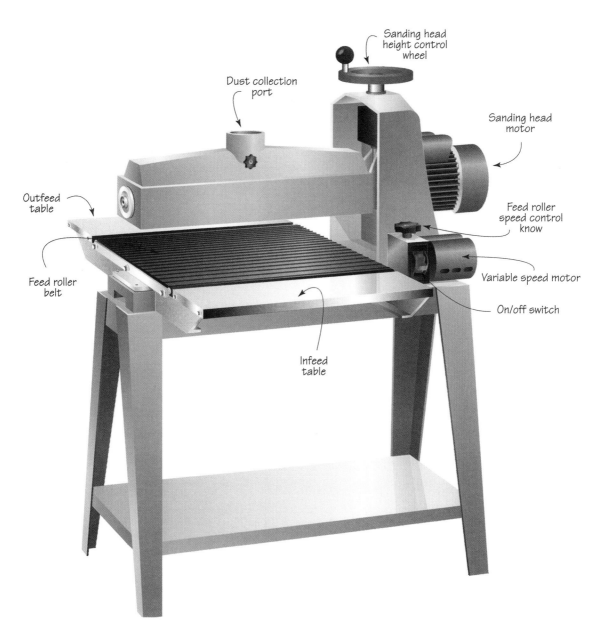

Sanding head height control wheel

Dust collection port

Sanding head motor

Outfeed table

Feed roller speed control know

Feed roller belt

Variable speed motor

On/off switch

Infeed table

AIR TOOLS

An air compressor and mating air tools can do an amazing amount of work around your home and shop. Regardless of whether your chores include woodworking, metalworking, mechanical jobs, or even simple home chores, a compressor is the tool. Many chores can be done at a lower cost than with comparable electric tools. The initial cost of the air tool is lower and the average life span longer. Campbell Hausfeld offers more than seventy air tools.

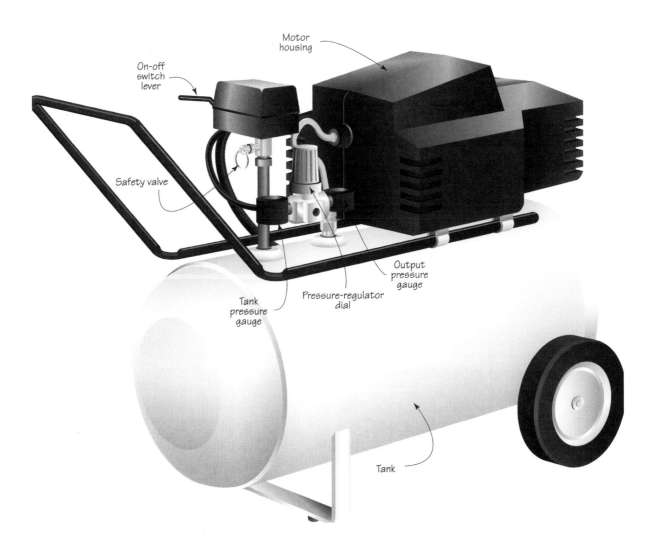

On-off switch lever

Motor housing

Safety valve

Tank pressure gauge

Pressure-regulator dial

Output pressure gauge

Tank

Air Compressors

To use all these air tools, you will first need an air compressor. These are available from a wide range of manufacturers in different sizes and styles. Homeowners and do-it-yourselfers may have different requirements than remodelers and contractors.

What to Look For

Air compressors are available in different sizes with different air delivery ratings, horsepower, and in single- and two-stage models. Single-stage models are the most common choice for the home shop needs. It's important to match the air compressor to the tool being used. Most air compressors feature an air-delivery rating. This signifies a specific model's output power. To ensure proper performance from your air tools, use only those tools with air requirement ratings less than the delivery rate of your compressor. These ratings vary according to manufacturer. Campbell Hausfeld models are available in Standard Duty, Serious Duty, and Extreme Duty. The Standard Duty line is designed for occasional use in the home, garage, or workshop. Serious Duty is designed for more frequent use on the farm, automotive garage, or work site. Extreme Duty is for commercial work. Other manufacturers have different rating systems.

Air compressors are also available in different sizes and types. Again, first choose the usage. Small portable compressors, including **pancake** styles, can run small tools around the house. Those with 2 horsepower can handle small jobs. Tank styles ranging from 5 up to over 6 horsepower can be used for most homeowner, contractor, or workshop chore. It's important to note the **peak** horsepower. The 6 horsepower models are about the limit in power for 120-volt homeowner and workshop operation and are available with horizontal or vertical tanks. Compressors with oil-free pumps require less maintenance.

Air Tools

Air compressors can be used for simple chores, such as inflating tires to basketballs and beach toys to air mattresses. With a blowgun, dust and debris can be blown off sanded furniture and cabinetry. A blowgun can also be used to clean out motors and other dirty problems.

Air Fasteners

Air nailers have become popular with woodworkers, contractors, and homeowners. These marvels can make many chores much easier, quicker, and safer. One of my friends, a long-time house framer (retired for about 20 years) still has tendonitis in his elbows and arthritis in his shoulders to the point he can't reach above his shoulders, all from years of swinging a hammer. And most roofers don't spend time driving roofing nails by hand. Forty-

some years ago, my dad would have loved today's finish nailers in his custom cabinet shop. And I wouldn't have been chastised for the occasional **hammer track** I made working for him. Air fasteners can make carpenters out of beginners. They eliminate the problems associated with driving finish nails in woodworking projects, installing house trim, or framing. My daughter Jodi learned this quickly helping me put up a building. Although she had no real carpentry experience, all I had to do was lay out a wall and turn her loose with a framing nailer. Within a matter of minutes she had the wall assembled. Although Jodi had helped build various things around the farm while growing up, she didn't have the ability or strength to swing a framing hammer for the time required to build one wall, let alone four walls. The air nailer evened out the playing field.

What to Look For

Air fasteners are available as pneumatic (driven by a compressor), cordless, impulse, or driven by a battery pack. Pneumatic fasteners are the most common, but

Compressors are available in a variety of sizes and tank types. A 2 to 6 horsepower model will handle woodworking, carpentry, and do-it-yourself chores.

It's important to match the compressor to the air tool and job. The Campbell Hausfeld model shown has a tool requirement chart.

The heavy-duty contractor-style compressor shown will handle multiple air tools.

A small compressor, along with a matching brad nailer, is a good combo that is perfect for installing trim.

cordless models are becoming popular. Air fasteners are available in a wide range of sizes, types, and for different applications. Air nailers and staplers run from models driving 23-gauge micro pins to larger models driving 3½" framing or decking nails. It's important to choose the air fasteners you need for your chores. Air fasteners are available in several price ranges, with the larger models being the most expensive. A professional house builder, remodeler, or roofing contractor will have different needs than the occasional homeowner user.

Regardless of the model or type, several features should be considered. First is weight. Air fasteners, particularly the larger types, can be heavy, and the trend is in weight reduction of the tools. This means more plastic or composite materials, which don't take away from the quality. Some high-end tools utilize aluminum or exotic metals, such as magnesium, to create weight reduction. Many top-brand names also feature isolation dampeners on the larger units to prevent fatigue from day-long use.

Air fasteners are also available as oil-lubricated or oil-free. The majority of the tools on the market are oil-lubricated, which means you must place a drop or two of lightweight oil in the tool each day before use in order to lubricate the cylinder. Excess oil can sometimes be blown through the exhaust, a problem when creating fine furniture or installing inside house trim. Oil-free tools do not present the problem but are more expensive.

How to Use

When the tool is operated, excess air is blown out the exhaust port on the top of the tool. A directional exhaust can be handy in keeping the exhaust from blowing where you don't want it, sometimes right in your face. It's important the fastener be driven to the correct depth. For framing this means flush; with finishing, slightly below the surface; with siding, protruding slightly. Although you can make the depth adjustment with the compressor, having a built-in depth adjustment allows for control right at the job site, rather than having to go to the compressor. A visible load indicator is another important feature. This allows you to see at a glance how many fasteners are in the tool.

Trigger control is also important. Air fasteners may have either sequential or nonsequential trigger control or a switch

Air naiters are available in a variety of sizes and types.

Air nailers can make instant carpenters out of beginners and are a work and body saver for construction chores.

Air nailers are available as pneumatic, or compressor driven.

that allows switching between the two. For the beginner, as well as when doing fine woodworking projects, a sequential trigger is the best choice. With this type of trigger control, the tool will only fire once when the trigger is pulled. As you can see, this is a safety factor as it prevents accidental firing if you happen to bump into anything. This also prevents the possibility of double firing, which can happen with a nonsequential trigger control. A double-fired fastener can easily mar a nice cabinet, bookcase face, or other project. On the other hand, a nonsequential trigger control is often the best choice for framing, utility, and roofing tools. This allows you to hold the trigger down and the tool fires when you bump the nose against the object to be fastened. This makes for much quicker work, as well as less finger fatigue over a long day's work.

Several safety features are available. The most common is a nose safety. With this type of safety the tool will only fire when the nose is compressed down on the surface. Another type of safety is a double trigger. It's less common, but more useful for getting into tight places.

Probably the single most important feature is the jam-clearing mechanism. Air fasteners will jam,

you can bet on it. The better tools have easy-to-clear mechanisms.

Air Drive Wrenches

Mechanics have long used air-powered fasteners, and they are still the ultimate in torque. Most job sites have compressors for quick-and-easy framing, roofing, and other carpentry chores using air nailers. A compressor and air ratchet or wrench can also be invaluable for many of the harder job site fastening chores, such as driving lag screws. These tools do not require a battery, are durable, and long lasting. Ratchets are available in ¼", ⅜" and ½" drive and produce between 50 and 70 pounds of torque. Impact wrenches are also available in ¼", ⅜" and ½" drives and can deliver torque from 20 up to 600 ft./lbs. They are larger and heavier and more commonly used for chores, such as removing lug nuts, loosening stubborn bolts, and driving heavy-duty steel fasteners. Auto-repair mechanics utilize air-powered sanders, drills, and angle grinders for working metal. These are not typically home or woodworking shop tools, but at times they can be helpful.

Air nailer magazines vary. This is a straight model shown on this finish nailer.

This is a coil nailer shown installing siding.

The nailer shown here is impulse-driven.

Finishing Tools

Three basic types of air-finishing tools or spray guns are available. High-pressure spray guns are traditional and are still often used in body shops and some production woodworking shops. However, high volume, low-pressure (HVLP) guns are now the most common and popular with woodworking shops because they can deliver a high volume of materials with low pressure, which means less overspray and reduced airborne pollutants. These are gravity fed with visible material containers.

How to Use

Air compressors and their tools are relatively safe but some considerations and rules must be followed. Air compressors should not be used with extension cords, as this can cause the voltage to drop and overheat the compressor. Rather than using an extension cord, use extensions of air hoses to reach the job. Make sure you read your compressor owner's manual and understand safe operation.

Before each use, place the start lever to off. Pull out the regulator knob, turn counterclockwise until it stops. Push the knob in until it locks in place. Attach the hose and tools. Always check the manufacturer's maximum pressure rating for air tools and accessories. The regulator outlet pressure must never exceed the maximum pressure rating.

Properly storing an air tank after operation is important. Turn the regulator counterclockwise and set the outlet pressure to zero. Remove the air tool. Pull the ring on the safety valve, allowing air to bleed from the tank until the tank pressure is approximately 20 psi. Release the safety valve ring. Drain the water from the tank by opening the drain valve on the bottom of the tank. Then close the drain valve. Note: Water condenses in the tank. If not drained daily, water will corrode and weaken the tank, which can increases the risk of the air tank rupturing.

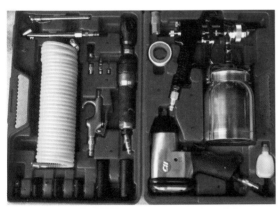

A wide variety of other air tools are also available.

Impact ratchet tools are great for job site chores, such as driving lag bolts.

Impact wrenches offer more torque and are used for tougher driving chores.

Air tools also include spray guns.

Sources

Avenger Products
www.avengerproducts.com
800-424-7633

Bench Dog Tools
www.benchdog.com
800-786-8902

Black & Decker
www.blackanddecker.com
800-544-6986

Bosch Tools
www.BoschTools.com
877-BOSCH99

Brownell's
www.brownells.com
800-741-0015

C.H. Hanson Pivot Square
www.chhanson.com
800-827-3398

CMT Orange Tools
www.cmtusa.com
888-CMT-BITS

Campbell Hausfeld
www.chpo wer.com
888-CHPOWER

Delta Machinery
www.deltaportercable.com
800-223-7278

DeWalt
www.dewalt.com

Dremel
www.dremel.com
800-437-3635

E.C.E. Primus Planes
Adria Toolworks
www.adriatools.com
604-710-5748

Eurekazone Inc.
www.eurekazone.com
877-877-1277

Freud
www.freudtools.com
800-334-4107

Gilliom Mfg. Inc.
314-724-1812

Grizzly Industrial
www.grizzlytools.com

Hitachi Power Tools
www.hitachipowertools.com
800-829-4752

Irwin Industrial Tools
www.irwin.com
800-GO-IRWIN

Jet, WMH Tool Group
www.jettools.com
800-274-6848

Kreg Tool Co.
www.kregtool.com
800-447-8638

Lansky Sharpeners
www.lanskysharpeners.com
800-825-2675

Legacy Woodworking
www.legacywoodworking.
com, 800-279-4570

Lee Valley Tools
www.leevalley, com
800-267-8735

Lufkin Tape Measures,
Alvin & Co.
www.alvinco.com
800-444-2584

Magnate
www.magnate.net
800-827-2316

Makita
www.makitatools.com
800-461-5482

McFeelys
www.McFeelys.com
800-443-7937

Milescraft
www.milescraft.com
847-683-9200

Milwaukee Tools
www.milwaukeetool.com
800-SAWDUST

Modified Square
www.modifiedsquare.com
412-331-7802

Plumb Hammers,
Cooper Industries
www.cooperhandtools.com

Porter-Cable
www.deltaportercable.com
888-848-5175

Ridgid Power Tools
www.ndgid.com
800-4-RIDGID

Rockier Woodworking &
Hardware
www.rocklerpro.com
800-233-9359

Roto-Zip
www.rotozip.com
877-ROTOZIP

Ryobi Power Tools
www.ryobitools.com
800-525-2579

Sears Craftsman
www.sears.com/craftsman
800-377-7414

Shop Fox Tools, Woodstock
International
www.shopfoxtools.com
800-840-8420

Skil
www.skil.com, 877-SKIL-999

Stanley Tools
www.stanleytools.com
800-262-2161

Vaughan & Bushnell
www.vaughanmfg.com
800-435-6000

Veritas Tools Inc.
www.ventastools.com
613-596-1922

Vermont American
www.vermontamencan.com

Wagner Safe-T-Planer,
Available from Woodcraft
Supply

Woodcraft Supply
www.woodcraft.com
800-225-1153

Woodline USA Eliminator
Chuck
www.woodline.com
800-472-6950

Woodmaster Tools, Inc.
www.WoodmasterTools.com
800-821-6651

Woodworker's Supply, Inc.
www.woodworker.com
800-645-9292

Woodworking industry information,
www.woodweb.com

Index